ELEVATING THE GAME

Black Men and Basketball

NELSON GEORGE

UNIVERSITY OF NEBRASKA PRESS
LINCOLN

Copyright © 1992 by Nelson George. Published by arrangement with
HarperCollins Publishers, Inc.
Manufactured in the United States of America

∞

First Bison Books printing: 1999
Most recent printing indicated by the last digit below:
10   9   8   7   6   5   4   3   2   1

Library of Congress Cataloging-in-Publication Data
George, Nelson.
Elevating the game: Black men and basketball / Nelson George.
p.   cm.
Originally published: New York: HarperCollins, c1992.
Includes bibliographical references (p.   ) and index.
ISBN 0-8032-7085-2 (pbk.: alk. paper)
1. Basketball—United States—History.   2. Afro-American athletes Biography.
I. Title.
GV885.7.G47   1999
796.323'0973—dc21
99-37582   CIP

This book is dedicated to two of my favorite Brooklynites: Bernard King, for a career that's been a testament to Black style and the largeness of his heart, and Ebony George, my niece, for surviving a brain tumor and still being so sweet.

CONTENTS

Illustrations follow page 104

A C K N O W L E D G M E N T S

Special thanks to Earl Monroe, Walt Hazzard, John McLendon, H. B. Thompson, John Salley, Tom Sanders, Hal Jackson, the late Chuck Cooper and Nat "Sweetwater" Clifton, Ken Hudson, Mel Reddick, John Thompson, Fred Slaughter, and Mark Jackson and family.

Also, thank you to Doug Simmons, Mike Curuso, Paul Solotaroff and Robert Christgau at the *Village Voice*; editor Wendy Wolf; agent Sarah Kazin; my mother, Arizona, sister, Andrea, and my nieces, Ebony and Amber; attorney Stephen Barnes; Melissa Clark, Pam and Tracy Lewis for the legwork; Michele Pierce for the inputting; Von Alexander for the hype; Anna Ponder, Ed Eckstine, and Sheila Eldridge for the hookups; Leah Wilcox for the NBA videos; Gary Harris for the basketball arguments; the guys at the St. George Health Club for the games; Bill Miles for access to his Black Champions research; Lem Peterkin for the conversation; same to *Newsday*'s Curtis Bunn; the librarians at the Schomburg Library in Harlem; and the Knicks fans at Madison Square Garden, whom I've sat among for parts of four decades.

A MOMENT AT THE HOLE

"There's a special lack of restraint ... best typified in certain
Black men. They may give him bad names and call him 'street
nigger,' but when you take away the vocabulary of denigration
what you have is somebody who is fearless and who is comfortable with that fearlessness. It's not about meanness. It's a kind of
self-flagellant resistance to certain kinds of progress, the lock-step
life, they live in the world unreconstructed and that's it."

—TONI MORRISON,
Black Women Writers at Work, edited by Claudia Tate, 1983

BROWNSVILLE, BROOKLYN, CIRCA 1971

The Hole was a basketball court located about ten feet
below street level in the middle of the Van Dyck Projects. Surrounding the court were long concrete slabs that served
as seats and no small distraction to players driving for loose
balls. But, truthfully, not many dived for balls. Most who
played in the tournaments there were too smart, too good, and
much too cool to be so foolish. The players sported bushy
Afros, goatees, thick head and wrist bands, and suede Puma
sneakers like that definer of 70s hip Clyde Frazier; a few still
wore, with equal pride, the more working-class Pro-Keds and
Converses. Underneath the basket major contact was being

made. Every rebound seemed an exercise in butchery. I remember one game vividly; it wasn't a thrilling contest really, but it had a "moment." Some skinny teen, with long bony elbows and knees, his Afro blowing in his self-created breeze, stole a pass and came whizzing downcourt. Sitting behind the metal backboard in the last row of the packed concrete seats, I watched his red Pro-Keds elevate above us as the ball, pressed on his fingers like a golf tee, moved through space and then disappeared behind the backboard. "Boom!" The backboard shivered, the ball smacked onto the ground, and the lanky teen stumbled on his descent. As the backboard vibrated slapped palms and laughed. Who won? Who cared? The game returned to its earlier level of mediocrity, the final results disappearing forever in yellowed records of some youth program that lost its funding during Nixon's second term. But that slam dunk—dramatic, unexpected, fantastic—that was the stuff of memory.

MADISON SQUARE GARDEN, FEBRUARY 21, 1989

The Knicks versus the Houston Rockets in a late-winter contest billed as the battle of the league's best centers, Houston's Hakeem Olajuwon and New York's Patrick Ewing. The next day's papers focused on the Knick victory and Hakeem's continuing domination of Patrick. On the subway home my posse rapped about how, while leading a two on one, Mark Jackson faked a behind-the-back pass to a trailing Charles Oakley and then dipped under Sleepy Floyd for two. Then, in a move that jogged an adolescent memory, Houston's 6´10˝ forward Otis Thorpe had taken off from the free throw line and flown to the hoop—pumping the ball twice on route in his massive right hand—before unleashing an explosive Dr. J-style rim-rocking dunk. On the subway home we laughed about those two moves, compared them to past moments, and savored these improvisational flights as intensely as any jazz aficionado might listening to a riff by Miles or Bird or Trane. Or any b-boy would be hyped by the rhymes of Rakim or Chuck Dee or L.L. Cool J. Or the righteously born again might shout "Amen" at the rigorous rhetoric of Dr. Martin Luther King or Jesse Jackson. What links these basketball moves with rapping, sermonizing, and soloing is that they all manifest a particular—and shared—African-American aesthetic. My unknown Brownsville dunker, like NBA players Mark Jackson and Otis Thorpe, didn't simply score, he personalized the act of scoring just as African-Americans, in everything from music to jump rope to slang, have put a fresh spin on activities elevated and prosaic.

Two-time Pulitzer Prize–winning playwright August Wilson defines this dynamic this way: "White American society is made up of various European ethnic groups which share a common history and sensibility. Black Americans are a racial group which do not share the same sensibilities. The specifics of our cultural history are very much different. We are an African people who have been here since the early-17th century. We have a different way of responding to the world. We have different ideas about religion, different manners of social intercourse. We have different ideas about style, about language. We have different aesthetics."

In all the analysis and observations about Black asethetics little of this thinking has been applied to sports. "Sportswriters and academics have examined sport as trap and safety value and escape hatch," wrote Robert Lipsyte, "usually in the context of an extraordinary hyper event, such as a Super Bowl or the Olympics, or in the progress of an individual from the ghetto to glory, and sometimes back." Sportswriters stick to bios; "analysts" talk sociology; Black historians undervalue sports. There have been some exceptions in boxing writing and in essays on certain stars—Willie Mays, Muhammad Ali—but nothing very extensive or systematic. In basketball, the prime arena after World War II for Black athletic innovation, this discussion has been swamped, muddled by the sociology Lipsyte refers to and by the fact that Black b-ball style has been saddled with the implicitly derogatory label "schoolyard," a phrase that covers some but hardly all of the story, or the style. It is, however, the focus of the story here.

Not all manifestations of this aesthetic are physical; but they are always aggressive. Verbal intimidation on the court (aka "the selling of wulf tickets") is a large part of the operating dynamic. Wulf tickets are intended to demoralize opponents by demeaning their intelligence, judgment, self-respect, manhood, and overall claims to humanity. Words like "sucker," "turkey," "lame," along with a constantly evolving variety of others, usually compounded by some artfully articulated obscenity, are employed to undermine the thin-skinned. Like "the dozens," a verbal trial by insult practiced among Blacks for generations, these taunts are essential to the game's component of one upmanship and to psychological combat. "In your face," the most celebrated bit of Black slang in recent b-ball lexicon, is about showing total disrespect for your opponent; it's an acceptably arrogant claim of excellence on the speaker's part. In fact, most Black ball expressions are about elevating oneself by embarrassing others.

"In your face" was originally coined to describe the impact of a jumper swooshing in over a defender, but since the seventies it's usually used to describe that most heightened of ball skills, the slam dunk. The ability to leap up and, with once two, now one hand, force (dunk, stuff, jam) the ball directly through the basket had been impossible for most players and frowned upon by coaches from basketball's inception in 1891 until the 1950s. Then, several Northern Black high school teams began to build reputations by using the slam dunk as a weapon of intimidation—even before the game actually started. Wrote Ira Berkow of watching the all-Black DuSable High team in Chicago, January 1, 1954: "The players came running in single file. They wore black and devil's red warm-up uniforms with flapping half-capes. They opened the drills with slam dunks. Some teams had no players who could dunk; a full one half of DuSable's fourteen players were tall enough or springy enough and with hands large enough to smash the ball through the hoop with one hand after a long bound and leap, or with two hands after circling under the basket and then jumping and stuffing the ball backwards."

The Black ability to dunk "with authority" became, in the wide-open American Basketball Association of the seventies, an integral part of professional basketball's tapestry. It is the unstoppable weapon that, when done with the rim-bending authority and flair Spike Lee dubbed "a 360 degree high flying, def-defying 360 Brooklyn Bridge slam dunk" ignites (or, on the road, deflates) a crowd, establishes a player's physical mastery of an opponent, and, as on that day in the park, affects the molecules in the surrounding air (see dunks by Charles Barkley, Dominique Wilkins, and Karl Malone for parallel metaphysical experiences).

Probably the most appropriate musical analogy to the African-American player's relationship to basketball is the African-American musician's affinity for the saxophone. The saxophone existed from the midnineteenth century to the 1930s before African-Americans took up Adolphe Sax's invention in large numbers. It was only when the improvising souls of these men were matched with this instrument that the saxophone assumed a prominent place in world music. Its expressive range and tonation liberated the psyche of African-Americans in a manner unique and beautiful.

The arrogance implicit in all this talking and dunking is,

alas, one of the elements in this style that brings down its practitioners. It can turn into a relentless egotism that makes every trip downcourt a testament to selfishness. The player is scorned for abandoning the team, for making a victory less important than a high personal score or showing off a remarkable playing flair. In basketball parlance a "schoolyard player" is, by definition, a selfish player. "Schoolyard ball" suggests an untutored, undisciplined, immature approach that works in opposition to standard or "classroom" ball. Classroom ball is implicitly a game that can be recorded in a textbook with strategies that, like any core curriculum, are the backbone of understanding. Classroom ball is defined by chalkboards, systems, and philosophies conspiring to become rituals.

A traditional reading of b-ball history, buttressed by the usual sociological observation about how sports teaches values to the underprivileged, is that only through indoctrination in classroom ball can the schoolyard player succeed indoors. In truth, the blend of schoolyard and classroom is much more complex than the old truism would have you believe; the schoolyard style has now enriched classroom philosophies so thoroughly that the differences aren't so easy to discern. Put simply—because of schoolyard experimentation *all* players now do things once thought impossible. When the aesthetic works in synch, the team, in fact, stands to benefit in every way. In the 1980s the Los Angeles Lakers were the world's best b-ball team precisely because their individual styles epitomized this complicated mesh. Blessed with speed on the wings (Norm Nixon and Jamaal Wilkes, later James Worthy and Byron Scott, and, always, Michael Cooper) and Earvin 'Magic' Johnson pushing the ball in the middle, coach Pat Riley fashioned a system that made the behind-the-back pass, the alley-oop, the jammin' dunk as essential as the pick 'n' roll and Kareem Jabbar's skyhook. But let me take this idea a step further. The genius was not in Riley's system, as sound as it clearly was, but in Johnson's game. It was his penchant for mating flamboyance with intensity, resulting in an ability to intimidate through his improvising, that raised his Lakers above the pack.

"Intimidation through improvisation" is crucial since it suggests how Johnson, going back to high school, has understood how to control a game's tempo—knowing when a no-look baseball pass or three-point shot would hype the crowd, energize his teammates, and dishearten the opposition. "Show time" perfectly described the Lakers' fast, entertaining brand of ball—it also told opponents the performance would be performed at their expense. In basketball improvisation is the ability to be creative on the move, and, while not limited to Blacks (see Bob Cousy, Pete Maravich, Larry Bird), there's no question that certain African-Americans execute their court magic with a funky attitude akin to that of the race's greatest musicians.

Arthur Ashe, the first African-American male tennis champ and author of the seminal three-volume history of Black athletes, *A Hard Road to Glory*, has observed, "In every sport we enter in large numbers we change how it's played and coached; be it Billy 'White Shoes' Johnson changing the idea of celebration in football to how Black players changed the use of speed in baseball. Within five years of Jackie Robinson's entry into the major leagues, Blacks took over the stolen base category and made it a weapon of intimidation it hadn't been since the Ty Cobb era. We're used to playing an in-your-face game." In boxing, track and field, baseball, and football Black men have broken rules and rewritten record books. But of all these outstanding sportsmen perhaps only boxers (Joe Louis, Sugar Ray Robinson, Muhammad Ali) have so radically remade a sport as African-Americans have basketball.

This Black aesthetic has not only changed basketball but, after a rough period in the seventies, has been the catalytic force behind the sport's extraordinary growth in popularity and profitability ever since. As basketball enters its second century the NBA and NCAA Division I are healthier than at any time in history. But *Elevating the Game* is not a history of the NBA or the glamour colleges. I look at most of the major post–World War II players whom I discuss at length primarily in the context of their local traditions; I'm interested in the way their styles developed when they were adolescents and teenagers, not necessarily in their more glittery professional careers. Much of the narrative focuses on the underdocumented African-American institutions of sports such as Black high school tournaments and college leagues. This material shows how so many Black educators in the years before desegregation saw athletics in general, and basketball in particular, as a tool for changing America. B-ball was used as a way to organize African-American higher learning institutions, draw attention to their overall educational mission, and build pride. Moreover, the sport was seen as a tool not to advocate pro athletics but to give the underprivileged but athletically gifted African-American a shot at a college education. Building race leaders was more important than promoting stars. We'll see this attitude was very much in keeping with the philosophies of many important white athletic institutions (such as the YMCA).

But in some ways the civil rights movement succeeded too well, resulting in an integration that weakened once hearty Black institutions and also perpetuated a destructive mentality among its youth. The white universities and NBA made b-ball glamorous with the promise of millionaire contracts, throwing out of whack the role of basketball in Black America and leading all but the top 2 percent of Black athletes down a road to frustration. The issues of Black and white athletic entrepreneurship, employment policies at universities and the NBA, and the value of role models all play crucial roles in tracing the evolution of Black men in basketball.

Let's be clear about what *Elevating the Game* is not. It doesn't make claims to be the definitive history of Black men in basketball since the subject is rich enough to fill three or four volumes. It doesn't deal with the fascinating saga of Black women in basketball, a story that dates back to the early 1900s and is worth a book of its own. This book is interpretive in the tradition of Black musical and cultural criticism. Be forewarned. This book is not "balanced"—the focus is on African-American history and African-American men. I consider certain European-Americans (Red Auerbach, John Wooden, Larry Bird, Bob Cousy), but only as they relate to the African-American experience. You've heard the term "Afrocentric." To the degree that an ethnic identity influences a writer's judgment (and that's quite a bit) this is an Afrocentric text.

Like music and comedy, basketball is one revealing prism for studying how a distinctive African-American ethos, in conjunction with the nation's evolving sociology and economy, has elevated an aspect of our culture.

In a very special way basketball has blended with our self-image. Black male arrogance, intelligence, greed, toughness, weakness, and innovation are all displayed in this sport. Since the sport's invention 100 years ago Black players have been depicted as clowns, role models, and threats to its survival and, ultimately, the game's very soul. *Elevating the Game* looks at how, why, and what, if anything, it has meant.

ELEVATING THE GAME

FREEDOM OF MOVEMENT

"Basketball was originally invented as a white man's game."
—MICHAEL NOVACK,
The Joy of Sports, 1988

n 1891, at the International Training School of the Young Men's Christian Association in Springfield, Massachusetts, students were instructed in five types of literature. Ranked in order of "seriousness" they were told to read Teutonic myths, legends, and folklore; tales of heroes with individual prowess like Hercules and Samson; stories of great leaders like Moses and patriots like George Washington; tales of love, family, and God. The underlying idea was to funnel the youthful enthusiasm for larger-than-life figures into a respect for Western traditions and religious institutions. An adjunct to this outlook was attention to physical fitness. "Bodily vigor is a moral agent, it enables us to live on higher levels, to keep up to the top of our achievement," wrote Dr. Luther Gulick, head of physical education at the Springfield Y.

Unfortunately, in the snowy winter of 1891 the student body's vigor was flagging. Gulick's students were bored with their reading and needed a new athletic outlet. With football season behind them and baseball many months away, the institution's contentious young charges were fed up with the regular regimen of gymnastics, calisthenics, and that ever exciting activity, marching. For Gulick, a distinguished-looking man with a silver head of hair and mustache, this restlessness was not an isolated problem but one that challenged his basic philosophy.

Gulick was a disciple of a philosophy that shaped his actions—the YMCA—and that dreary winter 100 years ago in Massachusetts would inspire basketball's creation. Quite simply, Gulick and his fellow adherents argued that the body's form "could be altered and perfected, and implicitly, their afterlife. Perfection of the body was an essential part of Christian morality in this system of thought." At midcentury nearly half the Eastern population lived in cities and towns, many working in "brain work" or, in contemporary parlance, that century's equivalent of white-collar jobs. Residing away from nature and the rigors of life these new urbanites saw in organized physical activity a way not just to be healthy but to achieve a "perfection of the body [that] was an essential part of Christian morality." The linkage of exercise (calisthenics, gymnastics, physical education, and more playful sporting activities) with spiritual development became known as "muscular Christianity." This worldwide movement, which first emerged in Great Britain, would, with its blend of physicality and moral certitude, be as important an underlying theme in white American aesthetics as the blues would eventually be to Black Americans.

In the 1870s Dudley Sargent, a Maine native interested in medicine and gymnastics, became muscular Christianity's guru. He opened his Hygienic Institute and School of Physical Culture in New York in 1878 and then became Harvard's first professor of physical training. He advocated use of pulley and weight machines designed to duplicate the activity of laborers, plus a philosophy that said physical education was essential for all people, not just serious athletes. Educators, athletes, and politicians all came to Harvard to study his techniques and seek ways to apply his ideas off the playing field. Teddy Roosevelt, President and noted health nut, was Sargent's most prominent disciple, though the torch may have been carried most high by a student named Luther Gulick.

While studying under Sargent at Harvard young Gulick was intrigued by the Greek philosophy that a sound mind and body were inseparable. Upon graduation Gulick became a powerful member of the Young Men's Christian Association hierarchy and in the 1880s joined the Springfield Y.

Confronted now with the dilemma of 1881 and being a forward-thinking citizen of the industrial age, Gulick reasoned some game could be invented to satisfy his winter-weary students. The shrewd Gulick believed that whatever game was conceived should include elements of already familiar sports. Then, like any good leader, he passed the ball to his subordinates. Two YMCA instructors failed in attempts to create a satisfactory game before the assignment fell to Dr. James Naismith, a thirty-year-old Canadian with degrees in medicine and theology. Naismith's face was dominated by a thick mustache that engulfed his lips and gave him a dour, melancholy look consistent with his intense manner. Gulick gave him two weeks to conceive "something," and, according to legend, on the fourteenth day Naismith "birthed" basketball.

Naismith made several key decisions in designing the game:

3

action centered around a ball rather than a stick and a ball because he felt requiring players to be proficient with a stick, as in baseball and hockey, would make the game more difficult to master; by prohibiting running he ruled out indoor tackling and encouraged multidirectional passing; to emphasize skill over strength, he put the goal ten feet up, forcing players to shoot from a distance to score. In addition, with an elevated goal one player or group of players couldn't stand in front and prevent scoring—at least that's what Naismith reasoned. He felt this sport needed a time limit, unlike baseball—two fifteen-minute halves with a five-minute intermission.

In his thirteen original rules Naismith decided "a player can not run with the ball ... allowance to be made for a man who catches the ball at a good speed if he tries to stop." But there is no mention of dribbling; that part of the game soon evolved through play. Nor is there any set number of players allowed per side, except to say, depending on the floor, "it may range from 3 on a side to forty," though he was forward-thinking enough to note that three on three was "more scientific." But Naismith's vision of basketball wasn't rigid—early contests at Springfield were often nine-on-nine affairs since his class consisted of eighteen students. Naismith invented basketball, but it would be players and coaches who would refine the game's rules over the next forty years so that by the late thirties its format would be recognizable to contemporary fans. At its inception, however Naismith was not concerned with refining this game but just figuring out what the elevated goal should be made of. Initially, Naismith envisioned it as a box. Luckily for the fingers of the future slam dunkers the Springfield Y's janitor had no boxes in his basement—just two empty peach baskets.

On January 15, 1892, basketball in its original incarnation debuted in the Springfield Triangle. It quickly caught the attention of Y branches around New England and New York. By October games were being played as far away as San Francisco. Women adopted basketball quickly—in fact, Naismith married an early woman player, Maude Sherman. The first known tournament was held in New York with Brooklyn's Central Y the victor. Three years later in Mount Holyoke, not far from Springfield, YMCA instructor William G. Morgan, inspired by basketball, created volleyball. Colleges soon picked up the game. An intercollegiate game in 1897 between Yale and Penn State in New Haven left the Yalies victorious, 32-1, in an unusually high score for the era. Earlier pioneering collegiate contests, such as the Minneapolis State School of Agriculture's win over Hamline University of St. Paul, 9-3, and Haverford College's defeat of Temple, 6-4, both in 1895, had typically lower scores. Semiprofessional basketball began to spread in 1898 with the inauguration of two leagues, the National and New England, which were both defunct by 1900.

Still, the game's appeal continued to grow. Vacationing Springfield students astounded locals in California and the Carolinas by hoisting soccer balls, coconuts, and even oranges up toward goals nailed to tree barks. Like Naismith, the athletic evangelist they strove to emulate, YMCA personnel preached the gospel of basketball around the country, so it's not surprising that in devoutly religious heartland states like Indiana and Kentucky that basketball became a secondary, though mighty, religion. The game's growth in the Midwest was solidified by Naismith's presence at the University of Kansas physical education department from 1898 until his retirement in 1937; he coached the team for nine years and inaugurated a historic basketball tradition.

Crucial to the game's increasing appeal during the late 1890s were refinements in its structure. Backboards were introduced to stop sneaky onlookers from leaning down from the elevated running tracks that circled most of the period's gyms and blocking shots. Backboards eliminated that bit of chicanery and made the bank shot possible. Baskets with chains that could be opened to release the ball were the norm until someone wondered, "Why don't we just leave the bottom open all the time?" and they did, paving the way for nets to replace chains. Then, in 1897, after much debate and experimentation, teams were standardized to five per side.

Of how the early players performed there is precious little useful descriptive evidence. The language of sportswriting wasn't as rich then in physical detail as it is now, and the vocabulary of basketball phrases we take for granted hadn't yet been created. H. B. Thompson, a Black man who played high school ball in West Virginia during the twenties, gives this account of practice and playing during that early period:

"I remember we never had more than two balls. And then you got about 15 to 20 kids out there. Can you imagine what we were doin' with 15 to 20 kids and two balls? You may get, maybe, 10 shots during the year. Now you look out there and there's one ball to every two boys. In other words you got ten kids out there and you got five balls. We had 15 with one ball so they have to learn to work together. So that's a big part of the difference then and now.

"All our plays stemmed from the center jump. Once the ball went through the basket it came back to center. Your center had to be the tallest man or you were in trouble, 'cause if you didn't get the tip it was hard to get the ball. So most of our plays started at center. You'd have plays going back to your point guard and you'd have plays developing for your forward. Your center had to be smart enough to tap the ball to the guy who you felt could get in the clear. See that was a lot of thinking. Right out of the center jump you get into your regular offense."

Naismith envisioned a nonphysical sport, but, as the game

spread during the new century, play quickly became combative and feisty. It got so bad that dedicated muscular Christian Teddy Roosevelt complained in the press that injuries in basketball, and football, were perverting athletics' wholesome purpose. In 1908 Harvard president Charles Eliot called for a basketball ban because it was "even more brutal than football." The problem was that most played the game as if it were football; a separate basketball mentality hadn't yet developed. Many referred to the game as "basket football" or "football in a gym" and made baskets as "touchdowns"—too many players saw it as a scaled-down version of the gridiron game. Thomas G. Bryant, who played for the University of Kentucky Wildcats from 1905 to 1907 remarked, "We didn't play for championships but for bloody noses." In a 1907 game versus Transylvania University, Bryant's opponent came on court in shoulder pads. In another contest, a 6´3˝, 250-pound football tackle stepped on his ankle. "He poked me with a left jab," Bryant said, "and I came back with a haymaker to the face." In those golden days a game without a fight was like a day without sunshine. And in various manifestations, this acceptance of aggression, even fighting, continues to be part of basketball's makeup.

The mesh and wire screens that were built to surround the court during the early 1900s and that survived into the 1940s were an outgrowth of this violence, protecting the fans from the players, players from fans—it wasn't unusual for a spectator to pinch the leg of players bringing the ball inbounds—and the poor referees from everybody. The reference to basketball players as "cagers" comes from this Roman Colosseum-like barrier between participant and participant spectator.

The chief beneficiaries of education, physical and intellectual, as preached by most institutions at the turn of the century were white males. White women, who actually played basketball in large numbers during this era, were very much second-class citizens. For Americans of African ancestry, freedmen since 1865, access to education of any kind was elusive. The saga of Black America's efforts to gain a toehold in this nation through education and the race's ever increasing involvement with athletics would, throughout the years, be strangely intertwined. Sometimes sports buttressed the battle for educational access. More often than many think, sports corrupted and sidetracked that process. In either case Gulick and Naismith's invention would eventually play a huge role in illustrating the pluses and minuses of the education/athletics dichotomy.

PLAYING THE BLUES

In 1891 the Blair Education Bill, named for New Hampshire's Republican senator Henry W. Blair, was rejected by the U.S. Congress in a decision that insured the shackles of legal servitude and its strengthener, ignorance, would restrain African-Americans for many years to come. First introduced in 1880, the bill proposed to earmark $77 million (a huge sum then) to combat illiteracy below the Mason-Dixon Line. Senator Blair conceived the legislation to aid "millions of Southerners, Black and white, who were growing up in absolute ignorance of the English alphabet" in the devastated post–Civil War South. Initially, the bill had a good shot at passage since in the troubled years of Reconstruction only federal aid to education received enthusiastic Southern support. Though Blair made sure its language was racially nonpartisan, Southern Blacks would have been its chief beneficiaries, as the bill aimed to pump federal dollars into education and mandate increased spending by state governments.

Blair's bill didn't challenge segregation—no white elected officials were that bold in the nineteenth century—but it did require equal spending on *all* schools, Black and white. It passed the Senate in 1886 and 1888 but died in the House of Representatives—both times a victim of political infighting and plain old Southern racism. "From 1890, when the Blair bill was finally defeated, onward into the 20th century, what was described as 'educational lethargy' settled all over the South. Millions of illiterate whites were sacrificed by Southern leaders whose main objective was to keep millions of illiterate Blacks ignorant, impoverished and politically impotent by denying them education," wrote Black historian Harold Cruse.

That same year Congress voted down Senator Henry Cabot Lodge's "force bill," which aimed to provide federal supervision of national elections so Black voters in the South would be protected. Lodge's bill actually made it through the House but was demolished in the Senate. As a result, these bills, one to upgrade the ability of Southern Blacks to compete economically through education and the other to allow Blacks to exercise their voting franchise without fear of violence, shut the door on two key avenues of empowerment and set the stage for the Supreme Court's 1896 *Plessy* v. *Ferguson* "separate but equal" decision that gave Washington's blessing to the domestic apartheid of Jim Crow. Conditions were bad in every Southern state, from Virginia to Florida and across to Louisiana. But, with the possible exception of Alabama, no state was as repressive as Mississippi. In its Delta region, a 200-mile stretch of land on either side of the Mississippi River that housed some of America's richest farmland, resided more African-Americans than any other region in the 1890s. Blacks outnumbered whites in the Delta by three to one. Picking cotton and cutting lumber for trips up the river to Memphis and St. Louis gave Mississippi Blacks employment but no economic upward mobility. They still lived in squalid one-room shacks shackled to white-owned land by sharecropping agreements, which was just slavery with less overhead for plantation owners.

Families had been terribly fragmented by slavery, while poverty fueled Black-on-Black crime and addiction (just as it does today). Yet these Delta residents, mostly descendants of people stolen from West Africa, displayed a willful creativity that couldn't be suppressed. During slavery work songs were rife throughout the plantations and were even encouraged by owners who, according to Frederick Douglass, saw the singing as "evidence of their contentment and happiness" when in actuality these field hollers "repressed the sorrows of his life." Spirituals celebrating Old Testament figures, turning their biblical tales into metaphors for stifled African-American aspirations, were the work songs' religious counterparts.

Around 1890 in the Mississippi Delta, a new sound emerged, one that owed much to earlier styles but that spoke directly to the pains and pleasures of post-Emancipation life. Folks started calling these songs "blues." Church people thought the music's unmistakable sensuality was the work of the Devil; others saw its will to self-expression and personal revelation as something new in American music. Whether it was a work of Satan or man, the power of the blues was readily apparent every time it was performed. Elements of Africa could be found in its rhythms and chords, in particular, the bending of certain notes on the diatonic scale that was similar to West African music and became known as "blue" notes. Vocal harmonies derived from European choral traditions; elements of work songs and field hollers were also prominent. Quickly the blues became the dominant musical expression of post-Reconstruction Black America and the focal point around which an aesthetic encompassing language, dance, mating rituals, and life-style coalesced. Just as slaves took foods discarded from the tables of slave masters (pig feet, chitterlings, pork chops) to develop a distinctive cuisine, the indentured freedmen of the Delta took old instruments and broken tools (many early blues were performed with a piece of broom wire tied at both ends by nails and hung from a wall) to give musical expression to the woes of oppression and the spirit of life. Early white commentators viewed the blues, as they had field hollers, as mournful wailing. Yet embedded in the blues was a rebellious sense of one-upmanship and verbal play suppressed in daily contacts with white authority. "It is the disposition to preserve," wrote Albert Murray, "(based on a tragic, or, better still, an epic sense of life) that blues music at its best not only embodies but stylizes, extends, elaborates, and refines into art."

The men who sang the blues in those perilous times weren't simply musical pioneers but, says William Barlow, "cultural rebels." In *Looking Up at Down: The Emergence of Blues Culture,* Barlow writes: "They were the makers and carrier of a music that resisted cultural domination in form and content. They used traditional African musical practices to spread the rebellion and to reinforce the powerful hold that African traditions had on African Americans living in the South. By choosing a life of travel and recreation rather than unrelenting labor and unrewarded abstinence, they signalled their alienation from the established cultural norms in their communities. To older and more conservative religious members of the Black populations their music was blasphemous and they were characterized as the Devil's disciples. And it is true that they acted as proselytizers of a gospel of secularization in which the belief in freedom became associated with personal mobility—freedom of movement in this world here and now, rather than salvation later on the next."

These early bluesmen loved performing songs that celebrated "bad men," defiant African-Americans who bedeviled plantation owners and sought legendary status for themselves:

I's Wild Nigger Bill
From Redpepper Hill
I never did work an' I never will
I's done kill the boss
I's done knocked down the hoss
I eats up raw goos without apple sauce

Humorous and rebellious, sassy and thoughtful, many blues presented a view of African-American heroism that whites feared but its singers and audiences craved. The Delta blues suggested an angry, innovative instinct in African-America that was a profound contrast with the blackface buffoonery popularized in minstrel shows. Many blues lyrics emphasized virility and a mythological boldness. Songs like these were irreconcilable with America's already contradictory images of Black males. These men were supposed to be lazy, silly, innocent, and childlike; at the same time Black men were sneaky, deceitful, and, in terms of their alleged lust for white women, frighteningly potent. Blues lyrics posed instead a vital, assertive view of these men, one defined by their values, their perspectives.

Not every blues song overtly challenged the racial status quo. In fact, some white listeners were attracted to this music purely for its musical quality and that "mournful" quality that they attributed to it. What they didn't often acknowledge was that impulse to express one's experience, which is integral to blues music, giving voice to a humanity otherwise suppressed by white authority. The emergence of the blues, as well as its tolerance (and later embrace), is a prime example of how Black music has always been able to overcome or at least muffle racism.

Most other avenues of Black expression in the late 1880s were stifled. Jim Crow, the profusion of laws that sprang up across the South to put a lid on Black aspirations, performed its evil duty well. In athletics, where after the Civil War many Blacks found employment and earnest respect, the discrimination was profound because the playing field was one arena Blacks could challenge white supremacy without benefit of a formal education.

GETTING IN THE GAME

Before the Civil War, the job of grooming, feeding, and training thoroughbred horses fell to slaves in the South. So it was natural that African-Americans were accepted as jockeys in the years immediately after emancipation. Fourteen of the fifteen jockeys at the first Kentucky Derby, May 1875, were ex-slaves, while fifteen of the first twenty-eight Derbys were won by brown-skinned riders. Then, in the 1911 Derby, a man named Jesse Conley rode the show horse and sadly became the last Black jockey to have a mount in America's premiere race for decades. By the 1920s there were virtually no Black jockeys riding in the Derby (or any other prestige races). The reason? Jim Crow. Turf and harness racing had, in America and around the world, traditionally been a sport enjoyed and promoted by the wealthy, who tended to view the jockeys more paternally since most were attached to rich breeders. As the sport's common-man appeal grew via lowered admission prices and parimutuel betting, the same pressure that denied Blacks the vote eventually usurped their right to ride.

In baseball, which in the nineteenth century was already the national pastime, exclusion came earlier. At baseball's 1867 National Association convention of amateur clubs it was agreed, "It is not presumed by your committee that any clubs who have applied are composed of persons of color, or any portion of them; [teams] unanimously report against the admission of any club which may be composed of one or more colored persons." Still, in the 1880s several Blacks gained entry to pro teams. For example, catcher Weldy W. Walker was signed by Toledo in 1884, but his career was star-crossed. Once, in Louisville, he was forced to sit out a game because the home team refused to play against him. More menacingly, in Richmond, Virginia, before a game six local whites warned that seventy-five "determined men" had sworn to mob Walker should he suit up. "It is a well known historical paradox that, as the Civil War receded, Jim Crowism in America became more pronounced," wrote baseball historian Harold Seymour. "Southern caste attitudes spread increasingly to the North and West, much to the alarm of liberals and reformers. This blight included professional baseball in its contagious advance. White players objected to the 'colored element'...So by the late 1880s the major leagues erected a solid, though unofficial, dam against Negroes, shutting off completely the tiny trickle, which had previously flowed through."

Of America's major professional sports only boxing maintained a consistent level of African-American participation through Reconstruction into the 1900s. In large part that's because the spectacle of Black men fighting each other was quite familiar to whites. Battle royals, where for prize money a dozen or so Black men were blindfolded, ushered into a ring, and told to fight until one man was left standing, were extremely popular. Straight one-on-one bare-knuckle matches between Blacks had long been part of Southern entertainment, while up North Blacks were often pitted against European immigrants. Lightweight Joe Gans, called "The Old Master" by his fans, was able to compete for and ultimately win his weight division in 1902. But purses for Black fighters were smaller than for whites, and some states and cities prohibited even Black-on-Black matches, much less pugilistic race mixing. The ability to compete for the heavyweight title, the sport's apex, would be withheld from Black challengers until 1908.

In 1891, when African-Americans faced limits on their rights in the voting booth, schools, and athletics and their postslavery culture was developing new expressions away from European-American eyes, it's not surprising that the newly minted sport of basketball would have very little impact on them for most of the decade after its invention. Basketball was the by-product of a very rational, very rigid, very white world of values and institutions far removed from the blues in the Mississippi Delta night.

So, appropriately, the crop of Black hoopsters who first appeared after 1900 were men who had to create a marriage of education and athletics. There weren't a lot of them, nor were these early African-American players in any way ordinary. Most were products of the talented tenth of Black America—the sons of Northern freedmen whose love of the sport was deep but whose use of and relationship to it fit neither the "noble primitive" stereotypes of the early 1900s or the "greedy jock" caricatures of the 1990s.

As Bryant Gumbel, founding editor of *Black Sports* magazine, wrote, these sportsmen "had all come from families that were, comparatively speaking, financially comfortable. In those days of no athletic scholarships, and sports as a sidelight, only the well-to-do could afford to go to college. Once there, the wise student knew better than to waste his rare opportunity of obtaining a college education. Above all, the Black man was in college to study, not to perform on the athletic field. The socioeconomics of the times went far to alleviate any possible grumbling concerning the participation of Blacks in college athletics. Those Blacks who were in college came from backgrounds and environments similar to their white counterparts.

And still later, after athletics had come under the auspices of college faculties, the primal objective academics, was still in force."

From the turn of the century to the end of World War I eight Blacks are known to have played on white basketball varsities. According to Arthur Ashe's *Hard Road to Glory* they were Samuel Ransom at Beloit College (Wisconsin), 1904–1908; Wilbur Wood at Nebraska, 1907–1910; Fenwich Watkins at Vermont, 1909; Cumberland Posey at Penn State, 1909, and Duquesne, 1916; Sol Butler at Dubuque (Iowa), 1910; William Kindle at Springfield University (Massachusetts), 1911; Cleve Abbott at South Dakota State, 1913; and Paul Robeson at Rutgers, 1915–1918.

Obviously the most celebrated is Robeson, a true Renaissance man. At Rutgers Robeson was the first Black football all-American (1917–1918); he also made all-American in discus and javelin. In all, he won fifteen varsity letters in four sports. Basketball was, along with debating and singing, a particular favorite activity. At 6´2˝, 190 pounds he was an early "wide body" center whose bulk took up plenty of court space. Robeson's love of the game is clear from the fact that along with the many activities crammed into his Rutgers years, he was a member of the basketball team at Harlem's St. Christopher's Club, where the future activist-entertainer played with two important future pros, Harold "Legs" Jenkins and his brother Clarence "Little Fat" or "Fats" Jenkins. St. Christopher's was, with Manhattan's Marathon Athletic Club and Brooklyn's Smart Set, part of the first Black club league organized in New York City.

For Robeson basketball was a pleasant diversion in a life filled with activity. But for several Black graduates of white universities, advocacy of basketball would be a tool of educational and economic empowerment. Black Harvard grad Edwin B. Henderson didn't play on his alma mater's varsity, but after returning to his native Washington, D.C., around 1905, he became a driving force in organizing the nation's first Black high school athletic association. In 1862 a bill passed in Congress that gave 10 percent of all taxes paid by D.C. Blacks to support education. This provided a stream of income unusual for Black schools in the South. Using the available money Henderson, who by 1906 was physical education training instructor for D.C. schools, joined with five other local Black high school and college educators to establish the Interscholastic Athletic Association (ISAA) of the Middle States. Two years later schools in D.C., Indianapolis, Baltimore, and Wilmington were competing against each other in track, baseball, football, and basketball. In the *I.S.A.A. Official Handbook,* Henderson and Howard University's W. A. Joiner wrote, "In two years over forty basketball teams, averaging eight players to a team, have trained and competed under the auspices of the ISAA. It is conservative to state that over 1,000 boys have played basketball in this city since the sport was introduced." Henderson was also active in forming club teams in D.C., such as the Crescent City Athletic Club, which lost to Brooklyn's Smart Set on December 18, 1908, in what was reportedly the first contest between "colored" athletes from New York and the District of Columbia. Henderson obviously liked to keep busy because he was a member of the YMCA's 12th Street branch, reputed at that time to be the city's best, a team that went undefeated in 1909–1910 against squads up and down the East Coast. In fact, when Howard added a basketball varsity in 1911 it recruited most of its players from that YMCA team. Henderson's role in the promulgation of Black sports didn't end merely with the games—in 1939 he wrote *The Negro in Sports,* the first work on the subject ever published. Its chief concern was sport's amateur aspects.

By 1905 many enterprising African-Americans had begun

designing ways to make money with the game. In New York Will Madden, who ran St. Christopher's amateur team, organized a semiprofessional offshoot called the Incorporators that featured ex-St. Christopher's star, Walter D. Cooper, a player renowned for his accurate underhand free throws. Legend has it that Cooper was so good the all-white Original Celtics, regarded as the sport's best early team, offered him a contract, but, Cooper, fearful of prejudice in traveling with the Celtics, reluctantly turned it down.

The Incorporators' biggest semipro competition came from a team run by a man, who, like Henderson, had attended a white college. The son of the first Black granted a chief engineer's license to operate a Mississippi riverboat, Cumberland Posey came from a respected Pennsylvania family. His admission to Penn State and acceptance on the basketball varsity suggested a young man of stature, a good candidate to prove the equality of his race on the playing field of academe.

But Posey got kicked off the Penn State squad for being academically ineligible in 1909, an unfortunate event that foreshadowed the relationship between Black college athletes and professional sports. He immediately set about organizing a semipro team, the Monticello Rifles. Operating just outside Pittsburgh, he and brother Seward ran a very successful operation, competing against, and defeating, mostly white teams throughout the East. In 1913 Posey inaugurated a new team that was even more successful: the Loendi Big Five. Based out of Pittsburgh, the team included Posey, James "Stretch" Sessoms, Williams T. Young, William "Big Greasy" Betts, and James "Pappy" Ricks. They were a big feisty group that never held the ball, quite aggressive and not afraid to rough up even the many white clubs they faced. In the spirit of the blues, Loendi was fierce on court and the consensus choice as the best colored cagers in the country according to the Black and white press.

Loendi might have grown into a major enterprise if the ambitious Mr. Posey hadn't moved on to establish one of Black sport's great franchises. When he wasn't playing basketball Posey was center fielder for the Murdock Grays, a semipro team that played for steelworkers in Pittsburgh's Homestead section. In 1910 Posey took over the team, changing its name to the Homestead Grays. The Grays became Posey's passion. Boasting the talents of Hall of Famers Buck Leonard and Josh Gibson, from 1937 to 1945 the Homestead Grays captured nine straight Negro League pennants. Posey's interest in Loendi naturally waned with the Grays' success, and the club eventually folded. Still, Posey's involvement with several Black entertainment entities is an excellent preview of the way different aspects of Black show biz and basketball would be linked in years to come. Cumberland Posey, a well-educated Black man, was one of the first to recognize the connection.

Posey and Henderson were dedicated, smart men who wielded their education like weapons. Henderson funneled his knowledge into athletics to mold young minds muscular-Christian style, while Posey was a businessman who made segregation work for him. Both, in their refusal to accept the limitations mandated by racism, worked as cultural rebels in a blues era. There were more to come.

INBOUNDS PLAY

"I had in mind the tall, agile, graceful and expert athlete, one who could reach, jump and act quickly and easily."
—JAMES NAISMITH

Nineteen fifteen was a terrible year to be Black in America. Booker T. Washington, the most powerful African-American at the turn of the century, died at his Alabama home. Whether you saw him as a pragmatic politician or a top-shelf Uncle Tom, Washington's presence on the national scene (a lunch with President Roosevelt was front-page news) gave him the ability to obtain federal employment for his acolytes and cultivate friendship with the likes of industrialist Andrew Carnegie. It also made him an unholy threat to racists North and South. And in 1915 there were plenty of them, which is maybe why *The Birth of a Nation*, director D. W. Griffith's innovative silent film, captured the hearts and minds of his countrymen. Griffith used the film to push the artistic limits of motion pictures. Its editing style, camera angles, and almost 3-hour length all brought new standards of excellence to the embryonic art form.

But in a way typical of white America, Griffith used state-of-the-art technology to dazzle audiences with a distorted vision of history. Based on the Reverend Thomas Dixon's propagandistic novel *The Clansman, Birth* celebrated the Ku Klux Klan as the true savior of whites and viewed the social reforms of the Reconstruction era as unnatural disasters that had to be, and in fact were, revoked. Historian Thomas Cripps bitingly summed up *Birth* and the context in which it thrived when he wrote that the film depicted "Reconstruction history as a Gothic horror tale haunted by Black brutes. The movie appeared as Black status had deteriorated. Lynching persisted in the rural South as life in Yankee cities worsened. Black sharecroppers remained trapped while Black migrants wasted in the cold daily round of poverty."

Just as Griffith's caricatures of Black men as brutal buffoons fed prejudice, the 1915 defeat of Jack Johnson cheered racists by removing from the scene the most frightening Black "buck" of all time. There had never been a widely known Black man, much less an athlete, who was as bold and openly contemptuous of the tenets of white male supremacy as this fighter. Big, bald, dark brown, and bodacious, John Arthur Johnson, the first African-American heavyweight champ, rose out of Texas with a style as reckless and fierce as the Delta blues. His boxing career began in 1894 when he was sixteen. By 1902 he was traveling throughout the South with a vaudeville troupe. When not boxing Johnson played harmonica and bass fiddle and danced for audiences—another early example of the show biz-sports connection. He beat Denver Ed Martin in 1903 for the Negro heavyweight belt and over the next two years successfully defended his title against all Black challengers. Johnson sought a shot at the white heavyweight belt, but champ Jim Jeffries declared, "If I am defeated, the championship will go to a white man, for I will not fight a colored man."

So for another three years Johnson cajoled, ridiculed, and otherwise campaigned for a title shot. Finally, in 1908, defending champ Tommy Burns gave in and agreed to fight Johnson in Sydney, Australia. Johnson towered over Burns and taunted him the entire fight ("I have forgotten more about fighting than Burns ever knew"), then battered him until police entered the ring to stop the pounding in the fifteenth round. Whites worldwide were enraged. They clamored for the retired Jeffries to be their Great White Hope. So, appropriately, on July 4, 1910, Johnson beat Jeffries in Reno, Nevada, shattering the mythology of Black male cowardice and stimulating a fear of Black potency that *The Birth of a Nation* exploited.

Johnson did more than just beat white men bloody before thousands of spectators. He brazenly flaunted his taste for white women—either marrying or having love affairs with many. His relationship with Belle' Schreiber finally got Johnson indicted under the Mann Act and led to his exile from the States. On April 5, 1915, when the thirty-seven-year-old boxer lost to Jess Willard in a match staged in Havana, he was easily one of America's most hated men. There is considerable evidence Johnson actually threw the fight, not just for money but because the promoters promised to ease his return to the States. Johnson, one of the first great African-American rebels of the twentieth century, went on to become a sad, bitter man who, in 1924, gave a well-received speech at a KKK rally in Danville, Illinois.

Johnson's career sent contradictory signals to the nation. Yes, a Black *could* beat a white man, but this Black man fit the stereotype by lusting after white women. An uneducated Black man *could* gain fame and fortune, but that didn't mean press and government would accept or celebrate him. The great boxer's career was a tale of athletic progress undercut by the quirks of personality and the relentlessness of hate.

Johnson's defeat, along with Washington's death and *Birth*'s popularity, are signposts that led into a new era of African-American organization in athletics. To combat racism and establish a framework for showcasing players and make money, a visionary crop of educators and businessmen stepped forward in this nasty era.

COLORED ONLY

On February 2, 1916, nine educators, coaches, and faculty members from Hampton Institute and Shaw, Lincoln, Virginia Union, and Howard universities formed the first Black collegiate conference. The gathering gave these all-Black schools, most of them founded after the Civil War, funded by liberal Northern philanthropists with little or no government assistance, and mostly scattered throughout the border states and the South, a much needed system of unified competition and rules. Until then an athlete could compete on a Black college team for as long, and as early, as the school allowed. It wasn't unusual for a talented local teenage player to play on a college team while still in high school. Under the guidance of Howard professor Ernest J. Marshal, one of the Central Interscholastic Athletic Association's first moves was to limit a player's athletic eligibility to four years. It was this sort of rules standardization plus other, more race conscious goals, that motivated the CIAA's founders. "The league is needed to unite area colleges in a common effort for athletic elevation," Marshal wrote. "It will serve to train students in self-reliance and stimulate race-pride through athletic attainment." The CIAA attracted national attention, which helped increase enrollment and created enduring rivalries. With no integrated college-level competition in the South, the CIAA schools also pulled together with the hope sports would encourage racial pride. They were not alone. At Atlanta's Morehouse College several colleges united to form the Southeastern Athletic Conference. The Southwestern Athletic Conference (SWAC) was formed in 1920, though it didn't have title competition until 1928; 1928 also saw the inauguration of the Southern Interscollegiate Athletic Conference (SIAC).

These conferences stimulated Black involvement in all sports, but its impact on basketball was quite profound. After World War I innumerable poor African-Americans from the North ventured South using their on-court prowess to attain an athletic scholarship and a college education. Because athletic facilities were available to Northern Blacks and basketball was already an established winter sport above the Mason-Dixon Line, the migration of these superior players to Black colleges inspired Southern youngsters to take up the game. The combination of up-North basketball know-how and Southern college exposure enabled superior teams and players to attain a national profile within Black America. The Morgan State basketball program from 1924–1927 is a prime example. Led by players Ed "Lanky" Jones, Talmadge Hill, and Daniel "Pinky" Clark, the Baltimore-based school tore up the CIAA. They went undefeated in 1927, and many hailed them as Black college basketball's de facto national champions.

Morgan State's coach during that invincible season was Charles Drew, better known historically as Dr. Charles Drew, the man who developed the medical use of blood plasma during World War II. A graduate of D.C.'s Dunbar High School, which since the twenties has produced excellent basketball players, Drew received personal instruction from D.C.'s Black phys ed activist Edwin Henderson. As an undergrad at Amherst University in Massachusetts from 1923 to 1926, Drew lettered in basketball, track, and football, winning the college's Ashley Trophy as its outstanding all-around athlete in 1923. Utilizing his sports training from D.C. and Massachusetts, Drew moved on to Morgan State, coaching the basketball team before attending Montreal's McGill University Medical School in 1928.

The tradition of excellence Drew inaugurated in 1927 was continued into the thirties by coach Eddie Hurt. From 1927 to 1934 Morgan State didn't lose a home game and from 1931 to 1934 won the CIAA crown each year. Indeed, the 1929 edition beat the top Black professional team, the Harlem Rens, 41-40, in Baltimore, the biggest victory for a Black college team in the twenties.

Another legendary collection was the unit from Xavier, New Orleans, which played together from 1935 to 1939. At one point during these four years Xavier had won eighty-two and lost only two. Key to the college's success was the fact that its entire starting five (Cleveland Bray, Leroy Rhodes, Tilford Cole, Charlie Gant, Williams McQuitter) came down South together, after leading Chicago's Wendell Phillips High to the Windy City schoolboy title. The concept of the starting five of a high school team traveling South en masse wasn't unusual. It guaranteed all five would get a scholarship and have moral support in adjusting to the Jim Crow South. Moreover, many Northerners felt they were too good to have country boys as equals on a college starting five—big-city b-ball arrogance was already apparent.

The 1939–1940 Virginia Union Panthers, aka "the Dream Team," were Black college ball's most celebrated club prior to World War II, compiling a forty-two and two record behind the play of two Northern imports, Wiley "Soupy" Campbell, who scored 269 points in twenty-five games in 1940, and the CIAA's best guard, Melvin Glover, who hit for 273 points. This inside-outside duo made history by leading Virginia Union to wins in two of three games with coach Clair Bee's NCAA champion Long Island University aggregation. It was a manifestation of Black athletic equality that is still savored by Black college-ball old-timers.

"From out of the dizzy, colorful swirl of courtdom ten great players have emerged during the past season to win coveted places on the Pittsburgh Courier first annual All-American basketball team," wrote the nationally respected Negro paper in 1940. The *Courier* list illustrates the dominance of Northern players at predominantly Southern universities: eight were from the North, four of them from New York, and the two from below the Mason-Dixon Line were natives of St. Louis and Marshall, Texas. None of the stars were from the Confederate States. At the time, Southern Black athletes were more interested in outdoor sports like baseball, track, and football. But that didn't stop a dedicated group of educators from below the Mason-Dixon Line from adopting the often frustrating struggle to indoctrinate basketball in the South, including the decade-long effort to maintain a Black high school basketball tournament.

THE VIRGINIA UNION

"Hampton Institute is proud to inform you that your school's basketball team has been selected to participate in the first annual National Interscholastic Basketball Tournament [NIBT]. Your team's meals and lodging will be handled by the Institute. You must be ready to play Friday morning, March 22, 1929 at 9 o'clock. Please send your team's roster."
—Charles H. Williams

Williams, physical education director at Hampton Institute, was a catalyst for the founding of the all-Black Central Inter-Collegiate Athletic Association. (CIAA) That conference's success in organizing Black educational institutions gave Williams the idea of inaugurating a national high school tournament. Williams and his Black educational peers, influenced by the ideas of muscular Christianity, saw sport as a tool for upgrading Black-only athletic facilities.

Edwin Henderson's pioneering work in founding the ISAA had bolstered Black schoolboy sports in D.C. and Baltimore. In Kansas, where there was no legal segregation but dual education systems still existed in most cities, indoor gyms had been available to Blacks since 1912, a vital ingredient in instigating that state's vibrant basketball tradition. The Missouri Valley Interscholastic Athletic Association was formed in 1918, enabling six schools to compete on a regular basis. Basketball's growth in West Virginia was chaotic due to conflicting rules used around the state and because most of its gyms were sub-standard.

In an effort to address these racial roadblocks fourteen schools formed the West Virginia Athletic Union in 1924, inaugurating the first Black statewide athletic association in the South. The farther South a state was, the slower the introduction of Black statewide schoolboy organizations. Mississippi didn't have one until 1940. It took Arkansas until 1942; last in line, as it would be in so many areas related to racial progress, was Alabama, which didn't have a Black state-sanctioned program until 1948.

So Williams's vision that basketball could help spark overall Black athletic progress proved correct. As Black high school basketball historian Charles Thompson observed, "It was the game of basketball that served as the catalyst for the growth and development of many Black high school athletic associations, for a number of these organizations were founded in conjunction with efforts to establish state tournaments. The tournaments were not only a means of bringing all concerned parties together, but they also generated funds necessary for the maintenance of the state association. By 1930 the states of Illinois, Indiana, Missouri, Kansas, West Virginia, Virginia, North Carolina and Florida had organized Black state high school athletic associations which were basically created to administer state basketball tournaments."

Unfortunately for Williams, distance and money would hamper his tournament. No teams from the Midwest, Southwest, or Deep South attended. The ten participants were comprised of three schools from Virginia, four from North Carolina, two from West Virginia, and the tournament favorite, Armstrong Technical High of Washington, D.C., which, not coincidentally, was one of the first Black schools in the country with an indoor gym. Due to scheduling and financial problems all games had to be conducted in two days. So Williams made it a double-elimination affair, with sixteen teams playing the first day and some teams being forced to play three times in one day. It didn't bother Armstrong, which won the title by besting Douglas High of Huntington, West Virginia. In the NIBT's second year, 1931, Armstrong again beat Douglas, this time, 34-23.

Nineteen thirty-one was a key year for Williams's pet project. Two Midwestern schools that would be crucial incubators of Black basketball style made the NIBT field in this year the most impressive to date: Chicago city champ Wendell Phillips and Gary, Indiana's top school, Roosevelt High. They brought the tournament total to fourteen teams and gave it a more national profile. In the final, Phillips crushed Genoa of Bluefield, West Virginia, by twenty-five and, according to the Chicago *Defender,* were "a team of brilliant individuals, well groomed in the fundamentals of the game and in effective team coordination. They were man-to-man equal to any who played in this tournament and as a team they blended their personal abilities into unbeatable offensive play and discouraging defensive play."

Unluckily, flooding in the mid-Atlantic states forced cancellation of the 1932 tournament. Compounding Williams's problem were Hampton officials' complaints about the tournament's cost. The physical education director held on this time, but sentiment was building on campus for the NIBT to be discontinued at Hampton.

So 1933 marked the end of Hampton's sponsorship of the tournament but also the start of a remarkable era of dominance for one Black high school team. In the finals Gary's Roosevelt Panthers stomped the Henderson Institute of North Carolina, 37-6, a score that magnified the disparity between Black basketball competence in the Midwest and the South. Furthermore, from 1933 to 1942 clubs from Indiana, notably Roosevelt, would dominate Black high school competition no matter where games were held. This domination wasn't hurt one bit by the fact that in 1934, 1935, 1937, and 1938 the NIBA was held in Gary and run by Roosevelt's John Smith, a black coach, who saw this shift as a showcase both for his team and the increasingly Black city he represented.

STEELTOWN BALL

In its new home in 1934 the tournament now had a victory trophy, a printed program filled with sixty-eight pages of ads from local businesses, and a new site: Gary's 7,000-seat Municipal Auditorium. Gary's mayor, superintendent of schools, and two local papers all voiced support for Smith's efforts. Visiting teams stayed at Roosevelt High, which had cots supplied by one of the major local employers, U.S. Steel, and free movie passes were given to players and a victory ball was held following the final. Because of this immense local support, 1934 was a high point in tournament history. But no matter who ran it or how well, there was no question who was taking home the trophy: Roosevelt beat Louisville's Central High, 30-24.

This win and the high profile of the tournament made Smith the best-known Black schoolboy coach in the country, and he sought to consolidate his position by forming a Black schoolboy sports organization, the National Interscholastic Athletic Association (NIAA). Jake Pearson, sports editor of the Gary *American,* wrote of the NIAA in his "Scop-O-Sports" column March 22, 1934, "The purpose of this organization should be to maintain just claims for Negro schools in the athletics and allow various colored prep institutions of the country to battle for sectional, state and national fame annually."

In 1935 Roosevelt won its third straight title after overcoming Kelley-Miller High of Clarksburg, West Virginia, 21-19, before nearly 3,000 Gary residents. It should be noted that this was the fourth time in six years that a West Virginia school had made the finals. Though these schools lost each time, there is no question that Black ball in this border state was at a high level. The formation of a statewide association eleven years before had surely had a positive impact on Black athletics, even though West Virginia did not have as large a black population as Maryland or Virginia. Overall attendance for the 1935 event reached nearly 12,000. Despite these numbers the NIAA board voted to move the tournament to Roanoke, Virginia's Lucy Addison High School for 1936, in part because that city's chamber of commerce pledged enthusiastic support. More important, the move back South was an attempt by the NIAA to attract more schools from that region.

TUSKEGEE POWER

Down in Alabama a venture was beginning that would eventually derail Charles Williams's tournament yet ironically fulfill his original dream. Behind this new tournament was Cleve Abbott, who while attending South Dakota State in 1913 was one of the pioneering Blacks on a white college squad. After graduation Abbott was named Tuskegee Institute's athletic director, and he went on to become one of African-American sports' behind-the-scenes giants.

Even after Booker T. Washington's death, Tuskegee was a showcase school, the jewel of a pragmatic, sweat-oriented approach to education and Black excellence. Athletic competition, a way to train minds and instill values, fit right into the Tuskegee philosophy. In fact, the school's athletic outlook suggested a sepia-toned version of muscular Christianity. In 1926 Abbott was one of only four Black college-level tennis coaches in the country and personally supervised the building of fourteen courts, able to accommodate 1,000 viewers at Tuskegee. The American Tennis Association, a Black group composed of amateur club and college players, held its championship there in 1931, with Abbott serving as ATA head. Tuskegee was the nation's first Black college with a golf course—though it consisted of only five holes. Abbott had it expanded to nine and in 1938 held the first Black intercollegiate golf tournament. In 1927 Abbott began a track-and-field event, the Tuskegee Carnival, that was the first sponsored by a Black college; and, a rarity for any track event of that time, Black or white, it included women's competition. (None of the CIAA schools had varsity competition for women at that time.) Under Abbott's coaching Tuskegee also had a tremendous football program that won nine of ten SIAC titles from 1924 to 1933. So when Abbott proposed that a high school tournament be held at Tuskegee, he had the clout to make it work. And no one squawked when he asked each participating school to pay a nominal entrance fee and, in keeping with his interest in women's sports, included girls' teams in the event. Starting with twelve schools in 1935, by 1942 the SIB hosted forty-seven teams, a growth spurt aided by declining interest in the NIBA.

From 1937 to its end in 1942 the NIBA shifted from Roanoke, back to Gary, to Fayetteville, North Carolina, and then Durham, North Carolina, losing teams to Tuskegee and, in some cases, to integration. A sign of the changing times came in 1938, when Roosevelt—which had won six straight NIBA titles—finally lost to a West Virginia school, Garnet of Charleston, 20-14. It was Coach Smith's first loss in five years of tournament competition. In 1939 and 1940 Roosevelt returned to the NIBA, but by this time Abbott in Tuskegee was calling his tournament the National Invitational Basketball Tournament. When in 1941 Eleanor Roosevelt's on-campus speaking engagement coincided with the tournament and caused a respectful pause in all play, it confirmed for many the importance of having the event at Tuskegee. One of the humorous aspects of Tuskegee's 1941 tournament was that both finalist schools were from Oklahoma and each was named after Tuskegee's founder, Booker T. Washington: one was from Sand Springs, one from Seminole. Booker T. of Sand Springs beat Booker T. of Seminole 38-24, and featured a promising teenage guard named Marques Haynes.

The Tuskegee era of high school ball ended with World War II. Following the victory of yet another Oklahoma school named in honor of Booker T. Washington—this one from Tulsa—42-19, over Southern University High of Scotlandville, Louisiana, the Chicago *Defender* of March 27, 1942, ran the following press release: "The Annual National Interscholastic Basketball Tournament for boys and girls has been cancelled for the duration ... Gasoline and tire rationing as well as other factors in the connection with the war efforts were reasons given by Mr. Abbott for the cancellation."

RUNNING RENS

"It don't mean a thing if it ain't got that swing."
—Recorded by the Duke Ellington Orchestra, 1932

Harlem during the 1920s experienced an explosion of Black thought and expression dubbed "a Renaissance" by historians. Poets Countee Cullen and Langston Hughes, musician-author James Weldon Johnson, bandleader Duke Ellington, author-folklorist Zora Neale Hurston, and their peers—a remarkable collection of painters, sculptors, party givers, and philosophers—resided in upper Manhattan. Street-corner orators addressed passersby on Lenox Avenue, selling religions, schemes, and always themselves. Many talked, but few swayed audiences like the Jamaican-born orator Marcus Garvey. Influenced by Booker T. Washington's advocacy of Black self-sufficiency ownership, Garvey raised funds for a back-to-Africa movement by telling Harlem's teeming masses, "Up you mighty race, you can accomplish what you will." Under his leadership Garveyites published newspapers, held meetings, and even purchased ships for the back-to-Africa trip.

Though Garvey himself was deported in 1927, his Afrocentric vision wasn't easily suppressed. The Jamaica-based Rastafarian religion made Garvey a deity, and its focus on Africa inspired an interest that still endures in America. At his height Garvey was the most visible representative of the business-minded men who left their native Caribbean for New York and the Eastern Seaboard. From Jamaica, Trinidad, Barbados, and

Haiti they, like their celebrated European contemporaries, chased the American Dream through Ellis Island during the twenties. From the British and French colonies with a majority Black population, West Indians brought an aggressive entrepreneurial spark to America's cities and, in one special case, to Seventh Avenue between 133rd and 139th Streets in Harlem.

William Roche came from the island of Montserrat to Harlem, where he started Sares Realty Company. In 1922, Roche turned an empty lot into the Harlem Renaissance Casino, a two-story entertainment center, which in its spacious first-floor showroom presented first-run films, while upstairs there was a ballroom available for banquets, concerts, and, at the behest of another Caribbean immigrant, basketball games. That man, Robert L. "Bob" Douglas, is today considered the "Godfather of Black basketball" and a key entrepreneur in the growth of professional basketball. Among Douglas's many innovations were monthly contracts with his players, a custom-designed team bus, and tours in the South, which he began before the region was considered a significant market for the game.

In 1901 Douglas arrived in New York, seeking his fortune like so many immigrants. What the St. Kitts native found, initially, was a doorman's job at 84th Street and Columbus Avenue. For four dollars a week Douglas worked from eight to eight, getting thirty minutes for lunch, thirty for dinner, and the day off every third Thursday and every third Sunday. He lived on West 52nd Street in the San Juan Hill area, which then housed most Black Manhattanites.

It wasn't until his fourth year in America that Douglas encountered basketball. "Where I was working at the time, one of the boys took me to see a game on 59th Street where we had to walk up five flights of stairs to the gym," he told the Amsterdam *News*. "I thought it was the greatest thing in the world.

That's when I started with basketball. You couldn't keep me off the court after that." Apparently more enthusiastic than skillful—Douglas cited swimming as his best sport—he began concentrating his energy on organizing athletic activities. He slipped away from his doorman's job to start a Caribbean athletic club that competed in cricket and basketball. Later he played on a team called the Spartans, which played other Black clubs from St. Philip's Church, the Alphas Club, and the Salem Church, whose boxing program later nurtured the brilliant middleweight Sugar Ray Robinson.

In the fall of 1923 Douglas approached Roche about allowing games in the ballroom Sunday evenings. As an inducement Douglas told Roche he'd call the team the Renaissance, making them a constant advertisement for the building. Roche agreed. The Harlem Renaissance, soon known locally as the Rens, debuted on November 30 of that year, beating the Chicago Collegians, 28-22. As was typical of the era, games were played right on the ballroom's dance floor with two portable baskets set up—one right in front of the bandstand—and portable wooden chairs on either side. Under a chandelier beneath which big bands usually played, the Rens took set shots and tried not to scuff up the floor too much. Douglas's original Rens were Leon Monde, Hy Monte, Zack Anderson, Clarence "Fats" Jenkins, and Frank Forbes. Years later Forbes was named the New York State Boxing Commission's first Black judge, while the six-foot Jenkins was an athletic wonder who would play professionally into his forties.

Under the direction of Douglas and coach-road manager Eric Illidge the Rens won an amazing 2,318 and lost only 381 contests in their history by utilizing a very team-oriented approach. "There is less team play because the big bucks are in high scoring and you have a more individualized game," Douglas said in the 1970s about the Rens style versus the NBA style. "Years ago a man wouldn't dare try to take a ball up-court without passing to a fellow player. If a player had started that one-on-one stuff you see so much of today, I would have yanked him right away. We called that hogging the ball."

Ball movement was essential in that era because of this resistance to "hogging" and because in the twenties the standard basketball featured big fat laces that made fancy dribbling difficult. Defensively, the Rens utilized their quickness to deny cutters passing and drives to the hoop. "When we played you had to check your man," recalled Hall of Fame Ren star William "Pops" Gates. "Make him take two steps to get one. Nobody guards nobody now ... If you watch close, you'll see guys actually get out of the way when a man's driving to the basket. When we played you had to earn your grits."

Attending a pro contest in the twenties and thirties was as much a social event as an athletic one. A game consisted of three fifteen-minute periods. Guys and gals showed up to see the Rens stomp some worthy opponent and afterward would dance to the big-band music of a Count Basie or Jimmy Lunceford.

"We had to have a dance afterwards or nobody would come to the damn thing ... the Renaissance (Ballroom) was right across the street from the Red Rooster (nightclub)," Eyre Saitch, a Ren of the '30s, told Arthur Ashe rather ruefully. "If you didn't get there by 7 o'clock you didn't get in the damn door. The big game didn't start until 10 o'clock." "Many a fellow met his wife there," pioneering basketball promoter Eddie Gottlieb said of the ball game-dance presentations of the era. "And I guess many a fellow met somebody else's wife there, too!"

The Rens' rise coincided with profound changes in the game: the center jump after every basket was eliminated, and the basketball itself shrunk, as did its laces, which made dribbling easier. These changes made speed and leaping ability more important—factors that favored Douglas's all-Black squad. During their first years of existence the Rens only played in New York City, then they expanded to the rest of the state, the Northeast, and, by the late twenties, the South and Midwest. Integrated competition, as we've seen, wasn't prohibited in pro basketball, so it's not surprising that the Rens developed rivalries with two legendary white teams: the first was with the Original Celtics of New York, run by the city's first widely acclaimed basketball genius, future St. John's and Knicks coach Joe Lapchick. Their second rival was a team from the South Philadelphia Hebrew Association, whose owners included Eddie Gottlieb. Douglas, Lapchick, and Gottlieb supported and trusted each other. "We never had a telegram or written letter or anything as far as a guarantee," Gottlieb told *Black Sports*. "Everything was done over the phone and never any problems. I have been associated with basketball for over fifty years and I have never found a better businessman than Bob. My various teams have locked horns with the Rens over seventy times and I can tell you we lost more than we won; but those good pay days sometimes take the hurt out of losing, and that's what we had when we played Bob's team."

Once in the twenties, while playing a local team in Louisville, the Rens were surprised to see the Original Celtics in the stands. Douglas remembered, "Joe Lapchick, who knew our center Tarzan Cooper, ran out on the court and embraced Cooper because he was so glad to see him. There was a silence on the court. This was Jim Crow country, and the races were strictly separated. The Celtics were put out of their hotel and a riot was narrowly averted. Lapchick was a fine man. Once when we played the Celtics, they offered to pay my coach Eric Illidge with a check. Lapchick said, 'No sir, pay him in cash.' That's the kind of man Joe Lapchick was."

The Rens prospered in the twenties, but it was in the thirties that Douglas's team created its legend with a squad composed of some of the best players found anywhere between world wars. The Rens' hub during this golden age was Wee Willie Smith, a strong, aggressive 6´5˝ center from Cleveland recruited by Douglas after he played against them for Cleveland's Slaughter Brothers team. In November 1932 Smith relocated to New York, where his defense and rebounding catalyzed the 1932–1933 team to eighty-eight straight wins. Original Ren Fats Jenkins remained, joining forces with James Pappy Ricks, Eyre Saitch, Bill Yancey, Johnny Holt, and future Hall of Famer Charles "Tarzan" Cooper. From 1932 to 1936, this edition had a 473-49 record and was so imposing that teams considered beating the Rens a career highlight. In 1988 SPHA's center Joel "Shikey" Gotthoffer still fondly remembered defeating the Rens fifty-three years earlier in New York by winning a tap over Cooper in the game's waning seconds. "There were plenty of brawls in that game," Gotthoffer told *Philly Sports,* "but we made up afterwards."

As rough as the Rens were on court, their Black manager was equally tough-minded on and off the court. When he was on the road Illidge carried a tabulator to count the gate and a gun to make sure he took home what he counted. Douglas stipulated that the Rens would never take the floor until Illidge had the Rens' money in his hand. He used that same savvy to give his team a boost off the court, when he purchased a customized bus they called the Blue Goose (perhaps a jokey reference to Howard Hughes airplane, the *Spruce Goose.*) In the thirties a private bus with reclining seats capable of carrying food was a major luxury for any team, white or Black. It meant the members rested better on the road and, as often as humanly possible, could avoid the indignities that confronted any group of Blacks traveling around America. Duke Ellington employed a similar strategy during one long Southern tour;

his band traveled in two specially outfitted Pullman cars.

In fact, it was Southern prejudice that brought the Rens a key player who would one day enter the Hall of Fame with Cooper. William "Pops" Gates was a New York schoolboy star who learned the game at the Harlem YMCA on 135th Street, just two blocks down from the Seventh Avenue Renaissance. He got his nickname not for basketball wisdom but by impressing older men he played stickball with in the streets. At East Harlem's Benjamin Franklin High, Gates first displayed the devastating two-hand set shot that led the school to the public high school title. Upon graduation from Franklin, Gates and many of his Franklin teammates decided to go to a college together as a unit just as, for example, the Wendell Phillips High team of 1935 moved from Chicago to New Orleans' Xavier. "We saw that most of the Negro ballplayers in the New York area were not offered scholarships to go to various colleges in this area," says Gates, so he and his friends chose Clark College in Atlanta. But Gates, unable to adjust to a more overtly racist Southern environment, headed home after only a few months.

Once back in New York Gates hooked up with the Harlem Yankees, a semipro club that practiced against the Rens. Quick to spot talent, Douglas gave Gates a tryout, which he passed easily, and then offered him $145 a month, plus $3 a day in meal money on the road. Once Gates agreed Douglas gave a small speech: "We travel throughout the country. We are respected by all, black and white, and we want you to carry yourself as a gentleman at all times."

"Pops had a lot of ability," Douglas said years later. "But he was hotheaded. Didn't take nothing from nobody. Not even referees ... Nobody was better cutting to the basket and nothing could stop him. He could shift and he was strong as the dickens." Playing backcourt at what we today call shooting guard,

Gates added scoring punch to a veteran squad that included Cooper, Jenkins, Smith, and Saitch. Along with Gates, Douglas recruited Johnny Isaacs, who "had more natural ability than any man to have ever played for me," Douglas once noted. According to Gates this lineup played approximately 140 games his first season with them, losing only eighteen.

During the thirties Douglas felt the Rens were the best team in America, but it wasn't until a professional tournament was organized in Chicago that he could prove it. Playing in Chicago Stadium—currently Michael Jordan's home court—the Rens breezed through a field of eight teams to win the "world champion" title March 28, 1939, against the all-white Oshkosh (Wisconsin) All-Stars, 34-25. The title game was memorable for its fierce contact—both Cooper and Smith fouled out—and Gates's uncanny two-hand set shots. Joe E. Williams, writing in the New York *Evening Telegram,* said, "They are the champions of professional basketball in the whole world. It is time we dropped the 'colored' champions title."

The Rens' story testifies to two ideas. First, an African-American could run a successful athletic organization, handling both the game's financial and on-court aspects; second, it made clear a Black professional basketball operation could survive without exploiting white racism by demanding its players clown for white entertainment. An irony of the organizing by men like Charles Williams, John Smith, Cleve Abbott, and Bob Douglas is that they nurtured an audience and developed players that helped inspire one of the most popular (and stereotypical) entertainment entities in U.S. history, one whose prominence would overshadow the more noble efforts of these African-Americans.

SCARCE QUARTERS IN THE

MAGIC CIRCLE

"How in God's name can you do that?"

"I needed a quarter and I got it," he said, soberly, proudly.

"But a quarter can't pay you for what he did to you," I said.

"Listen, nigger," he said to me, "my ass is tough and quarters is scarce."

—RICHARD WRIGHT,
Black Boy, 1945

T|he Harlem Globetrotters' story perfectly captures the hypocrisy and brilliance that are emblematic of America's tortured history of race relations. The financial and cultural promotion (and exploitation) of African-American artistry, a staple of U.S. (and European) business, is one key element in the Globetrotters' story. So is the formal inventiveness of Blacks in taking Naismith's game and laying the groundwork for the kind of athletic aesthetic that would come to dominate the game after World War II. In the nineties the Trotters are merely inconsequential, even embarrassing showmen; once they were arguably the most talent-laden, finest basketball organization in the country. From World War I to the late fifties the Trotters had first pick of every Black player who wanted to make a career of roundball. If you were a Black kid with b-ball talent, from the Roaring Twenties until the era of the student sit-ins, the Trotters were basically your only shot at making money playing. One team. Twelve spots on the main squad. All sought by a nation of gifted, excluded men. That desire drove some to greatness, making them not merely "legends of the game" but artists who reshaped the sport to their taste. But by virtue of the man who owned them and the way comedy was used to reinforce prejudice, the Trotters were a definitive example of white paternalism and Black male submission. The Trotters represent innovative Black basketball and the compromise of dignity to acquire a few scarce quarters.

The Trotter tale begins at Chicago's Wendell Phillips High, which had outstanding basketball teams in the twenties and thirties (as we know from its success in the Black high school tournaments). At that time schoolboy sports in Chicago weren't divided into varsity and junior varsity but lightweight (freshman, sophomore) and heavyweight (junior and senior). The heavyweight team made the city title game in 1924, losing to the integrated Lane Tech, whose high scorer was an African-American named William Watson. After making the finals in 1926 Phillips's lightweight team was even more successful winning the 1928 Chicago title in its classification over Harrison, 23-10, and becoming the first champs from an all-Black school in Windy City history.

From these Phillips squads came the nucleus of the semipro Savoy Big Five in 1926. In a team photo from that year five of the eight players were from Phillips, including four ex-heavyweight team members—forward Tommy Brookins, guards Lester Johnson and Walter "Toots" Wright, center Randolph Ramsey. The center was a lightweight alumnus, Inman Jackson. Lane's Black star, Watson, had befriended his championship opponents and was a Big Five member as well. The team, run by a Black ex-football star named Dick Hudson, played on Sundays at Chicago's Savoy Ballroom for twenty-five dollars a game. The Chicago Bears, a team owned by future pro football legend George "Papa Bear" Halas, were an early opponent. Games, as was typical of the time, were scheduled in conjunction with shows by performers like bandleader Cab Calloway and one-legged dancer Peg Leg Bates.

At this point the evolution of the Savoy Big Five into the Harlem Globetrotters is clouded by conflicting stories. There is the official history and a recently revealed revisionist version of the Trotters' roots. The less charitable version is based on the recollections of ex-Phillips player Tommy Brookins, who claims the Savoy Big Five first changed its name to Tommy Brookins' Globetrotters and then to the Original Chicago Globetrotters. He cites Hudson as the man who brought Abe Saperstein into the picture. Hudson felt a white man could more readily obtain bookings in Wisconsin and Minnesota than he could. The deal, according to Brookins, is that the twenty-six-year-old Saperstein promised to seek out competition and book ten games in exchange for $100 and a 10 percent booking fee. It was at this time that a dispute over rental fees for the Savoy between Hudson and Savoy owner I. J. Fagan forced the team to move games over to the 8th Regiment Armory, where they played against Black college teams from Clark, Morgan State, and Wilberforce, as well as Black club squads, such as the Cleveland Elks.

Saperstein got the Chicago Trotters those ten games in the winter of 1926, but that wasn't all he used his $100 to arrange. Unknown to most of the Savoy Big Five or Hudson, Saperstein booked more than ten games. In fact, he committed them to so many contests that he decided to organize another team, which he labeled the Harlem Globetrotters, to fulfill these obligations. It became clear to Brookins and company that Saperstein's color gave him a huge advantage in expanding the business. Within a few months of Saperstein's involvement, the Chicago Trotters disbanded and three of the players, Lester Johnson, Inman Jackson, and Randolph Ramsey, had signed with Saperstein.

Not surprisingly, the "official" story makes Saperstein look both smart and benevolent. The story goes, in the Trotters' official video history, that in December 1926, Abe Saperstein was made coach of the all-Black team. Though only five-foot-three, Saperstein was said to be a pretty good high school point guard. Born in London around 1900, Saperstein moved with his family to Chicago in 1908, and by the early twenties he was hanging around the city's Black South Side when the "coaching" offer was received. All agree it was Saperstein who thought of calling his team the Harlem Globetrotters, using the Harlem tag to capitalize on that neighborhood's identification with colored style and put him in direct competition with the then better known Rens. Saperstein packed his original team members (Walter "Toots" Wright, Byron "Fat" Long, Willis "Kid" Oliver, Al "Runt" Pullins, Andy Washington) in his Model T Ford around the Midwest, where the players, due to segregation, often slept in the car. It's not clear whether Saperstein slept with them. In the early days the Trotters were guaranteed twenty-five dollars and half the gate. Later in the twenties they received seventy-five dollars per game, the players earning ten dollars apiece and Abe twenty dollars, with five dollars left over to cover expenses and promotion.

By all accounts Saperstein was a very complicated man. The motivations and methods of Saperstein's Trotter enterprise may be disputed, but the imagination and energy he used to construct it into an empire is unassailable. He was a smart man.

He had, if not a racist, then a profoundly paternalistic, conde-scending view of African-Americans. He bristled at being called prejudiced, yet he referred to his employees as "chil-dren." He had the vision to see the game's international appeal—in 1950 and 1951 he sent the Trotters on a ground-breaking first American pro basketball tour of Europe, North Africa, and South America. The man also had the blind ego to instruct his players in the nuances of basketball style, demon-strating how to protect the ball in the pivot but not noticing the contemptuous smirks he mistook for good humor.

Saperstein should be viewed not just as an individual busi-nessman but as part of a generation of entrepreneurs who built enduring institutions through entertainment; many of them were, not incidentally, Jewish. In their end run around institu-tionalized anti-Semitism, which kept them off a lot of businesses' main streets, a great many Jews found themselves operating in areas with largely Black populations. They peddled groceries, furniture, shoes, jewelry and owned real estate. The entertain-ment industry, a sometimes disreputable world of quick wits, backslapping, and imaginative hucksterism, embraced Jews and granted them great power.

In his insightful history of Jews in the film industry, *An Empire of Their Own,* Neal Gabler makes observations about Hollywood that paralleled the experiences of the movers and shakers in Black sports: "There were no social barriers in a busi-ness as new and faintly disreputable as the movies were in the early years of this century. There were none of the impediments imposed by loftier professions and more firmly entrenched businesses to keep Jews and other undesirables out ... having come primarily from fashion and retail, they understood public taste and were masters at gauging market swings, at merchan-dising, at pirating away customers and beating the competi-tion. For another, as immigrants themselves, they had a peculiar sensitivity to the dreams and aspirations of other immigrants and working class families."

Combine the Jewish involvement in show biz with the proximity of their stores to Black consumers and you find in Abe Saperstein, the rich, adventurous, basketball equivalent of Hollywood's Louis B. Mayer and Samuel Goldwyn, men who made movies that affirmed America's most wholesome, clean-cut view of itself. Saperstein's role in basketball also paralleled that of two South Side Chicago furniture salesmen turned record makers, Phil and Leonard Chess, who in the fifties, by recording Chuck Berry, Bo Diddley, Muddy Waters, and others, made available a dynamic form of African-American music, yet never fully compensated its creators for the revenue they generated.

For Saperstein and his Philadelphia-based friend Eddie Gottlieb the key to opportunity was Black sports. Aside from their basketball business, the duo were also the key agents for booking Negro League teams into major-league ball parks (the Yankees made $100,000 a year from such rentals). For these services Saperstein and Gottlieb demanded, and got, 40 percent of the gross receipts for the games—no small cut.

Black sports, in the cases of Negro Baseball Leagues and the Trotters, were easy for Jews to enter because most WASP businessmen wanted nothing to do with managing any Black athlete beyond the occasional boxer. And while Bob Douglas and his Rens were formidable on-court competition, the team was still Black-run, which made it vulnerable not simply to fan abuse but to institutional racism—they couldn't get booked in certain halls; they were often offered less money for engagements than a white-owned club would be. Quite simply, it was easier for a little, roly-poly Jewish man to do business in this country than an aggressive West Indian. Saperstein, knowing both the Rens' success and their racial roadblocks, saw an opening and walked through it.

THE TROTTER WAY

How Blacks who knew Saperstein viewed him says as much about them as it does about the Trotter founder. In 1947, one-year-old Chicago-based *Ebony* magazine, the vehicle of enrichment for a bright, Black businessman named John Johnson, praised Saperstein for "scurrying around the country digging up obscure Negro athletes and building them into top bracket stars" and promoting match races that pitted Jesse Owens against horses, heavyweight champion Joe Louis, and baseball speedster George Case. *Ebony*'s description was the kind of fawning adulation that saw almost any white use of Black talent, no matter how condescending, as a step toward integration. Meadowlark Lemon, who would become one of the Trotters' most famous clowns, felt affection and resentment toward Saperstein, usually at the same time. Lemon, who twice attempted to form his own barnstorming teams, admired Saperstein's ability to keep the Trotters fully employed and paid on time. At the same time he admits, "We never knew what was going on with the finances. There were a lot of people around the team making more money than the ball players ever were." Saperstein was at the top of that list. Wilt Chamberlain, a political conservative with a survival-of-the-fittest business philosophy, thought Saperstein a "dear friend" and called his time with him in 1958 and 1959 the "most fun of his career." Appropriately, perhaps, his archrival Bill Russell disliked Saperstein, noting in his first autobiography, *Go Up for Glory,* that the Trotter chief told the press he'd pay Russell $50,000 to go to the Olympics and then join his fiefdom. But when they met, Saperstein spoke to Russell only of the "social advantages" of being a Trotter, while he talked business with University of San Francisco coach Phil Woolpert. Russell, a man with pride and intellect, decided, "If I'm not smart enough to talk to, then I'm too smart to play for him."

It was Saperstein's instincts for the prejudices of the white working class, in many regions largely immigrants, and their stereotypical attitudes toward Blacks that led him to make comedy the centerpiece of the Trotters, turning the team from players into performers. In the official Trotter video history narrator Lou Gossett says the genesis of Trotter clowning was a winter game in Iowa. The gym was ice-cold, so the locals circled the court with several potbellied stoves. Inadvertently, Willis "Kid" Oliver leaned his backside on one and his shorts caught fire. Oliver's butt burn sent him screaming across the court, stopping play and making the predominantly white audience guffaw.

Clowning, according to Trotter lore, subsequently became an integral part of Trotterdom as a way to rest tired players. As one player dribbled around befuddled opponents, the others relaxed and even slid over to the bench for a drink. In addition, because the Trotters were so much better than the competition the clowning kept scores down and fan interest in games up. In his 1987 autobiography Meadowlark Lemon says the ball-handling technique became institutionalized during a game the Trotters were up, 112-5. All of this makes sense and is, no doubt, technically factually true.

But all official discussions of Trotter jokes or "reams," as the players called them, are viewed within the narrow confines of Trotter games. We have to remember that Saperstein's Trotters played and were hired in a world where the lynching of Black males for "reckless eyeballing" of white women was still commonplace in the South and more prevalent in the North than is generally acknowledged. The idea of five Black men rolling into a Midwestern town, kicking ass, and getting paid could not have been the easiest sell ever (nor, as the NBA found in the seventies, would it ever be). Clowning Black men have always been more popular in this country than stern no-nonsense brothers. It's no accident that the Trotters' antics found favor with white fans at a time America's favorite Black movie star was Lincoln Theodore Monroe Andrew Perry, also known as Stepin Fetchit. This Florida-born actor embodied every vicious stereotype of Black men—cowardly, comic, and lazy with a capital L. Not coincidentally, his performances were brilliant. As a comic actor Perry's timing, intonation, and the physicality of his character were truly superb. When you watched Fetchit move on-screen, you suddenly felt lazy yourself. As Joseph Boskin wrote in *Sambo,* his study of racist Black comic images, "[he was] the most prominent practitioner of the Black fool in films. It is more than an act; it becomes an art form." Fetchit, along with Willie Best, Mantan Moreland, Eddie "Rochester" Anderson, and Hollywood's other sambos, coons, and fools, was clearly an inspiration for Saperstein's cooning brand of ball, though the owner was smart enough never to say so.

It's impossible today not to view the way the Trotters adopted comedy as good business and an affirmation, no matter how skillfully done, of racist attitudes toward Black males. And the Trotters were not alone. Louis Armstrong, the greatest jazz innovator of the pre–World War I period, often wore the coon's mask in films and lived with this duality of artistry overlaid with crap. As a national star during this era—he regularly appeared at Chicago's Savoy in the late twenties—Armstrong made an eloquent defense of musical clowning, one that could also be applied to the Trotters: "The best band in the world is the clown's band in the circus. You gotta be a good musician to hit a bad note at the right time." Amplifying Armstrong's view, Wilt Chamberlain wrote in his autobiography: "They [the Trotters] had—and have—highly developed skill for comedy, for making people laugh at them. It's the same skill that guys like Jerry Lewis, Charlie Chaplin and Jackie Gleason have.

They're clowns, actors playing a role Jews would call the 'shlemiel' or a 'shlimazl.'" Without the Trotters' existence, Wilt argues, many players might have "become janitors or gone on welfare." Whether you agree or disagree with Wilt's view, Saperstein's commercial judgment was sound. Playing against the primarily white semipro clubs around the country, the Trotters, much like many Black entertainers and Negro League baseball teams, utilized comedy laced with racial stereotypes to please white fans and spread their fame. In 1940, the Trotters defeated the Harlem Rens, taking the world championship title from the first great all-Black team to start a decade of clowning professional b-ball supremacy.

During the forties the Trotters set up housekeeping at the Evans Hotel, a seven-story Black-owned establishment at Evans and 61st Street on the South Side. Players received a room, a bath shared with an adjoining room, a telephone, a dresser, but no radio. During the tryout periods no one beefed because the players' only concerns were basketball and sleep. Tryouts consisted of two separate four-hour practices with over 100 prospects bidding for spots on the "A" or Eastern Unit, the secondary Western or Southern units, or, barring that, a place on one of the traveling opposition outfits. "I saw all those young guys flying, and I mean flying, through the air, slam dunking, rebounding, dribbling, shooting long jump shots, doing everything spectacular," wrote Meadowlark of his first camp. "It looked like a waterfall of balls going through baskets."

Survivors were instructed in "the Trotter way," a style that had developed two important structural quirks. As in basketball strategy since the center jump era, the pivot man was key. Only in Trotter ball he didn't simply rebound and score. The center position, a spot held by Inman Jackson for fourteen years, was designated court jester. From a position in the high post area near the top of the key the center told jokes, made funny faces and sounds, and starred in most of the reams, from shifting suddenly into baseball to throwing water on the referees. Opposing players were allowed to guard the Trotters closely except during the breaks for the Trotters' more elaborate skits. As part of the ground rules for playing then, the Trotters were also allowed uncontested passes into the post area since most of their reams were designed around the center position.

Another Trotter signature was their lack of traditional guards as such. Both guards and the small forward all had ball-handling responsibilities. With the center at the high post and the other big man in one corner, the three other players went into a weave of dribbles, behind-the-back passes, and clever ball exchanges. This flash-and-dash, done with more rapidity than almost any other team of the day, pro or college, was showcased in the Magic Circle routine before every game.

GOOSE AND MARQUES

The contrast between Trotter clowning and innovation, innovations that have impact on the game in the nineties, is illustrated by the careers of the two most important players in Trotter history: Reece "Goose" Tatum, the classic clown center, and Marques Haynes, the most influential ball handler in this game's first 100 years. Goose joined the Trotters in 1942 and, with a colorful nickname (gained as a football receiver), a seventy-four-inch reach, and an elastic face, he quickly won the lead clown gig. He had an uncanny, looping hook that he could shoot with magical accuracy from over twenty feet out. That he often did this flat-footed, wearing an undersized jacket, and cackling at the top of his lungs is testimony to his blend of comedy and talent. Unlike his successor, Meadowlark Lemon, whose on-court obsequiousness and off-court careerism made you see the gears turning, Tatum had an easy charm that made his more outrageous reams less objectionable than they probably should have been.

Tatum, more often than any other player, epitomized the childlike qualities that made even intolerant whites comfortable with the Trotters. If any other forties figure paralleled this humorous, graceful man in appeal it was the dancer Bill "Bojangles" Robinson, who, like the Trotter, funneled his extraordinary physical gifts into mass entertainment for whites yet remarkably, considering the time, avoided cooning. Tatum was a fine player and the comic heart of the team. From the long-range hook to the eatable ball to the fake free throws, Tatum's reams remain Trotter staples.

But Marques Haynes was the Saperstein employee who catalyzed Black interest in the game. From 1946 to 1953, with the Trotters and later with his own barnstorming teams, the Oklahoma-bred guard elevated dribbling into a spellbinding sleight of hand a decade before the celebrated Bob Cousy.

Talk to serious ballplayers about the Trotters' impact on their game and Haynes is the name that recurs. His Trotter gift was the one with practical applications; his gift was the one that allowed him to frustrate, dominate, and intimidate; his gift was a manifestation of African-American improvisation. In other words, Haynes was the first player who, based on eyewitness testimony, embodied the modern black athletic aesthetic.

Walt Hazzard, great Philadelphia high school guard, star of UCLA's 1963 NCAA champions, one-time NBA all-star, and former UCLA head coach, remembers the first time he saw Haynes: "It was at Convention Hall in Atlantic City. On the court were Sweetwater Clifton, Goose Tatum, and Marques Haynes. Up until then I had never seen anybody dribble the ball like that before. He'd be on the floor, on one knee and people couldn't take the ball from him ... I was seven or eight years old, and Marques had an immediate impact on me."

Earvin Johnson, star of Michigan State's 1979 NCAA champs, ten-time NBA all-star, and three-time Most Valuable Player, remembers the first time he saw Haynes: "Marques Haynes was my hero when it came to dribbling; he would get lower and lower until he was lying on the floor, still dribbling the basketball ... Marques never looked at the ball; he always kept it away because every time the defender made a motion one way or the other, Marques would be able to evade him just as quick." That Hazzard and Johnson, representing two different generations, both cite Haynes as, if you will, their artistic inspiration shows how his legacy endures. Haynes's flamboyance, a product of the forties, is echoed in the best player of the eighties and nineties much as the bebop innovations of a post–World War II player in another game, Charlie "Bird" Parker, still resonate in contemporary jazz.

Haynes's facility and background strengthen the strong argument that the romantic notion of the Eastern street player as the epitome of basketball style is simply big-city chauvinism. Time and again we'll see that the most enduring African-American contributions to the game came from players not reared on Northeastern asphalt but the Midwest, West, and, in the eighties, even the South.

Haynes is a pure product of the segregated Black basketball world. Growing up in Sand Springs, Oklahoma, he picked up the game from his brother Wendell, himself reputedly a fancy dribbler and passer. Considering Magic Johnson's reverence for Haynes, it's an amazing coincidence that Haynes's family called their flashy brand of ball "show time" back in the thirties just as the Johnson's Lakers called their style in the eighties. Haynes led his team, Booker T. Washington High, into the finals of the Black high school tournament in 1941. From 1942 to 1946, he attended Langston University in Langston, Oklahoma, where, under coach Zip Gayles, Haynes says he learned to wed his flamboyance to fundamentals. Langston was in the Southwestern Conference, so he competed against Texas schools, Wiley, Sam Houston, and Texas College; Southern, Xavier, and Grambling in Louisiana; and Arkansas State. With Haynes handling the ball Langston won 112 of 115 games during his four years.

At Langston he majored in education, figuring, quite correctly, that for a 1940s Black college grad teaching at a segregated public school was a great gig. The direction of Haynes's life shifted when, at a 1946 contest in Oklahoma City, Langston beat the Trotters, 74-70. Haynes and company so impressed their celebrated competition that he and several teammates were offered spots in the Trotter organization. Instead of jumping at the opportunity to turn pro—as most college kids do today—Haynes decided to stay in school and receive his diploma.

That summer Haynes attended a Kansas City Monarchs game and ran into Ted Strong, a multitalented athlete who played with the Trotters and the Monarchs. Strong remembered Haynes and urged him to contact Trotter management. Haynes wrote Saperstein and was offered a tryout. Along with two other former Langston teammates Haynes traveled to Chicago. He performed well and was placed with the Kansas City Stars, one of the Trotters' traveling opponents and a de facto farm team. Jesse Owens, who after his 1936 Olympic triumph spent years capitalizing on his prominence through various promotions, traveled with the Stars as an announcer, gave track demonstrations, and signed autographs. Haynes stayed with the Stars only three months. "During that time, I created somewhat of an uproar with my dribbling and ball handling," he told Art Rust, Jr., modestly. "The Globetrotters did not have a fancy type of ball handler and passer that I was."

Looking at tapes of Haynes in the early fifties in games

against college all-stars I'm struck by the fact that by 1980s standards he seems somewhat limited in skills. First of all, he's overwhelmingly right-handed. Haynes only used his left as a change of pace or escape hatch when cornered by defenders. Haynes's between-the-legs and behind-the-back moves aren't that quick to contemporary eyes. You don't realize how radical Haynes's approach is until you study his opponents, players whose robotic ball fakes and stiff chest passes look ancient. In the context of his time Haynes's moves, keying the Trotters' flowing weave, were shocking.

Most impressive was the way Haynes used his low center of gravity as a weapon. He'd start his dribble waist-high and then get as low as six inches from the ground, making the ball virtually impossible to steal. Down on one knee, he'd spin like helicopter blades, delighting viewers and frustrating opponents. The teenaged Magic Johnson was so impressed by this ability he developed a "six-inch drill" during which he lay down on his side and dribbled low à la Haynes to sharpen his ball control. Others have taken Haynes's techniques further, but he was the catalyst who popularized show-time dribbling as a manifestation of Black style.

In business Haynes proved equally progressive. In 1953, Haynes found out Saperstein was renegotiating with longtime pal Eddie Gottlieb to sell him to the NBA's Philadelphia 76ers. Haynes blocked the deal and then asked for a higher salary, which Saperstein refused. So he split to form the Harlem Magicians in Elk City, Oklahoma. The first two years were a struggle, as large arena owners were reluctant to book the Magicians, no doubt in large part to Saperstein pressure. Then, in 1955, Tatum left the Trotters to join Haynes as full partner, pumping new excitement into the Magicians and cutting into the Trotters' action, though Saperstein found a replacement in Haynes clone Pablo Robertson.

The exit of both Haynes and Tatum in the midfifties ended the Trotters' years as a significant force in American basketball. Other fine players would wear the Trotter uniform—some, like Wilt Chamberlain and Connie Hawkins, are of major historic import. But the world was changing, and Saperstein's domination of Black ball ebbed with every passing year. He'd helped popularize sport as entertainment, using Blacks' ability to entertain to spread basketball around the world. In that sense Saperstein was a pioneering marketeer of the game and in some aspects anticipated the NBA's successful selling job of the eighties. Of course, the gap between Trotters' jokey reams and today's assertive style are as wide as that which separates the comedy of Stepin Fetchit from Eddie Murphy. The Trotters' visibility in the forties obscured for many the fact that African-Americans did more in basketball than grin, dribble, and whistle "Sweet Georgia Brown." Black basketball was evolving its own personality, one that differed in speed from white ball and in intensity from the Trotters. With the Trotters, Haynes's hands articulated a bluesy, idiosyncratic attitude, but he was not alone in speaking the new improvisational body language.

IN TRANSITION

Before he made history with the Brooklyn Dodgers and while he was an all-American halfback at UCLA, Jackie Robinson found time for basketball. As a member of the Bruins' basketball squad in 1939, the future basketball great set a Pacific Coast Conference scoring record with 148 points in twelve games. The next year, while also excelling at track, Robinson again led the PCC in scoring, with 133 points. Maybe in the nineties someone as determined as Robinson might, like Bo Jackson, play a number of professional sports. At the very least he would have been able to pit the basketball, football, and baseball leagues against each other in the pursuit of million-dollar contracts. But in the 1940s this athletically gifted, academically able Black man knew, even before he broke the baseball color line, in which sport there was definitely little future. Today it's unimaginable that a UCLA basketball star wouldn't consider a career in the pros. But can you imagine the intensely competitive Jackie Robinson as a clowning Globetrotter? In the 1940s that was still his only significant option. But basketball, like America itself, was about to enter a period of profound change.

Entering 1940, approximately fifty years after its beginnings in Springfield, basketball had outgrown its image as "football on wood" and had become a faster, more extroverted sport than Naismith or any of its early devotees could have envisioned. This new tempo was sparked in part by the game's ever changing rules. During World War II the goaltending rule was altered to prevent the blocking of shots on the way down, an attempt to neutralize the height advantages of big players—in particular, De Paul University center George Mikan, who, at 6′10″, was considered a giant at that time. In addition, Mikan's domination of college ball (and later the pros) instigated the widening of the foul lane from six to twelve feet. Equally important was that the number of fouls allowed per player rose from four to five, which kept star players on court longer. Mikan wasn't the only white player to have such a crucial impact.

From out West, Stanford's Hank Luisetti caused a sensation in 1936 simply by jumping when he shot the ball. By contemporary standards Luisetti was no skywalker—he elevated maybe a foot above the floor. Yet that rejection of the set shot was radical enough to confound defenders accustomed to guarding ground-based opponents. When Luisetti arrived at Madison Square Garden, palace of the Eastern game, where a style close to that of the early Celtics that emphasized passing and cutting in the half court was celebrated, he shocked Long Island University by scoring fifteen points in a 45–31 upset of a team that had won forty-three straight. Though traditionalists abhorred the jump shot (what we, in this more sophisticated time, call a "J") Luisetti started a revolution that eventually drove up scores.

While Luisetti's introduction of the jump shot is well documented, a slick-handling white guard from Harrisburg, Pennsylvania, named Robert Davies, made a significant, if underappreciated, contribution as well. Davies, who attended Seton Hall University in South Orange, New Jersey, and played from 1945 to 1955 with the Rochester Royals, followed Marques Haynes as the next figure strongly associated with the behind-the-back dribble. Certainly he was the first white to utilize it extensively. In Charles Salzberg's *From Set Shot to Slam Dunk* Davies provides a succinct survey of ball circa 1940s and the impact of Blacks on his style: "In the Midwest, which was considered just outside of New York, it was full-court basketball. In the East, they were bringing the ball down slowly, which made it half-court basketball. When I was a kid I couldn't afford to pay to see the high school team, so we would look through a crack in the door. The only thing I could see was the foul lane area and the basket on the other end of the court. I'd see these great Black players jump in the air, throw the ball, hit somebody with a pass or shoot the ball, and I guess that stuck in my mind."

Davies, like Luisetti, rebelled against Eastern conservatism and sought to play a more liberated game. A famous tale is that a behind-the-back move by Davies so shocked a Seton Hall priest that he suffered a heart attack. Even if it never happened, the story aptly conveys the violent reaction to innovation among traditionalists. There was a strong belief that such unorthodox moves unduly embarrassed opponents, so even if crowds loved it, the game's gatekeepers felt it was poor sportsmanship. This attitude, as much about aesthetics as race, was one reason serious basketball fans hated flamboyant playmakers.

Good sportsmanship was an essential part of the mainstream athletic philosophy preached in schools and YMCAs where the game was taught to white youths. African-Americans saw the world, much less basketball, differently. Flamboyance as fun, as self-expression, as a way of ridiculing the slow-witted or venal, was at the heart of a culture so growing in its potency that it would eventually force white America to pay attention. As African-American players slowly flowed into the basketball mainstream this conflict would get more pronounced.

NATIVE SONS

In 1940, 12,865,518 people, or approximately 10 percent of the U.S. population, were Black. And since the twenties the Black population had been fleeing toward big cities: Southern and Western centers such as Memphis, Atlanta, and Los Angeles and the Northern metropolises of New York, Philadelphia, Detroit, and Chicago. They came searching for better jobs, better housing, and freedom from Southern apartheid. The concentration of Blacks this created on Chicago's South Side, New York's Harlem, Los Angeles's Central Avenue, and elsewhere led to the creation of businesses to cater to their needs. Publisher John Johnson, for example, saw opportunity in these burgeoning neighborhoods and in the forties created *Ebony* and *Jet* magazines to service the teeming Black populations of the big cities with role models for success and understanding.

But too often African-Americans were confronted with new twists on old prejudices. Packed tightly in substandard housing and harassed by police, who, just as they had down South, defended the status quo, many residents exploded in violence. In *Native Son,* published in February 1940, Mississippi-born and Chicago-based writer Richard Wright made the first commercially successful literary attempt to depict the sorry conditions and agitated state in which the new urban Black existed. Wright was particularly concerned with alienated young men; he called his Black Everyman Bigger Thomas. While working at a South Side Boys Club Wright felt "for the first time that rich folk who were paying my wages did not really give a good god damn about Bigger, that their kindness was prompted at bottom by a selfish motive. They were paying me to distract Bigger with ping pong, checkers, swimming, marbles and baseball in order that he might not roam the streets and harm the valuable white property which adjoined the Black Belt."

While Wright's observation speaks to the particulars of his employment, it also serves as a critique of what happened when the tenets of muscular Christianity were applied to Black youth. From his viewpoint this philosophy was a Band-Aid on a brain tumor, a pathetic attempt to camouflage American racism. Wright's Bigger, however, was not successfully distracted by Boys Clubs or his chauffeur's job, and it is his unfulfilled dreams that eventually destroy him.

Wright's and Johnson's visions of life up North were certainly different, yet both were accurate, depending on family background, income, and life-style. The big cities up North could be a grand opportunity or a bitter trap, or both at the same time. African-Americans were in transition from a rural to an urban environment and in this time of change developed new languages to describe their evolving condition. In music this period saw the creation of the two key musical styles of the century's second half—bebop and rhythm & blues. Bebop advanced the art of improvisation by, in the manner of saxophonist Charlie Parker and trumpeter Dizzy Gillespie, making chords, not melodies, the point of departure for soloists. Instead of big-band dance rhythms its young players performed rapid, intense flurries of notes. Bebop was a virtuoso, self-consciously "arty" music that reflected the pretension and sophistication of city life.

Bebop's dance-floor counterpart, rhythm & blues, was a mutt music that fused elements of gospel, blues, and swing into a sound more urban than its church and country cousins but one not as harmonically rich as jazz. Small brass and reed sections replaced the large big-band sections, while thick boogie beats superseded swing dance rhythms. Technology, in the form of the electric guitar and bass, made R&B propulsive, and its vocalists embraced a wide range of approaches. Few American postwar musicians of any color created music of significance without referring to either R&B or bebop.

With these musical manifestations of big-city Black culture came new modes of behavior. Many Southern boys now wise to the concrete jungle started to move with a fluid, no-sweat attitude everybody called "cool." Cool came to define a certain sartorial elegance, smooth charm, and self-possession that in the hurly-burly of the city suggested a dude that controlled not only himself but his environment. Cool, wrote music critic Joe McEwen, "for one, meant you didn't have to answer to anyone. For two, it meant you had what it takes." Though later many whites, particularly musicians, would copy the attitude, cool was clearly an African-urban thing.

Bebop, rhythm & blues, and cool were complementary concepts that interacted with each other. The rhythm & blues band saxophonist often played bebop at after-hours clubs following his regular gig, and he always acted as cool as possible. Sometimes a neighborhood's Bigger Thomas was cool, hiding his hostility under a guise of distance, which made him both alluring and dangerous. It is in this context of creativity and anger that Black athletes began displaying a new approach to basketball.

"A distinctive 'Black' style of play developed that featured speed, uncommon jumping ability and innovative passing skills," Arthur Ashe wrote in *A Hard Road to Glory*. "Though this style was frequently at odds with white coaches' philosophies of the late '40's, it produced results and was extremely exciting to watch." African-American style would change basketball "from stationary strategy and deliberation [to one that] unleashed the individual player for improvisation and virtuosity," wrote Michael Novak in *The Joy of Sports*. "The music of the game was discovered to be jazz."

From 1940 through the mid-fifties basketball and the African-American influence on it grew. But just as Black aspirations were locked in a struggle with white racism, the desires and aesthetics of Blacks in Washington, D.C., Chicago, New York, and Nashville would constantly be confronted with road-blocks that, for the most part, they would surmount.

THE WASHINGTON BEARS

The short, active life of the Washington Bears is one of the forgotten stories of pro ball. In their brief existence the Bears were successful, though they never entirely escaped the chaotic conditions that stunted the growth of pro basketball prior to the NBA. On the court the D.C.-based squad fared well, but as one of the last nationally known all-Black pro teams its confrontations with racism, from businessmen, fans, and even gangsters, doomed them to obscurity. Hal Jackson, a graduate of D.C.'s Dunbar High and later a beloved deejay in Washington and New York and a music entrepreneur, was the catalyst for the club's formation. During the early forties Jackson was a jack-of-all-trades—he covered sports for the Baltimore *Afro-American* newspaper, ran a dump truck for WPA construction projects, tracked down venereal disease among Black soldiers for the Health Department, all while taking night courses at Howard University. Jackson, years later a founding partner of the country's largest Black-owned radio empire, was always on the lookout for ways to make a buck. Noting the strong support Black Washingtonians gave Negro League baseball and the fact that there was no white pro ball team in the nation's capital, Jackson decided to start a local all-Black basketball team.

Joe Turner, owner of a small, self-titled local boxing arena, let Jackson book games there on otherwise empty Sunday afternoons. He then wooed several ex-Rens (the team was then on a World War II–instigated hiatus), including player-coach Tarzan Cooper, Pops Gates, Johnny Isaacs, Zack Clayton and Puggy Bell, as well as the recently graduated Long Island University star Dolly King. During the week, most of the players worked for Grumman Aircraft, either in D.C. or New York, so they were only available on weekends.

Jackson had an arena and players. What he needed now was money. So, in the ongoing tradition of Black entertainment, Jackson sought and received aid from a local Jewish businessman. Abe Lichtman was the perfect funding source. He owned ten theaters catering to Blacks in D.C., including the city's answer to Harlem's Apollo, the Howard, so his interest in Black entertainment was deep. Lichtman put up money for the uniforms and advertised the Bears at his theaters in return for a healthy cut of all proceeds and his name being plastered on the back of their jerseys.

Under Cooper's guidance the Bears rounded into a powerhouse that went 66–0 in 1943. But despite that record, Jackson's club wasn't invited to the annual pro basketball championships in Chicago. This annual tournament, in existence since the 1920s, was the same event the Rens had captured in 1939 and the Trotters in 1940. In the absence of one stable national league this tournament was the only real way to test the relative strengths of the nation's many barnstorming teams. A good showing confirmed a team's quality and would generate more bookings for the next season. So the week before that year's tournament, Jackson took a train to the Windy City and, at the last minute, wangled the Bears an invitation. Arrangements were so hurried that the Bears arrived by train from D.C. at 10:00 A.M. and had to drive straight to the Chicago Stadium for a game. While their start was hectic it didn't deter them from defeating Sheboygan, Rochester, and others before moving into the finals versus Oshkosh of Wisconsin.

On game day Jackson received word that four white hoods were looking for him at his hotel. Later, at Chicago Stadium, they found him and offered him $20,000 to have the Bears throw the game. According to Jackson's unpublished memoirs, he refused and withheld word of the offer from his players until just before the final quarter. On clutch shooting by Gates and Clayton the Bears defeated Oshkosh by two. Still in uniform, the Bears sprinted out of Chicago Stadium, dived into eight waiting limos, and took off. Fearing reprisals, Jackson had contacted some "tough" friends of his own in Chicago to arrange rapid transportation out of the arena and up to Wisconsin, where the Bears lay low for a week. Once back in D.C. the Bears were honored with a Pennsylvania Avenue parade and a White House visit with Franklin Roosevelt.

The Bears, unfortunately, didn't last very long after their triumph. White teams weren't crazy about playing a team this good that performed without jokes. Bookings were slow, and when they did come white teams demanded exorbitant fees to take on the Black team. And to Jackson's dismay, contests opposing other Black clubs attracted no whites. Moreover, the war had driven up the price of gas, food, and lodging, and the increased cost of travel made all forms of entertainment difficult. Big bands, for example, began scaling down during and after the war because of the changing economy. Of all the barnstorming teams only the unserious Trotters emerged from the war still healthy.

Within two years the Washington Bears were dead. Jackson went on to a rich career in broadcasting, and the players, as was typical for Black pros then, scattered: some signed with the Trotters, some joined a reassembled postwar Rens team, others joined local semipro outfits.

While the Bears' reliance on Jewish backing was typical, organized crime's threatening presence at the championship game foreshadowed its coming involvement with basketball and Blacks. As African-Americans moved closer to the sporting mainstream, these athletes, most from poor backgrounds, became increasingly vulnerable to bribes from gamblers. In addition, the chaos of the championship game reflected pro ball's second-class sports citizenship in America. This lack of structure affected whites as much as Blacks because teams and leagues were perpetually unstable.

OPENING TIP

The organized professional leagues of the forties didn't pay well, had poor training and playing facilities, and initially were segregated. In 1946 there were a dozen leagues. A remarkable number were Pennsylvania-based, for instance, the Pennsylvania, the Philadelphia, the Western Pennsylvania, and the Eastern; others, like the Inter-State, the Metropolitian, and the Hudson, covered the Northeast and New England. The National Basketball League, started in 1937 and based out of the Midwest, was the soundest league of the era because of the robust Minneapolis Lakers and their dominating star, George Mikan. Yet Mikan's presence couldn't offset the fact that the NBL was composed of too many small cities like Sheboygan, Wisconsin; Waterloo, Iowa; and Anderson, Indiana. Recognizing the NBL's weakness, the Basketball Association of America was formed in 1946 by large arena owners like Walter Brown, whose Celtics played in Boston Garden, and Ned Irish, whose Knicks were based in Madison Square Garden.

Because the Trotters and Rens had already competed for nearly two decades against whites and integrated schoolboy fives were not unprecedented in the North, Blacks were regularly employed by white teams in the 1940s. Pops Gates and Dolly King, refugees of the Washington Bears, spent the 1946 season with the Basketball Association of America (BAA)'s Tri-Cities Blackhawks, though both were let go at season's end because, Gates contends, of an on-court scrap with a white opponent. Two years later another BAA team, the Chicago Stags, hired an unprecedented six Black players (Leon Wright, Irving Ward, Henry Blackburn, George Raby, Arthur Wilson, and Leonard Jordan). But again, this relationship lapsed after only one campaign. It was during that same 1948–1949 season that Bob Douglas's Rens played their last game. Things had gone badly for the Rens since winning the 1939 title. The ABL's presence and World War II hurt the Rens' business and forced Douglas to discontinue the team for a time. During those years many Rens either joined the Trotters or local operations like the Washington Bears. Following the war Douglas petitioned for entry into the ABL and, after much negotiation, was allowed in but with two eventually fatal preconditions— the Rens had to take on the defunct Dayton (Ohio) Vagabond Kings' two and seventeen record so as not to unbalance the league schedule, and they had to play home games in Dayton.

Maybe if these were the Rens of the twenties they might have persevered. But the players were old (Willie Smith was thirty-seven, Johnny Isaacs thirty-three), and the squad was short—no man on the roster was over 6′5″. Twenty-six-year-old Hank DeZonie was high scorer with a 12.4 average, but he missed the last seventeen games due to injury. Player-coach Gates, at thirty-one still a threat, averaged 11.2 points, and Jim Usry, later Atlantic City's first Black mayor, hit for nine points a contest. Ripped out of Harlem, possibly because the Knicks didn't want the competition, and shoved into a hostile white working-class industrial town, the Dayton Rens, a Black squad playing against all-white teams, were a disaster, drawing flies and losing forty-three of fifty-nine games. The Rens, born of the Harlem Renaissance as a by-product of Black entrepreneurship and pride, played their last game on March 21, 1949.

Later that year the Midwestern teams of the NBL and the big Eastern city clubs of the BAA merged to create the National Basketball Association. The sad irony is that in the deal almost all the franchises from both leagues were admitted into this new entity—New York played Sheboygan, Philadelphia battled Anderson. If Douglas's Dayton Rens had held on for one more season they, too, would have received a free ticket into the NBA. The presence in 1949 of a Black-owned team in the first real national basketball professional league would have clearly altered the sport's history and, more important, the course of race relations in America.

PANTHER POWER

Known around Chicago as the "young Globetrotters," the 1954 DuSable Panthers were the first all-Black, Black-coached squad to reach the finals of an integrated mainstream scholastic competition—Illinois's state high school tournament. Not only was coach Paul Brown's team a pioneer but—in the tradition of the school's most famous basketball alumnus, Sweetwater Clifton—was flamboyant.

DuSable's historic success wasn't due just to the fact that it won but how it won. To Brown, a Gary, Indiana, native, who had attended Michigan State on a football scholarship and played baseball in the navy with Larry Doby, the American League's first Black, an aggressive approach was essential to helping his players overcome the Uncle Tom attitude he felt school authorities encouraged. "Second is nothin'," he told the Panthers, "especially if you're Black. If you're first, then maybe you get a chance." Brown designed some half-court plays for the team, but the Panther hallmark was a gambling full-court press keyed to converting turnovers into easy baskets. Brown labeled his style "free-lancing." Whites ridiculed Brown's coaching and the Panthers' "lack of discipline." Yet in the 1953–1954 Chicago high school season they averaged eighty points per game, when most schools rarely scored seventy, and they hit the century mark in a quarter of their contests. Between stealing, shooting, and tenacious rebounding the Panthers averaged ninety-five shots in thirty-two-minute games or one field goal attempt every twenty seconds.

The Panthers had street nicknames (Sugar Lump, Sweet), wore unusually high numbers (60, 63, 68, 75), and sported long, slick red and black kneepads. Coach Brown was a sight, too, stalking the sidelines in a bow tie and his lucky plaid vest. When the Panthers ran on court for warm-ups they didn't set up a lay-up line but a dunking line where players stuffed with one or two hands at a time some teams still considered a jump-shot radical. Duster Thomas, coach of Pinckneyville High's all-white downstate team, spoke for many when he cracked, "DuSable ain't nothin' but a five-ring circus," a reflection of the conservatism of coaches in a state historically dominated by classroom ball.

The Panthers' stars were center Reggie "Big Red" Henderson, number 63; guard Curly (his given name) Johnson; Paxton "Sugar Lump" Lumpkin, number 13, the squad's flashy ball handler; and Charlie Brown, number 68, a deadeye shooter from thirty feet and in. Upon graduation Henderson and Johnson became the first Black starters at Bradley University in Peoria, while Lumpkin and Brown were recruited by, and then flunked out at, Indiana University (due, they asserted, to a redneck head coach). Henderson, Johnson, Lumpkin, and Brown would all play pro ball at some level. But that 1954 season marked the high point of their athletic lives.

After crushing all competition on their way to the Chicago city title and in early tournament contests, the Panthers and a busload of supporters from the South Side ventured down to Champaign for the finals against Mount Vernon, a traditional classroom team with one very important wild card—its key player was Black. Albert Avant had already played on Mount Vernon's 1952 state titlist and was widely regarded as the best athlete in Illinois. In addition to starring in basketball Avant was also Mount Vernon's starting shortstop, quarterback, and a track star, too. But in 1954 Avant still couldn't eat in white-run restaurants nor did he socialize off court with his teammates. Of Mount Vernon's 700 students only six were African-American; Avant was the only male.

As pioneering as DuSable was in style and attitude, Avant's position as the Black standout in a white environment made him a forerunner as well. He was like a Sidney Poitier movie character, a Black man who wore the double burden of being a good player on any terms *and* being an example of his race's competence. On court Avant sublimated his aesthetic interest—he would have loved to run and gun like the Panthers—to mesh with the effective, yet more methodical approach of his white teammates. Off court he navigated the ironies of being an African-American star in a European-American environment. His mother was a domestic, and his father, Prince Albert Avant, worked for the Department of Public Works. Avant's father didn't encourage his son's athletic activity. He couldn't understand why his son subjected himself to verbal abuse from rival players and fans.

The title game, one of many on-court style wars that would define Black basketball's evolution, was won by Mount Vernon, 76–70. In the game's last four minutes two DuSable stars fouled out and the Panthers had four made baskets disallowed. Avant hit for twenty-three points. The Panthers, to a man, felt they'd been screwed. That bitterness endured. In April 1974 the Illinois high school coaches' Hall of Fame voted Lumpkin, Brown, and Henderson in as individuals and the 1954 DuSable Panthers collectively. The plaque inducting the team cited them for "pioneering the fastbreak, the full court press and pro socks in Illinois basketball." Coach Brown attended the ceremony, but, still mad two decades later, the entire 1954 team boycotted the affair.

UPTOWN

In the postwar years a new kind of building began to dot urban landscapes: high-rise housing projects. Outgrowths of the Democratic New Deal philosophy of public works for the common good, these government-owned buildings were designed to save the poor from crowded tenements and place them into standard-issue apartments with refrigerators, not iceboxes, and incinerators that took garbage off the street—even if they spewed thick clouds of black smoke into the air. Though intended to help the poor, these projects also worked as tools of social control. The building of these huge complexes in African-American neighborhoods, for example, encouraged Blacks to live in these self-contained areas (soon to be labeled ghettos) out of sight (and mind) of the cities' white inhabitants. In the long run, they were as effective as a weapon of segregation as Jim Crow laws had been in earlier decades.

Projects often had community centers where public health care was usually available—a great many polio vaccines would be given in them—long rows of metallic mailboxes, oblong parking lots, and green lawns that told city kids to "Keep Off the Grass." Instead, youngsters were encouraged to use asphalt as a playing ground for jump rope, touch football, Johnny-on-the-pony, stickball, and a game played with hoarded bottle tops called "skelly."

And there was basketball, a game that worked better on asphalt than grass. With the help of some yellow paint, a few hollow steel poles, a couple of slabs of sheet metal, and metal rings painted orange, empty stretches of asphalt metamorphosed into courts. On long days and nights, whether it was spring, summer, fall (and on more snowy weather days than made sense), the impulse to play spread. Like the changes the city had made in the blues, the way brothers played ball absorbed the quirks and characteristics of the urban scene surrounding them. The "new" ball was about putting one's personal stamp on any given contest, about using a team sport as a way to tell your story just as the beboppers did on bandstands nightly up North in every major city. City ball was faster, louder, more stop-and-go, and like bebop defiant of established standards of performance.

Appropriately, a park adjacent to a housing project in Harlem would become a temple to this new sport style, but one with a most unlikely high priest: Holcomb Rucker, a slight, sickly Department of Parks employee with little recorded athletic talent. In 1946, the twenty-year-old Rucker was assigned to the public park at Harlem's St. Nicholas Projects, 127th Street and Seventh Avenue. Operating out of a red-brick Parks Department building "Ruck," as the players called him, grew from an obscure city functionary to a legend in American sport. Rucker was the catalyst who gave this new urban ball, this Black athletic asethetic, a spiritual home.

Rucker believed in two now sadly abused notions: sport was one of the quickest tickets out of the ghetto for African-Americans, and even lesser players would, through sport, learn positive lessons in life that would aid them in rejecting crime, alcohol, and drugs. In the late forties narcotics (as all manner of addictive substances were then labeled) were not yet mass-market commodities, but working in the heart of Harlem Rucker saw firsthand the rising use of marijuana and heroin. Years before the rhetoric "To get a good job, you need a good education" became a part of the American scene, Rucker preached a stay-in-school sermon in the shadow of the St. Nicholas Projects.

"I used to go down to his park every day when school was over," ex-Knick guard and Harlem native Fred Crawford said of Rucker in *Black Sport*. "He was always there rappin' with the guys. He was the type of guy you could really talk to, know what I mean? Today, school is the thing, but at the time, it was just beginning to catch on—getting a scholarship and going to college was not very common. He kept education on your mind. That's all he talked about ... When I went home at night, I couldn't wait for the next day so I could get to practice and get my game together at school. Then it would be down to the park and another shot of Rucker's adrenaline." In fact, after years of advocating education, Rucker himself went back for his college degree at thirty-five.

Though time tends to soften the hard edges of memory, there

are few longtime Harlemites who wouldn't nominate Rucker for sainthood. In an era before funding minority-youth sports programs was fashionable Rucker started a tournament in his park. Sometimes he had to borrow basketballs from local teens, and at other moments he was forced to loan money to coaches and kids, all the while working from sunup to sundown recruiting referees, wooing sponsors, and lugging around a long slab of oaktag paper to record an ever changing schedule of games.

His teen-targeted summer league was an immediate success that soon attracted scouts as well as players. The ghetto express that would begin to transport New York City's best players to universities across the land had his park as a major depot. One of the great romantic images of urban ball—of a schoolyard hero dominating an NBA star and his getting signed by a college or pro recruiter—is a legacy of the Rucker environment. The key to this imagery and Rucker's fame was the inauguration of professional competition in 1955 and the expansion of the tournament to several Harlem parks. This meant Wilt Chamberlain and Roger Brown and Walt Hazzard and, later, Willis Reed and Julius Erving, pro stars of three decades, would all compete on concrete against dropouts, junkies, and criminal-minded players. Press clippings and paychecks didn't matter at Rucker. You could gain or lose a reputation in the time it took to say, "In your face!"

Moreover, simple competence wasn't enough. Only ballplayers with a certain élan satisfied crowds that stood six deep and dangled from trees for big games. At Rucker you played fly, flashy style (or at least tried to); otherwise you were just taking up space. This wasn't traditional New York ball as practiced by the Irish and Jewish stars of the twenties and thirties, symbolized by the Original Celtics and its players. Despite the gloss of harmonious brotherhood sports scribes have always put on Gotham ball, the style that had been promulgated by European ethnics until now wasn't the same as that played by these brothers. Pre-Rucker Big Apple style was, as Davies pointed out earlier, often half-court or full-court, peppered with the give-and-go, the back door, the pick 'n' roll—names given to tricky plays utilized in half-court offense and associated with the Original Celtics and its famous alumni, Joe Lapchick and Nat Holman. To Eastern players basketball was a series of tightly choreographed patterns that encouraged passing from the pivot man to perimeter shooters through and around the defensive. Eastern teams on all levels ran through these patterns endlessly, seeking to lull opponents into mistakes, fatigue, and lassitude. Each coach and team had its idiosyncrasies, but this approach was the essence of New York ethnic ball and is still employed successfully by Pete Carril's Princeton team.

Basketball at Rucker wasn't about weaves, patterns, or anything approaching the standardized means of deception. The tales told of Rucker are not of team ball but of individual forays, not of careful geometric designs but of gravity defied and good sense ignored. The Rucker tournament was special because of the ball and, as novelist Barry Beckham eloquently described in *Double Dunk,* the atmosphere: "They [the fans] are here to see theatrics, something rhythmic, something astonishing, some expression of a natural ability loosened spontaneously, something that goes naturally with the dude under the tree who is practicing a bop and the little girl standing under the basket with a fried chicken wing dangling from her fingers and the poor kid wearing plaid wool pants in this August heat because, you know, his parents can't afford to buy him anything else, and the smiling old dude with a gold tooth in the top of his mouth who tilts a paper-wrapped bottle to his lips and the colors of all the clothes and the energy and the feel and the sound of the voices."

Rucker was where the extraordinary was ordinary: players

rising aloft to pick quarters off the top of backboards or slamming their palms against the backboard not to block shots but to make the bucket vibrate just enough to send lay-ups off course. Pinning a shot to the backboard meant nothing unless the pin was made up high and the offending shot was then heaved back at its perpetrator or into the crowd. Players "double-dunked," stuffing the ball and then, before landing, grabbing the ball and stuffing it backwards. Years before Jordan, Dr. J, or "hang time" entered basketball's lexicon, the Rucker was, at least among its best, a place where the game belonged above the rim. Many a player did a 360-degree dunk in the vertical plane before the existence of Nike ads. The point wasn't simply to have leaping ability. Rucker was also a place where philosophy and aesthetics were discussed via body language.

"Just as white college basketball was patterned and regimented like the lives awaiting its players, the Black schoolyard game demanded all the flash, guile and individual reckless brilliance each man would need in the world facing him," thought a gawky 6'10" teenager named Lew Alcindor (later Kareem Abdul-Jabbar), who played in and watched many a Rucker contest. "This was on-the-job training when no jobs were available. No wonder these games were so intense, so this was as good as it was ever going to get, and it was winner-stay-on. Who says the work ethic didn't live in the ghetto, that Calvinism and social Darwinism were outmoded credos? These were philosophers out there, every one-on-one a debate, each move a break through concept, every weekend another treatise. I took the seminar every chance I could."

One essay Alcindor remembers was composed by a bald-headed jumping jack named Jackie Jackson. One summer day Jackson was guarding Wilt Chamberlain when Philadelphia's favorite seven-footer shot his famous fall-away jumper. Alcindor says Jackson "looked like he was climbing stairs, and at the top of his arc, his arm above the white box over the rim as it reached the backboard. Pinned! ... It was the most exciting play I've ever seen on the court and the whole place went crazy." Jackson, Helicopter Knowings, Joe Hammond, and so many others are legends documented only in anecdotes: there are no highlight films that replay their greatness.

Among Ruckerites few names are more magical than that of a stocky, 6'1" guard named Earl "The Goat" Manigault. Manigault's rep is so immense that during a rare return trip to New York from his Charleston, South Carolina, home in 1988, the *New York Times,* by no means a dedicated chronicler of nontraditional African-American heroism, printed a long feature on him in its sports section, "A Fallen King Revisits His Realm." A quarter century after his peak the paper of record noted he walked "with a cigarette hanging from his mouth, carrying a can of beer in a brown bag and sipping through a straw" through an Upper West Side playground. In Rucker lore Manigault is "the man" who did everything described in my catalogue of Ruckerisms and more. The story is told that Manigault, to win a sixty-dollar bet, dunked backwards thirty-six times in a row, which is striking not only for the feat as a test of endurance for a 6'1" man but as testimony to the culture of challenge that spawned him. He starred briefly at Benjamin Franklin High and then, between incredible feats of on-court prowess, slipped slowly into the heart of heroin-induced darkness. When Rucker started his tournament in the forties, "horse" was primarily a diversion of hipsters and jazzmen. But by the time Manigault arrived at Rucker as an adolescent, heroin was a tool of evil that undermined many of the civil rights movement's legal victories.

The irony, of course, is that Rucker inaugurated the tournament with an eye toward saving the Earl Manigaults of

Harlem. Yet in Manigault's celebrated case and countless others it was shown that preaching, even local adoration, didn't, couldn't, and can't save a man from the social and personal demons that feed drug addiction. To think so is to be somewhere between naive and foolish, but that's a lesson that America still doesn't understand. None of this invalidates Rucker's dream. But it did suggest that as time progressed the roadblocks to Black achievement in basketball and elsewhere wouldn't always be overt racism but the moral degradation of drugs.

From the Rucker tournament's first home park you can dribble up St. Nicholas Avenue to 135th Street and the City College of New York campus, where in 1949 the integration of big-time college ball was occurring under the supervision of a classroom-ball taskmaster. Nat "Mr. Basketball" Holman, coach of the City College of New York team, was one of the game's most respected theorists. In books, lectures, and in practice Holman advocated a half-court offense based on minimizing turnovers and geared toward taking the high-percentage shot. But the fast break popularized by Western teams in white college ball, as well as the one-hand push shot and Luisetti's jumper, had increased scoring while spreading the court. So for the 1949–1950 season Holman adopted the fast break and, reluctantly, even allowed jump shooting. But just as crucial to Holman's revamped offense was his recruiting of two swift African-Americans, 6´4˝ forward Ed Warner and 6´3˝ guard Floyd Layne.

Among New York City schools—Long Island, Manhattan, New York, Columbia, St. John's, Brooklyn—Black athletic recruitment began in the early forties. But at no other school did Blacks have such an immediate radicalizing impact as they did at CCNY. Along with jump shooter Ed Roman, summertime Ruckerites Warner and Layne made CCNY much quicker, especially on defense, where Layne's foot speed and Warner's leaping (opponents claimed he played like he was 6'9") denied opponents easy access to the lane. An early complaint of Black players at white colleges was that coaches downplayed their offensive roles. Into the late fifties white schools usually showcased one Black scorer at a time—any other Blacks on the club were utilized as defensive specialists. CCNY was typical. Holman ran plays for Warner, while Layne's points came mainly from offensive rebounds or the fast break.

At the time they entered CCNY Warner and Layne were academically substandard by the school's then rigorous admittance policy. But Holman got the duo, as well as point guard Al "Fats" Roth, admitted as "special students," aka ballplayers. With these sophomores in its lineup CCNY became fan favorites at Madison Square Garden, where they and other city colleges played home games. But there was an evil undercurrent to the action at basketball's self-proclaimed mecca. Betting on college ball was so widespread at the Garden that cheers in the smoke-filled arena were said to be louder for point spreads than victories. For example, a CCNY fan might bet his team would win by four points or more. He'd then lose money if CCNY won but by only two points. Shrewd gamblers, if they could get one or two players to cooperate, would bribe them to keep the score down. At various times CCNY's entire starting five, poor, working-class kids all, took money to shave points. Just as Holman had compromised the academic integrity of his school for victories, the players worked in a gray area where they gave up cheap points or missed easy shots, yet still tried to win.

CCNY finished the 1949–1950 campaign seventeen and five by outscoring their opponents thirteen points per game, sixty-eight to fifty-five. In a historic two and a half weeks in the spring of 1950 Holman's integrated team went undefeated in the NIT and NCAA tournaments to bring their titles back to Harlem. Perhaps their most impressive victory was an 89–50 demolition of Adolph Rupp's Kentucky squad in the NCAA semifinals. Not only were the Wildcats two-time defending NCAA champs, but Rupp had always gone out of his way to avoid playing teams with African-Americans. Sweeter still was how Holman utilized Warner to outsmart Rupp.

Kentucky's hub was the immobile seven-foot Bill Spivey, whose brutish, slo-mo style helped create the enduring stereotype of the Leviathan white-boy center. CCNY's regular middle man, Ed Roman, was too short, too skinny, and too slow to deal with Spivey. Warner wasn't. Playing center Warner went around and over Rupp's huge protégé for twenty-six points as CCNY inflicted Kentucky with the worst thrashing of the Baron's career (though, as we'll see, Rupp's role as a segregationist foil for Black achievement wasn't over).

For Warner and his comrades this glory was relatively short-lived. During the 1950–1951 college season Junie Kellogg, a Black player from Portsmouth, Virginia, attending Manhattan College, told coach Kenny Norton of a bribe offer from local gamblers. Norton and Kellogg in turn alerted Manhattan district attorney Frank Hogan to the situation, triggering a twenty-three-city point-shaving investigation that in February 1951 led to the indictment of many, including the CCNY shavers. Not only was Warner dropped from CCNY, but the NBA barred him and all others implicated in the scandal. College basketball in New York was mortally wounded. The NCAA banned regular-season college contests from the Garden for many years, and, while St. John's was spared involvement (many claim due to Hogan's Catholic background), all other top New York schools decided to deemphasize the sport.

In retrospect, the scandal had an unexpectedly positive impact on basketball nationally. Once it was unusual for New Yorkers to attend college outside the city. After the scandal it was highway or no play for players unless they went to St. John's or New Jersey's Seton Hall. As a result, the richness of New York's postwar street ball as it was evolving under Rucker and Holman would spread and cross-fertilize with styles from around the nation.

DOWN SOUTH

"The white man ain't gonna let you get nowhere with that football no way. You go on and get your book-learning so you can work yourself up in that A&P, or learn how to fix cars, or build houses or something, get you a trade. That way you have something can't nobody take away from you."

—Troy Maxson to son Cory,
in August Wilson's *Fences*, a play set in 1957

Say "Nashville" and most people think "the home of country music" or "Grand Ole Opry." Say "country music" and the image of a rural white Southerner comes to mind. Because the country music's equivalent of the Apollo is located there, as well as innumerable publishing companies that cater to country music, Nashville, Tennessee, is so strongly identified with country music and, as a result, rural whites that the city's African-American presence is often overlooked. In the fifties WLAC, a 100,000-watt station with a signal that reputedly stretched from Mexico to Canada, was one of the nation's best-known rhythm & blues broadcasters. At the urging of returning World War II GI's, WLAC not only programmed this new Black popular music, but because of the reluctance of white retailers to stock rhythm & blues, WLAC became a clearinghouse for sales of rhythm & blues records. If WLAC played a record, you could usually order it by writing or calling the station—sort of precomputer musical telemarketing.

While WLAC reached the masses, three Black colleges were centers for educating African-America's most promising young minds. For several generations, if you met a Black doctor in the South there was a good chance he had attended Meharry Medical College, one of the first schools in the country with the mission of training African-Americans in medicine. Across 17th Avenue North in northern Nashville is Fisk University, considered one of the elite Black colleges since the days its Jubilee Singers brought the redemptive sound of Negro spirituals to the European continent in the 1800s. The best and lightest—Fisk was celebrated for its careful selection of light-skinned African-American women as students—attended the school, whose campus was dominated by a large statue of scholar-leader W. E. B. Du Bois.

Tennessee A&I (now Tennessee State), located ten blocks from Fisk and Meharry, didn't have the classy pedigree of its cousins. It was a state-run school for Black students that, in the tradition of Washington's Tuskegee, emphasized agricultural training. Fisk was identified with the talented tenth of African-America; Tennessee A&I was designed to be a more working-class institution. Fisk aimed to train leaders; Tennessee A&I sought to produce solid citizens. Their philosophy toward sports was then profoundly different. During the Eisenhower years the administrations of both schools, particularly Tennessee A&I, used basketball as a tool for uplifting the race—and the school's reputation.

As the war was ending in 1945 Tennessee A&I president Walter Davis and school athletic director Henry Arthur Kean decided to revive the Black high school tournament that had been discontinued in 1942. The Nashville-based educators, as had their predecessors at Hampton and Tuskegee, saw it as a vehicle to draw attention to Black athletics and help standard-ize instruction. Davis's involvement was crucial since it meant all the resources of Tennessee A&I would be available to make the idea work. On March 29, 1945, this version, labeled the National High School Athletic Association, debuted in Nashville. It would last nine years.

The NHSAA eventually provided the best-run and most stable Black schoolboy competition to date. Its Nashville orga-nizers managed to expand the number of teams participating to sixteen from twelve states in 1946, despite the absence of Indiana, Kentucky, and Illinois, which were allowed to play in their state's white tournaments. Just as Jackie Robinson's entry into the Dodger lineup led to the inevitable fall of the Negro Leagues, the Supreme Court's desegregation ruling in *Brown* v. *Board of Education of Topeka, Kansas* in 1954 would signal a slow decline in the vitality of most Black-run scholastic events that mirrored integration's impact on other valued institutions of this community, including the colleges themselves. While its intentions were the same as previous tournaments, times were changing.

Once star players only had one professional option after attending college, and that was playing for the Trotters. For example, it wouldn't have surprised postwar spectators that James Fitzpatrick, high scorer of Somerset, Kentucky's Dunbar High, would later join the Trotters. After all, that's what Black hoop stars did. But few would have been bold enough to dream that Sam Jones, in 1951 the leading scorer of Lauringburg Institute of North Carolina, would within the decade become a Boston Celtics fixture. And they would have been plain crazy to think that Elston Howard of St. Louis's Vashon High and lead-ing scorer in the 1948 tournament would, years later, be the first Black on baseball's lordly lily-white New York Yankees. Jones and Howard, in the vanguard of groundbreaking Black athletes, and later fixtures on championship teams, got their first taste of national competition at the NHSAA.

In the 1950s Black basketball was already being seen as a big-city game, but at the NHSAA schools from Marques Haynes's home state of Oklahoma dominated. From 1945 to 1954 five champs were Sooners (Dunbar of Oklahoma City in 1945, Booker T. Washington of Cushing in 1946 and 1951, and Booker T. Washington of Tulsa in 1947 and 1948, a team that barely lost in 1949).

Imagine a squad of players with the size and quickness of Atlanta's pint-sized star Spud Webb and you have Middleton of Tampa, Florida, a team of small players who were runners-up in 1946 and 1947. The NHSAA's most intriguing tournament winner, however, was St. Elizabeth of Chicago. St. Elizabeth was a Roman Catholic school, which, because it had an all-Black student body, was barred from the city's Catholic school league—this despite Chicago's long record of integrated public school competition. Blessed with the finest African-American Catholic athletes in the Windy City, the Ironmen barnstormed like pros throughout the South and Midwest. At the urging of tournament commissioner Frank Young coach Clarence Cash's team was made an associate NHSAA member in 1948. They didn't do well in '48, but in '49 the Chicagoans defeated Tulsa's Booker T. Washington, 57–36, and in 1950 beat Ballard-Hudson of Macon, Georgia, 56–49. In fact, the Ironmen won the 1951 title on the court but lost it due to recruiting violations. After beating Cushing's Washington, 46–40, it was discovered that the Ironmen's Jim Dorsey had already completed eight semesters of high school in June 1950, almost a year before the tournament. The school apparently let some players overstay their eligibility, figuring no one was monitoring them during their barnstorming sweeps. But after two NHSAA titles they came under new scrutiny.

And what happened to Coach Cash after St. Elizabeth violated NHSAA rules? In 1952 host college Tennessee A&I named him head basketball coach, suggesting that, even among African-Americans in the forties, winning had become more important than a coach's duty to enforce rules. Cash's Southern shift suggested how the NHSAA tournament aided Southern recruiting. For example, Nat Taylor, who had seventeen points for Oklahoma City in its 36–33 victory over Elkhorn, West Virginia, in 1945, went on to college stardom at Tennessee A&I.

Hosting the tournament was part of a grand design shared by Kean and Davis. In the wake of Jackie Robinson's integration of major-league baseball in 1947, the Tennessee A&I brain trust felt a similar breakthrough was possible on the collegiate level. By cultivating the talented tenth of Black athletes, they sought to build powerhouse teams that would both increase overall school enrollment and build an athletic program equal to that of white universities. In the fifties Tennessee A&I had a yearly ninety-dollar student activity fee, which was a lot of money to ask of Black kids then, but the Tennessee A&I motto was "A Number 1 in a Deluxe Fashion."

The money was spent to build dorms and a top-notch gym known nationally as Kean's Little Garden. Track-and-field coach Ed Temple supervised a team that would produce Olympians Wilma Rudolph and Ralph Boston, while football coach John Merritt cultivated future National Football League standouts Claude Humphrey, Ed "Too Tall" Jones, and Joe Gilliam. But the university's pride and joy was its basketball program. In 1954, Tennessee A&I made a key addition when it hired John McLendon as an assistant coach to Clarence Cash. But this Kansas City native would eventually be more than just another aide.

FAST BREAK BASKETBALL

When he joined the Tennessee A&I staff, McLendon was already known in Black athletic circles as the "coach of champions" for his ability to build winning basketball programs by utilizing the fast break. In 1962 McLendon published *Fast Break Basketball: Fine Points and Fundamentals,* making him the first African-American to document his coaching philosophy in book form. McLendon began developing his ideas at the University of Kansas, where, after studying under basketball's creator, James Naismith, he graduated in 1936, making him the first African-American to earn a degree from the school's physical education program. "Naismith believed you can do as much toward helping people become better people, teaching them the lessons of life through athletics, than you can through preaching," says McLendon. "So he had that in the back of his mind that a coach is supposed to make a difference between what a person is and what he ought to be. Use interest in athletics as sort of a captive audience type thing, you've got him, now you have to do something with him."

After earning a master's degree in physical education from the University of Iowa, McLendon landed a teaching gig at North Carolina College for Negroes (now known as North Carolina Central University) in Durham, where from 1942 to 1952 he dominated the CIAA, winning the conference title in 1941, 1942, 1944, 1947, 1949, 1950, and 1951. During that remarkable period McLendon and his players made several breakthroughs. Under his guidance Rudolph "Rocky" Roberson became the first African-American to break a national basketball record. His fifty-eight points against Shaw University of Raleigh in February 1943 eclipsed Hank Luisetti's record of fifty points set in 1938. Fired up by McLendon's fast-break attack, NCC set a national record for most points in the second half, with sixty-seven versus poor Shaw in January 1944. McLendon's belief in the fast break was an outgrowth of his study under Naismith.

"I got the idea from Dr. Naismith himself," McLendon says. "Dr. Naismith was not a basketball-class teacher. He was just a teacher. In class, no matter what the subject was, you might end up on any subject. The subject he liked to end up on most was fast break basketball. He was not a tactician, and he didn't really think basketball should be coached that much. He invented basketball as a recreation sport. He coached two years at Kansas, in the early twenties, and they often referred to it as the only two years Kansas ever had a losing season. We were going through the gymnasium and, after class, I was walking with him through there and a whole bunch of kids were playing in the gym. He asked them for the ball. 'Whenever on the court you had it, that's there where your offense begins. And whenever the other team has the ball that's where your defense begins,' he said. I took that to mean that you played basketball on the entire court. Your offense started off the boards or whenever you got possession, that's when your offense begins. You don't come down the court, stop, and decide 'O.K., now I'm going to run and play this and that.' The same on defense, if you get the ball anywhere on the court, you don't retreat, you attack. So that's where I got the press-and-run game from."

Off court McLendon was also a force, writing for the Pittsburgh *Courier* and Carolina *Times* to increase interest in Black college sports. In 1946 McLendon, along with Morgan State's T. C. Hill, Howard's John Burr, and Virginia State's Harry Jefferson, organized the Central Intercollegiate Athletic Assn. tournament, which grew into one of African-America's most enduring athletic social events. His Eagles played and defeated a marine team from Camp Lejeune in 1950, believed to be the first integrated college-level game in North Carolina.

It was during this time that McLendon, the leaders of Tennessee A&I, and others in Black athletics united in a battle to integrate one of the national white postseason tournaments. The National Collegiate Athletic Association, whose roots go back to 1905, was affiliated with the larger, more prestigious conferences (Big Ten, Ivy League). Its basketball tournament began in 1939 to compete with Madison Square Garden's National Invitation Tournament and, by the early fifties, largely as a result of the 1951 betting scandal, would grow to overshadow the New York-based event. Their small college counterpart was the National Association of Inter-annual Association (NAIA) basketball, which had gathered in Kansas City since 1937. In 1950 McLendon, and other representatives traveled to New York, where they got the National Association of Basketball Coaches to endorse their proposal that Black schools be granted entry to national tournaments.

But after a promising start, this move toward athletic integration hit roadblocks. The 1951 NCAA Convention was being held at a segregated hotel in Dallas, which, of course, prevented African-Americans from participating. The Black colleges formed the National Athletic Steering Committee (NASC) to continue pursuing their integrationist goal. Despite two years of correspondence and meetings, the NCAA rejected the idea of accommodating Blacks. The NCAA, according to McLendon, expressed the prejudices of the time by stating, "Fans may not accept or appreciate the kind of game you play," and "your coaches may not be competent enough."

In contrast, the NAIA, particularly executive director Al Duer, was very supportive. After several false starts, in March 1952 a decision was made to allow NASC teams into the NAIA tournament the following season. But the NAIA executive committee didn't totally embrace equal rights. It forced all Black colleges, no matter where they were located, to compete against each other by creating Division 29. In essence, the NAIA created a national Black college tournament. In February 1953, the Division 29 tournament was played at Tennessee A&I (where else?) with Tennessee emerging victorious over, ironically, McLendon's NCC club. In the NAIA tournament Tennessee A&I lost to East Texas State in the third round. In 1954, Kean and Davis's school again won Division 29 but this time lost in the NAIA first round.

■ ■ ■

At this point Tennessee A&I's administration wooed McLendon from Virginia's Hampton Institute, where his two-year record was thirty-one and twenty. McLendon's presence made Cash uncomfortable, though his hostility was really directed at Davis and Kean. A conflict over the addition of another assistant coach led Cash to resign, placing McLendon in charge of a strong program he was about to make better.

From 1956 to 1959 McLendon led one of Black basketball's legendary teams, Skull & the Whiz Kids. "Skull" was the nickname given Richard Barnett, known later as Dick "Fall Back, Baby" Barnett, the fifth starter of the New York Knickerbockers' celebrated 1969–1970 champs. As a Knick, Barnett was viewed by the media as aloof, private and the least essential member of that squad (he was the last of the starters to have his number retired by the franchise). In the many books chronicling that famous team, journalists like Lewis Cole and Pete Axthelm rush past Barnett's collegiate accomplishments as if they are automatically less important than the white college stardom of Princeton's Bill Bradley or Southern Illinois' Walt Frazier, a reflection of how unappreciated Black college ball has traditionally been to white observers.

For McLendon, Barnett's flair was essential to the team's competitive chemistry. "I had to cool him down," says McLendon. "He thought basketball was supposed to be played behind his back. He was kind of a hot dog, let's put it like that. I told him, 'The first time you make a bad pass going behind your back I'm going to pull you out.' He said, 'I don't make bad passes.'" McLendon strove to balance a coach's natural desire for fundamentals with the idiosyncrasies of players as gifted as Barnett. In the fifties it was rare for a white coach to be as willing to bend over for a Black star as McLendon was with his top scorer. For example, McLendon recalls that Barnett "had a shot that couldn't be imitated; up and back at the same time. Falling away and falling down. Some of them backwards and he made them." Did McLendon attempt to "fix" Barnett's game? "I didn't care what he did as long as they went in."

Tennessee A&I was as confident off court as on. "Tennessee State was the powerhouse, they were killing," recalls then Central State University student Ken Hudson, later to make his own mark on basketball history. "I can remember the first time they came to Central. They strolled on campus, arrogant, cocky, etc. They knew they were something. Barnett was the leader. He went around talking stuff, but they could back it up." Statistics back up Hudson's memory: Tennessee A&I beat Central six times from 1956 to 1959, and the closest Hudson's school came to beating McLendon was a fourteen-point loss in 1957.

A big part of the Tennessee A&I story was its continuing cultivation of Indiana-bred players. Even after Cash's departure the Indiana-Nashville connection remained strong. Barnett had been a star at that great Black high school power, Roosevelt High of Gary, Indiana, while Tennessee A&I's other star was John "Rabbit" Barnhill, a product of Evansville, Indiana, who captained the squad all three of his varsity years. Led by Barnett and Barnhill, McLendon's team won eighty-seven and lost eight those three seasons, averaging ninety-one, eighty-nine, and ninety-six points per game each season, numbers not matched by white college teams until the 1960s. The shooting of forward Barnett and guard-forward Barnhill, along with center James Satterwhite and guards Ronald Hamilton and Henry Carlton, made Tennessee A&I a team whose wide-open offense put it ahead of its time.

So it was a great shock to white fans, most of whom knew little of Black college ball, when McLendon's boys took Southeast Oklahoma in an easy 92–73 win in the NAIA title game March 1957 in Kansas City before 8,000. Tennessee A&I was the first African-American college team to win a national title against white competition in any sport. Even a bomb threat against Tennessee A&I's flight back to Nashville didn't dampen McLendon's coaching excellence, his team's greatness, and BAA's growing impact on white college athletics. Before UCLA and the Boston Celtics, Tennessee A&I used the fast break to build a dynasty.

THOMPSON TIME

In the Atlanta *Daily World,* March 21, 1950, John McLendon wrote that Morris Brown coach H. B. Thompson "is a shrewd coach and a hard task master, a real leader of young men who demands respect by his own manhood. He is fair and will not stoop to conquer." McLendon thought Thompson, who had led the Wolverines to their second straight Southern Intercollegiate Athletic Conference title, was "coach of the year" for 1950. High praise for Thompson, praise that didn't go unnoticed in Black college circles.

Thompson had come to Morris Brown's campus from Morristown Junior College in 1945 and turned the program around. The Atlanta school had previously been known for its football team, "but they hadn't won any championships or anything like that, so then we got busy in basketball," Thompson remembers. Pulling players from his old schools, Kimball High and Morristown College in West Virginia, under Thompson the Wolverines were so immediately competitive that the school constructed the Joe Louis Arena, an on-campus training facility, in 1946, where Morris Brown won four straight Southern Intercollegiate Athletic Conference (SIAC) titles from 1947 to 1950. A series of exhibitions against McLendon-coached teams at NCCC and Hampton in the late forties helped Thompson generate interest in basketball throughout Georgia since several of these games were played in Macon. Thanksgiving battles against archrival Clark College became annual events.

Despite his success in Atlanta Thompson wasn't known outside the Black community because there was no interaction between the Black and white athletic worlds. He recalls, "I remember Dr. Graves, our athletic director, went over with a few friends to see Georgia Tech play and people there wanted to know what these niggers were doin' coming in here. That was it. That was the forties. So I never went to a Georgia Tech game. I don't ever remember seein' any whites at our games either." In the summer of 1950 Fisk University recruited Thompson, offering him the football and basketball coaching positions at $4,000 a year, more than twice what Morris Brown was paying, plus a brand-new home. For a Black college coach of that era it was a sweet package. Fisk president Charles S. Johnson, a distinguished historian-social scientist and author of *Patterns of Negro Segregation,* told Thompson, "We're not going to give you scholarships. We're not going to do anything out of the ordinary for the players. What we want you to do is make men." Moving from Morris Brown to Fisk was the contemporary equivalent of a successful coach shifting from Ohio State to Dartmouth, going from an environment where sport was important to the school's self-image to a place where it took a backseat to academics. And that's precisely why Thompson made the move.

"In those days Fisk was it," Thompson says. "You see, you're talkin' number-one schools in the country, Fisk and Howard. They were the ones that had Phi Beta Kappa. So that's how it all started, and we never really had scholarships. We had a boy as a student, and we took care of him. He had to be a student. Our players at Fisk wanted to be lawyers and doctors, not players. We had guys turn down pro contracts because you didn't go to Fisk just to play ball."

Thompson often used more elemental desires to stock his varsity: "I used to tell them, 'I don't have a lot of money. But I promise you you'll get a good education and a pretty wife.' Just about all my players met their wives at Fisk." Don't get the impression that all Fisk players were bookwormish middle-class kids. In 1963, Thompson led Fisk to its first SIAC title and, looking at photos of that team, he points out a Detroit gang leader who was "tough as nails" and a New Yorker who was "a bad dude." In his eyes, "There is no question that hungry street kids make the better athletes. Many of my guys were thugs, but they all got an education. They were boys who came from rough streets." Thompson's charge, as part of Fisk's overall philosophy, was to funnel their energy into productive pursuits, turning ambitious home boys into race leaders.

In addition to his coaching achievements Thompson was an important advocate for the integration of intercollegiate sport. In the 1950s he was made a member of the NAIA's nine-member board of directors, serving in that capacity for four years. The larger NCAA ignored Black colleges until the NAIA reached out to them. "They didn't give us a second thought until then," Thompson says. He claims the creation of NCAA Division III was a direct result of the attention schools like Tennessee A&I brought to Black basketball. "Division III was born right here in Nashville," he says. "We had thirty-five to forty athletic directors here at the Holiday Inn at Trinity Lane. There was a week of meetings, and I invited all the white AD's up to my house. Had thirty crackers in my house and you could tell they didn't believe a nigger lived like we lived. That was funny, boy." Later, Thompson was one of two Blacks on the eighteen-member NCAA Basketball Advisory Committee, where many votes went sixteen to two against Black interest.

Despite his role as a pioneering spokesman in the corridors of white athletic power, Thompson now sees the dark side of integration. Opportunities were surely gained, but many things weren't replaced by legal equality. He says, "It makes me sick to see how it's changed things. Used to have four or five high schools in Nashville that employed Black teachers. Not anymore. At the start of integration the Black municipal college was eliminated by the state and only one fellow got a job at the University of Louisville. Most teachers had to move and sell their homes." In his eyes the role the African-American educator and college has played in molding character has been undervalued, and too many jobs squandered, since integration began in earnest.

A turning point in Fisk's program, and a perfect example of how Black collegiate athletics were subverted by integration, was Vanderbilt's recruitment of Perry Wallace, a star at Nashville's all-Black Pearl High, which made him the first Black at that prestigious university and in the Southern Collegiate Conference. "Pearl is right down from Fisk—right down from Fisk—and I knew him," Thompson says. "I remember I spoke at the Frontiers Club one day, and they had all the Black players in the city there. Yet when that boy got to be a senior you couldn't get to him at his house. Now here I am, a Black coach and couldn't get to him. Vanderbilt kept him covered all the time. So he went to Vanderbilt.

"You see, we used to get all the local players. When Mac [McLendon] was coaching at Tennessee A&I he'd get most of his players from Gary and Chicago with a few from here. Others came to me, if they were students. Then all at once it got to a point when Tennessee A&I couldn't get the few blue chippers. They were either going to Vanderbilt or Tennessee or Memphis State. They sure wasn't going to either of us." Looking back at that golden era of Black ball in Nashville, Thompson remembers a time when Tennessee A&I used to play, back in the fifties and sixties, and "you'd have to go there at six P.M. for a game at eight P.M. Man, you'd be standing on top of each other because that old gym only held six thousand. You couldn't find a seat. Now I don't think there's more than two thousand in any game."

THE FIRST THREE

Earl Lloyd, Chuck Cooper, and Sweetwater Clifton all have a valid claim as the first African-American in the National Basketball Association. At a Chicago hotel on April 25, 1950, Celtics owner Walter Brown selected Duquesne's Cooper in the second round of the college draft. According to *New York Times* columnist George Sullivan, this announcement silenced the room. Finally, another owner inquired, "Walter, don't you know he's a colored boy?" Brown responded, "I don't give a damn if he's striped, plaid, or polka-dot! Boston takes Chuck Cooper of Duquesne!" In the ninth round of that same draft the Washington Capitols picked Lloyd of West Virginia State. Within a few months the Knicks purchased Clifton's contract from the Trotters. So while Cooper was the first drafted, Clifton would be the first to sign an NBA contract. But it was the little-known Lloyd who, in an October 31, 1950, game in Rochester, New York, became the first of the trio to step on court as a player in uniform in the NBA.

When Brown picked Cooper he did more than break the color line: he challenged Abe Saperstein's stranglehold on Black talent. According to Wilt Chamberlain, when the Trotter honcho heard Brown selected Cooper, "Abe went crazy. He threatened to boycott the Boston Garden." During the NBA's early years Trotter appearances as an opening act guaranteed a large house, so Saperstein's threat carried weight. Other owners put pressure on Brown to back down on integration, but he held his position and that resolve decided the Trotters' future. Given the opportunity to play fewer games for more money with no clowning required, the best Black players started to ignore Saperstein's blandishments against the NBA. It didn't happen overnight—the Trotters were established, the NBA relative upstarts. But an irreversible trend had begun.

Earl Lloyd is the least remembered of that pioneering trio, in large part because of what happened to the Washington franchise. That October 31 game in Rochester, in which Lloyd pulled down a game-high ten rebounds, was supposed to be the first of sixty-eight. Unfortunately, on January 9, 1951, after compiling a 10–25 record, the Caps disbanded, a victim of the same basketball apathy that killed the Bears. Lloyd, a wiry, brown-skinned twenty-two-year-old, 6´6˝, 220-pounder nicknamed Big Cat, had appeared in only seven games, scoring forty-three points for a 6.1 average before being drafted into the army. For the 1952–1953 season Lloyd signed with the Syracuse Nationals, where he toiled as a hardworking rebounder or, in today's jargon, power forward for six seasons and then two more in Detroit before retiring in 1960. His best season was '54–'55, when he posted career highs in minutes (2,212), field goals made (286), rebounds (553), assists (283), points (731), and point average (10.2), this last statistic his only season in double figures. It was a career year for Lloyd that, not coincidentally, was the year Syracuse, perennial bridesmaids, won the NBA title against Fort Wayne in seven games.

Syracuse teammate Dolph Schayes recalled that Lloyd "got the poor end of the stick as far as playing was concerned. He was always doing the dirty work, fouling out of the game. Actually, he helped me a great deal because with him in there I was free to rebound and get a lot of glory, since his game was to guard the other team's offensive ace." Because Lloyd didn't play in a big city and wasn't a high scorer or flashy on the court, his career is little noted today. Yet he was unquestionably the first Black actually to suit up, and as such he probably deserves the title of NBA African-American pioneer more than Cooper or Clifton.

By some trick of fate both Lloyd and Cooper wore number 11. They both also spent time at West Virginia State—Cooper for only a year and a half before entering the navy for two years. But these similarities aside, Lloyd and Cooper had very different careers. While Lloyd developed into a valuable role player on championship-caliber clubs, Cooper never fulfilled the promise he showed in college. The barrel-chested, light-skinned, 6'5", twenty-four-year-old guard-forward was a star at Duquesne, a Pittsburgh school with a history of Black athletes in football and basketball, though Cooper was its first Black roundball starter. His presence inspired racist reactions several times in college: the University of Tennessee, after traveling all the way up to Pittsburgh for a game, canceled just before tip-off when they found Cooper didn't merely have a tan; Duquesne couldn't book any games against schools from Alabama and Mississippi; as players lined up for an inbounds play against the University of Cincinnati, a Cincy player shouted, "I got the nigger!" to which Cooper replied, "And I got your mother in a jockstrap!"

In four years in Boston, Cooper made a modest impact,

mostly playing forward, though Red Auerbach used him a bit at guard. His rookie season was his best, as he recorded what would stand as career highs in rebounds (562), assists (174), and point average (9.3). In two years with the St. Louis Hawks Cooper posted decreasing numbers in all areas and in 1956 left the NBA for good. "The major thing I had to adjust to upon entering the pros," he told the Amsterdam *News* in 1978, "was the stationary pivot. In college, with my size and agility, I liked to go down low and utilize that space, but in the pros a big man in the middle would clog that area." Cooper also complained that his career was marred by coaching decisions that, similar to those made for Layne at CCNY and Lloyd at Syracuse, limited his offensive role. "There were things I had to adapt to throughout my career that I wouldn't have had to if I were white," he recalled. "I was expected to play good, sound intensified defense and really get under the boards for the heavy dirty work. Yet, I never received the frills or extra pay of white players."

Another problem that nagged Cooper, and dogs Blacks in pro ball to this day, was the perception that they exaggerated injuries due to a low threshold of pain or plain old laziness. "If I was hurt, they got suspicious," he remembered. "Auerbach, in fact, had me labeled a hypochondriac. In my four years in Boston, I never had an x-ray—lots of stitches, but never an x-ray. There were one or two white players on the Celtics that if they jammed a finger it was a cause of great concern. But then you know how strong Black skin is. We don't hurt. Ha!"

After his exit from the NBA Cooper joined Marques Haynes's Harlem Magicians for a few years. His salary rivaled what he made in the NBA, but Cooper was getting tired of the road. An auto accident in the late fifties led to his retirement. In the years between the end of his career and death in 1984 Cooper made a comfortable life for himself as a Pittsburgh businessman. Still, even after his playing days were over, Cooper confronted other roadblocks. "I would have liked to get into coaching," he said. "I felt I knew how to handle young men. But there were no opportunities for Black coaches then. I got one offer from a school in Piney Woods, Mississippi, but they were still killing Black people down there then. When my alma mater was looking for a coach, they approached me in a very roundabout way, but it was only for a position as an assistant coach."

The best and most colorful of the NBA's original brothers was Nat "Sweetwater" Clifton. Clifton, a soda-pop fanatic whose passion for the liquid led to his nickname, was a Chicago cabbie from his professional retirement in 1965 until his death in 1990. Of the NBA's original Blacks Clifton was the one with the kind of leaping ability and flair we now associate with the contemporary game. The combination of Clifton's above-the-rim jumping and Trotter gamesmanship made him the NBA's first proponent of the Black athletic aesthetic.

His story began on the same Chicago streets he later cruised as a cabbie. After his family left Little Rock, Arkansas, in the 1930s, it settled on Chicago's South Side. By the time he entered DuSable High he was 6'5", and in the 1940s that made him a dominating schoolboy center and the foundation for a rich postwar basketball tradition at the school. After fielding offers from several prominent Black colleges (Morris Brown, Clark, Tuskegee) Clifton chose Xavier in New Orleans because his DuSable teammates had already committed themselves to go there (just as the squad from Chicago's Wendell Phillips had in 1935). For three varsity years, led by Clifton, these Chicagoans terrorized the Southern Conference. In 1943 Xavier took the conference title and Sweetwater was the league's most valuable player. Upon graduation he served in Europe with the army's all-Black 369th Battalion from 1944 to 1947. Back home he joined the Dayton Metropolitans, an integrated bunch (three Blacks, nine whites) composed primarily of ex-Big Ten players. The Dayton experience led Clifton to a year as round-ball gypsy: he moved from Dayton to the Harlem Rens for about six months before settling in Chicago with the Trotters in late '47. For the next three years Clifton was a member of the Trotters' best-ever lineup; playing beside Marques Haynes and Goose Tatum, Clifton's agility and good-natured personality meshed well with the team's style and comic reams.

A dispute over money ended his Trotter tenure. In the summer of 1950 Clifton found out that the white college all-stars the Trotters played in a very lucrative barnstorming series were making more per game than the Trotters. Clifton shared his knowledge with his teammates, which enraged Saperstein. So Saperstein, knowing the Knicks were interested in having a Black player, sold his contract to New York. "He told me he sold me for $5,000," Clifton remembered, "so he got $2,500 and gave me $2,500 ... But later I came to find out that it was something like $20,000 he got, you understand what I mean?"

During his seven years in New York Clifton did well on court (averaging 10.3 for his career there, playing in the 1957 All-Star Game) and in salary negotiations (going from $7,500 in 1950 to $10,000). Still, Clifton felt his game was inhibited by Knick management: "When I first came to the Knicks I found I had to change over, you know. They didn't want me to do anything fancy or do anything like that. What I was supposed to do is rebound and play defense ... I would have been happy playing with the Knicks, but the thing is all the time I played there they never did get another good Black ballplayer to play with me, somebody who knew what I was doing, you understand. And that kinda held me back 'cause you can't do something with the other guys because they played the straight way. I felt like I was sacrificing myself for some guy and I don't think other guys would have done that. I'll put it this way: at that time they weren't making any Black stars. You already had to be made."

Even mere flashes of Clifton's sweetness could cause trouble. Indeed, in an early fifties preseason game it even caused a fight. Boston's Bob Harris, a good old boy from Oklahoma, got upset when Clifton did "a little Globetrotter stuff to him and he said where he came from people didn't do him like that." After some cursing Clifton threw the fight's first and only blow, decking Harris with a right. Referee Norm Drucker remembers, "Harris lost several front teeth. The Boston bench started to come toward Clifton, and when Sweetwater started to meet them, they all retreated." In 1958 Clifton, then wearing a Detroit Pistons uniform, got into a major melee in St. Louis backing up seven-foot Black teammate Walter Dukes. Dukes had stumbled into the crowd on a lay-up attempt. "Suddenly Dukes is in a fight with some fans," says Drucker. "At this point Clifton runs toward the stands and with his humor yells, 'Walter, you take the first row, I've got the second row.'"

Clifton stayed with Detroit one season before reuniting with Haynes and Tatum for four years with the Harlem Magicians. Ironically, he ended his career back with the Trotters. He played for Saperstein until 1965, when his career was ended by a knee injury. Clifton wasn't a major star, but his occasional flourishes and refusal to be intimidated made a lasting impression on his peers. In terms of Black basketball history Clifton symbolizes the introduction of urban Black attitude into the NBA and, of equal long-term importance, the arrival of Blacks from Black colleges to the pros. As a Northern-bred African-American who attended a Southern Black college and moved on to the NBA, Clifton was a prototype for many African-American athletes of the next decade.

Clifton, and to some degree Cooper, were victims of a double standard based on race. While they were criticized for showboating, the first celebrated white show-time player was revered. At this point in NBA history the prime exponent of what is now considered Black style was a skinny, white Catholic kid from Queens. Bob Cousy, a teammate of Cooper's, was a star precisely because of his use of the behind-the-back dribble and no-look pass. Cooper, a clear victim of this skewered perspective, had no beef with the Holy Cross College alum. "Cousy is about as free of the affliction of racism as any white person I've ever known," Cooper said. Unfortunately for this pioneering trio, the Celtic legend was in the minority.

IN THE STREETS, THEN
ABOVE THE RIM

U ntil the fifties basketball stars had been on the second rung of Black sports heroism. Joe Louis and that ultimate icon of pugilistic style Sugar Ray Robinson, along with baseball greats Jackie Robinson, Willie Mays, and Hank Aaron, were held in the highest regard in barbershops from Harlem to Compton, California.

Then five men emerged in the 1950s to take basketball to amazing new levels. They came out of segregated neighborhoods during the years that rhythm & blues started to be called rock 'n' roll, Freedom Rides were spreading across the South, and Lorraine Hansberry's *A Raisin in the Sun* lit up

Broadway. By the time this quintet retired there was a Black mayor in Cleveland, Sidney Poitier was Hollywood's biggest draw, Afros were the official hairstyle, and everybody knew that basketball was as Black as the blues.

Open up any college basketball reference book and turn to the section on the fifties. In 1955 and 1956 you'll see that the University of San Francisco Dons, led by a local kid named Bill Russell, won the NCAA title two years running. The next year a gutsy bunch of transplanted New Yorkers carried North Carolina to an upset of a Kansas Jayhawks squad that starred Philadelphia-bred seven-footer Wilt Chamberlain and four guys never heard from again. Twelve months later Adolph Rupp's lily-white Kentucky outfit ousted Seattle and its star, Washington, D.C., native Elgin Baylor. Then, in '59, Cincinnati began an era of basketball excellence by reaching the NCAA semifinals with Indiana-born Oscar Robertson playing forward. That same year Connie Hawkins took Brooklyn's Boys High to its second straight New York schoolboy title. From 1955 to 1959, years marked by acceptance and infamy for Blacks, these five were standard-bearers for the Black athletic aesthetic.

Though the way was opened up by the Rens, the Trotters, the Rucker tournament and several individual teams, games, and players, it would be in the NCAA's Division I that the African-American attitude toward basketball would burst through the locked doors of integrated national competition. While the tales of their professional careers are well documented, it is in the way the styles of Russell, Chamberlain, Baylor, Robertson, and Hawkins evolved before they turned pro that the basis of their influence is found.

In their impact and personal dramas these five Black men led basketball flying, faking, blocking, and dunking into the present.

The Harlem Renaissance, the pioneering black-owned basketball team of the 1920s. *(Courtesy of the Naismith Basketball Hall of Fame.)*

The Rens in action at Harlem's Renaissance Ballroom. *(Courtesy of the Naismith Memorial Basketball Hall of Fame.)*

Harlem Rens founder Bob Douglas. *(Courtesy of the Naismith Memorial Basketball Hall of Fame.)*

Reece "Goose" Tatum, the
Harlem Globetrotter's trendsetting,
comic pivotman. *(Supplied by
The Harlem Globetrotters to the
Basketball Hall of Fame.
© 1991 Harlem Globetrotters,
a division of International
Broadcasting Corporation.)*

Rens star and Hall of Famer,
William "Pops" Gates. *(Courtesy
of the Naismith Memorial
Basketball Hall of Fame.)*

Marques Haynes, the innovative Harlem Globetrotter guard demonstrating his much imitated one-knee dribble. *(Supplied by The Harlem Globetrotters to the Basketball Hall of Fame. © 1991 Harlem Globetrotters, a division of International Broadcasting Corporation.)*

Coach H. B. Thompson *(standing in suit)* with his Morris Brown team in the 1940s. *(Courtesy of H. B. Thompson.)*

Chuck Cooper, first black Boston Celtic, while attending Pittsburgh's Duquesne University in the 1940s. *(Courtesy of the NBA.)*

Fast-break advocate, Coach John McLendon. *(Courtesy of the Naismith Memorial Basketball Hall of Fame.)*

Ex-Trotter Nat "Sweetwater" Clifton in his Knickerbocker uniform in the 1950s. *(Courtesy of the Naismith Memorial Basketball Hall of Fame.)*

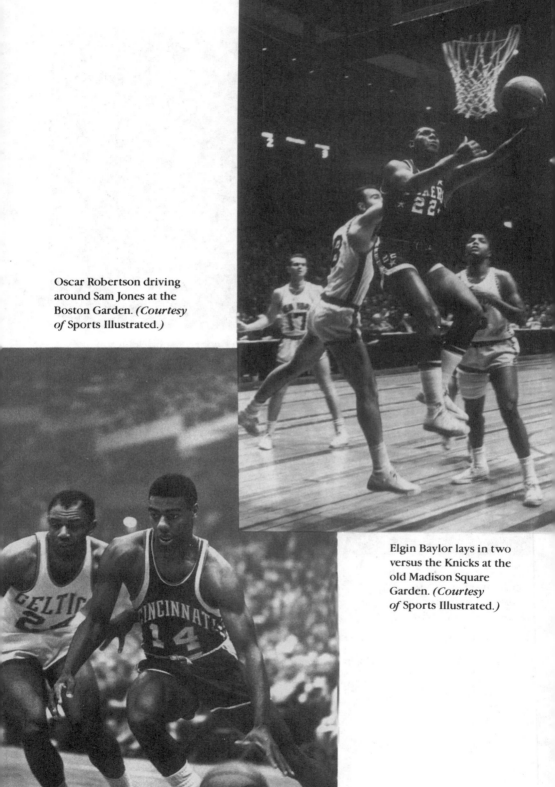

Oscar Robertson driving
around Sam Jones at the
Boston Garden. *(Courtesy
of* Sports Illustrated.*)*

Elgin Baylor lays in two
versus the Knicks at the
old Madison Square
Garden. *(Courtesy
of* Sports Illustrated.*)*

Bill Russell: The Hunter. *(Courtesy of* Sports Illustrated.*)*

Wilt Chamberlain during the 1972 NBA playoffs. *(Courtesy of* Sports Illustrated.*)*

Connie Hawkins while with the Phoenix Suns. *(Courtesy of* Sports Illustrated.*)*

Red Auerbach and his cigar.
(Courtesy of Sports Illustrated.*)*

John Wooden, as usual, victorious.
(Courtesy of Sports Illustrated.*)*

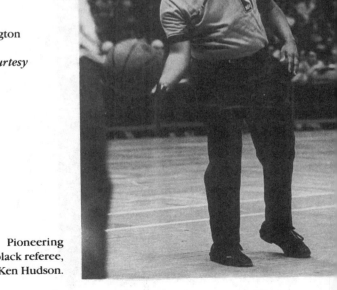

UCLA's Kenny Washington
rebounds in the 1964
NCAA title game. *(Courtesy
of* Sports Illustrated.*)*

Pioneering
black referee,
Ken Hudson.

Loyola's Jerry
Harkness scoring
against Cincinnati
in the 1963 NCAA
title contest.
*(Courtesy of
Sports Illustrated.)*

Bernard King's troubles
at the University of
Tennessee foreshadowed
the problems black
stars would face at
predominantly white
schools. *(Courtesy of
Sports Illustrated.)*

Elvin Hayes shoots over
Lew Alcindor in 1968
Houston Astrodome battle.
(*Courtesy of* Sports
Illustrated.)

Arkansas's Sidney Moncrief was one
of the black stars who changed
the complexion of Division I
basketball in the 1970s.
(*Courtesy of* Sports Illustrated.)

Julius "Dr. J" Erving jams at the
1976 ABA All-Star Game.
(*Courtesy of* Sports Illustrated.)

UCLA's dynasty-building centers
Bill Walton and Kareem Jabbar
battle in the pros.
(*Courtesy of* Sports Illustrated.)

Larry Bird and Magic Johnson in
the 1979 NCAA championship game.
(Courtesy of Sports Illustrated.*)*

Larry Bird shoots over Julius Erving.
(Courtesy of Sports Illustrated.*)*

Basketball's most famous drug
victim, Len Bias, with Celtic
executives Jan Volk and K.C.
Jones the day before he died.
(Courtesy of Sports Illustrated.*)*

New Jack Swinger,
Kenny Anderson.
(Courtesy of
Sports Illustrated.*)*

Lenny Wilkins, an
NBA Hall of Famer,
coached at Seattle
and Cleveland. *(Courtesy
of* Sports Illustrated.*)*

John Thompson instructs his star
guard, Eric "Sleepy" Lloyd,
at Georgetown in the 1980s.
(Courtesy of Sports Illustrated.*)*

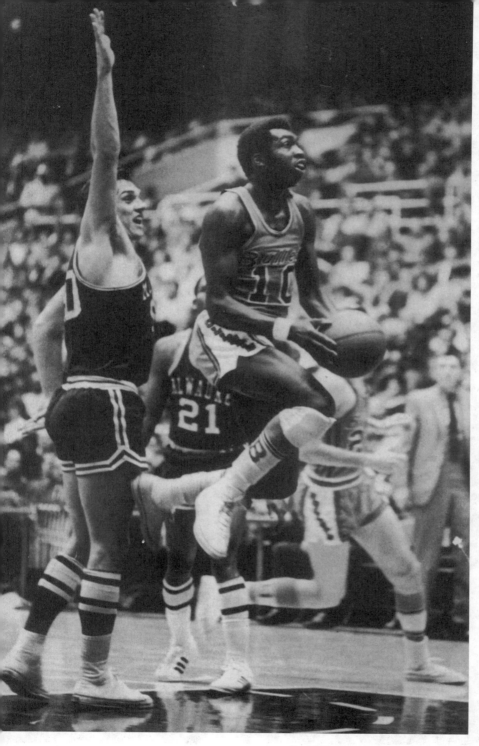

Earl "The Pearl" Monroe. *(Courtesy of AP/Wide World Photos.)*

Magic Johnson. *(Courtesy of* Sports Illustrated.*)*

Basketball Buppie
Michael Jordan.
*(Courtesy of
Sports Illustrated.)*

Basketball Bad Boy
Charles Barkley.
*(Courtesy of
Sports Illustrated.)*

THE HUNTER

"He is all alone and very handsome
Handsome even in quality of voice
Vital, he arises in the morning
Bow and arrow already about his neck
Oshoosi quickly unleashes his arrow
We see him only to embrace a shadow."
—A traditional Yoruba legend

"Oshoosi is the deity of the hunters, the fabled archer of the gods.
The power of this deity is manifest in the speed and accuracy of his
arrow, in prideful assertion of mind and muscle that have been won-
derfully honed by the disciples of forest hunting."
—Robert Ferris Thompson,
FLASH OF THE SPIRIT: African and African-American
Art and Philosophy, 1984

The first NBA game I ever attended was the first half of a
1968 preseason doubleheader at the spanking-new Madison
Square Garden. I sat behind the basket at the Eighth Avenue
end. The first game was a contest between the Boston Celtics
and Atlanta Hawks. I don't remember how I got there, what I
ate, who took me or even the second game with my beloved
Knicks. All I recall is Bill Russell, his back to me, his white
number 6 in bold relief against his kelly green jersey, and
arms—long, brown, muscular—spread wide like an eagle, as
he crouched low and anxious in the lane. When Russell turned
sideways his goatee, a symbol of cool rebellion, stood out and
little droplets of sweat fell from it. To my youthful eyes Russell was all a man could hope to be—successful, determined,
cool—a man whose defensive posture set the tone for the
action around him.

Emblematic of Russell's persona is this comment in *Go Up for Glory:* "I can honestly say that I have never worked to be liked. I have worked only to be respected. If I am liked, then that is an extra valued bonus of the world we inhabit. If I am disliked, it is the privilege of those who wish to dislike me—as long as it is not based on prejudice."

Russell spent his early life in Monroe, Louisiana, during the thirties, a time and place where Jim Crow reigned supreme. On several occasions his parents, Katie and Charles, were threatened due to their "arrogance." In one instance Russell's father, tired of being ignored by a white icehouse attendant, started to drive off. The attendant ran over and shouted at him, "Don't you ever try to do that, boy, unless you want to get shot." With a disregard for the consequences that apparently was a family trait Charles Russell grabbed a tire iron from under his seat and proceeded to chase his white tormentor.

It wasn't long before the Russells migrated West and, like so many Blacks from Louisiana and Texas, settled in California and, ultimately, Oakland, where the concentration of military bases meant jobs. They believed and were to some degree correct in thinking that racism wasn't as violent on the West Coast, though this was more a matter of relativity—contrasting the South's overt repression with the measured openness some found on the West Coast. Following a pattern set by many migrant families, Charles Russell left the South first, later sending for his wife and two sons. Though employment at a war plant earned the Russells good money, living conditions for Blacks in north Oakland was squalid. Things got even worse when, first, his parents separated and, then, when his mother died.

These trials forced Russell to be self-reliant, intense, and committed to keeping his own counsel. After his mother's death Russell began to pass time at the Oakland Public Library.

The book he remembers best from childhood was Richard Halliburton's *The Seven Wonders of the World* because of its detailed portrait of Haitian leader Henri Christophe. "He was mad," wrote Russell of Christophe. "He was a despot. Yet, in my mind, this was the first identification with a Negro who was a leader ... A Black man who became the dominant force in a power structure." The ability to make his own independent interpretation of events and a fascination with power would be two recurring themes in Russell's career.

At Oakland's McClymonds High he experienced a growth spurt that transformed him from bench-warming string bean to sturdy starting center. Because physically he was a late bloomer it wasn't until after his senior year, while on a California schoolboy all-star tour, that his skills matured. A teammate's offensive rebounding technique became the model for his own. Another teammate, whose dribbling and moves he couldn't mimic, inspired Russell in a different manner. The young center began imagining how he'd go about blocking his teammate's shot and, soon afterward in practice, Russell started blocking shots for real. This interest in the nonglamorous disciplines of rebounding and shot blocking made Russell both an anomaly and an innovator. In the midfifties, a time when the jump shot was still disdained by classroom-ball coaches, the idea of leaving your feet to attempt a block was equally heretical. No one was blocking shots and keeping them in bounds or, more extraordinary, tipping the blocked shot toward a teammate. On this tour Russell began rejecting shots so deftly that his tour mates dubbed the action "Russell moves." A factor in his shot blocks was that he was a lefty playing against predominantly right-handed opponents. This meant that when opponents drove the basket they unintentionally flowed straight into his flyswatter of a left hand.

Russell found the final piece of his game in an exhibition

game that same tour. In his perceptive memoir *Second Wind,* Russell describes his first moment in a place few get to experience—above the rim. "I got the ball near the basket on offense, went up as high as I could to take a short jump shot, and suddenly realized I was looking down into the basket. For an instant I was looking over the front edge of the rim to the back, and the basket itself looked like a skinny oval from this perspective. The sight was so strange that I missed the shot by a couple of feet." Initially fearful and then intoxicated by these leaps, Russell learned to mate this new jumping ability with the rebounding and defense he relished already. This synthesis earned him a scholarship to the University of San Francisco, a Jesuit school with no gym and an undistinguished sports history.

At San Francisco, in tandem with two African-American guards, Hal Perry and future proteammate K. C. Jones, Russell led the Dons to NCAA titles in 1954–1955 and 1955–1956, the second season with a 29-0 record. In the process Russell elevated the art of defense. In both his books Russell spends many pages chronicling the observations he and K. C. Jones shared on every aspect of defense, from blocking shots (his advice is to jump straight up, don't lean forward, and anticipate the ball's path) to finding a dribbler's "blind" spot when seeking a steal. Defense to Russell was applied science—observation and experimentation turned into practical application. While Russell's leaping ability was God-given, his analytical powers were consciously developed, and it was that intellectual process that made him a lethal weapon.

UCLA basketball guru John Wooden said of Russell at San Francisco that "[he] was the first master of the defensive aspect of college basketball ... I'll never forget one occasion when Willie Naulls, who later played with Bill on the Celtics, going up for a shot, had faked one way and Bill had gone for the fake.

Willie went by him, driving for the basket, obviously bent on dunking the ball with both hands. Just as Willie began to drive the ball down for the dunk Russell's hands went over the basket. Willie nearly dunked the ball but Russell blocked the shot. I contended that this was goal tending but the official insisted the ball never left Naulls's hands. The move was so incredible and surprised everyone so much that no official knew what to call."

Crucially, Russell's ability to dissect a situation didn't end at courtside. His relationship with coach Phil Woolpert was often strained—Russell saw whites get handed starting jobs over Blacks without any competition, he saw white guard Jerry Mullen named captain one season when he felt the honor was due to K. C. Jones. And early on he realized that white reporters often slanted stories to emphasize Blacks' physical abilities over their knowledge of the game.

As noted earlier, Russell had rejected Abe Saperstein's offer to play for the Trotters. Instead, after graduation in 1956 he played on the Olympic team in Melbourne, Australia. Coached by Henry Iba, whose basketball strategies were ancient even when he was young, the team had only three Blacks: Russell, Jones, and Iowa's Carl "Sugar" Cain. Russell was brilliant as the United States swept to gold. Still, he chafed at the Olympic team's segregated training facility. Following the Olympics he joined the Celtics a third of the way into the 1956–57 NBA season. Twenty-two years old, making a salary of $22,000, and with a then unique basketball philosophy, Russell entered the Celtics lineup and shifted the NBA's balance of power.

THE GIANT

"Mr. Big Stuff/Who do you think you are?
You're never gonna get my love."
—"Mr. Big Stuff," a hit for Jean Knight, 1971.

In 1968 Jim Murray, an award-winning Los Angeles *Times* columnist, made these two sterling observations about Wilt Chamberlain: "He was put together in a laboratory by a mad doctor with a pair of pliers, a screwdriver and a Bunsen burner. If you look close, you can see the bolts in the forehead. You don't feed it, you oil it baby." And: "Even in summer Wilt has snow on top. If he ever gets tired of basketball, he could rent himself out as a community antenna. To rush him to the hospital, you'd need a hook and ladder."

When Wilt Chamberlain went from being an unusually tall kid to a giant 6'11" student attending Philadelphia's Overbrook High, this African-American man had no chance at receiving fair treatment from white fans and glib sportswriters. There had been seven-footers before Chamberlain like hulking Bob Kurland of 1946 NCAA titlist Oklahoma A&M. There were Black seven-footers who were Chamberlain's contemporaries like Seton Hall's Walter Dukes. But Kurland was a slow slab of humanity with no agility or speed, and Dukes was a chronic underachiever who lacked the consistent intensity to dominate a game. Chamberlain was a new kind of seven-footer, a forerunner of the future who had no true peer in all-around athletic ability until Lew Alcindor a generation later. At 7'1" and, at his heaviest, 310 pounds, he towered over all he surveyed.

Because of his size no player in the history of Naismith's game would be the target of more hostility than this city of Brotherly Love native. His career, in fact, serves as a symptom of a problem that would grow in the coming decades—judgments made of African-American superstars based on unfair criteria, criteria that minimizes their individuality. If Chamberlain was the "loser" so many claimed, it wasn't because he lacked heart. Throughout his career Chamberlain was cursed with coaches and teammates who didn't or couldn't complement his skills. Management too often stood back and failed to build a self-sustaining system around him. In big games throughout his career too often it came down to Chamberlain versus five opponents determined to stop him. No single man, no matter how strong, could beat those odds consistently.

That was a lesson Wilt-watchers could have learned back in 1953 when Chamberlain, as a sixteen-year-old sophomore, led Overbrook High to the public school title in basketball in Philadelphia. During the regular season he averaged thirty-seven points a game and in one game hit ninety. High school games lasted only thirty minutes then, so you don't have to be a statistician to know he got busy.

But in a confrontation with the Catholic school champs, West Catholic, Overbrook was defeated, 54-52, as West Catholic's six-foot center Bill Lindsay had a career day, scoring thirty-two points on twelve of thirteen shooting. Lindsay's shooting was a surprise, but West Catholic's defense wasn't. After a week of practicing against a player standing on a chair, West Catholic was ready for Chamberlain. During the game four men clogged the lane on defense, daring Overbrook to hit from outside. Unfortunately, no one stepped forward to provide the needed perimeter shooting. It was an omen easily forgotten when in Chamberlain's next two years Overbrook won the city title and both annual battles against the Catholic champs. (Let the record show that in Chamberlain's senior year his school thrashed West Catholic, 83-42.) In those three years Overbrook was fifty-eight and three.

It is significant that Chamberlain, a great natural athlete who excelled in the javelin, high jump, and sprints, had to be talked into playing basketball. When he was an adolescent, a quartet of friends convinced him to join the Shoemaker Junior High team. At his friends' urging, Dip—so named for the way he had to bend down to enter rooms—and company enrolled at Overbrook together. Chamberlain never professed a deep passion for basketball. As a teen he preferred track-and-field events; after retiring he'd proclaim volleyball a superior sport. The significance of this is that Chamberlain wasn't—and honestly didn't need to be—the student of the game lesser mortals like Russell did. The center made light of his lack of high school instruction in his autobiography, noting, "My coach didn't teach me that you should pass the ball out quickly on rebounds, don't waste time banging it in your palm, or that you should try to keep shots inbounds when you block them to give your teammates a chance to get the ball, so I just went my merry way, smacking the ball on rebounds and knocking it into the bleachers on blocked shots."

In addition, Chamberlain claims that when it came time for him to select a college, his Overbrook coach steered him toward the University of Kansas. Chamberlain claims to have received $15 to $20,000 (in 1950s dollars, too!) from boosters while attending Kansas. At other schools he might have gotten even more. Over two hundred schools solicited Chamberlain in the biggest recruiting effort for any player, Black or white, up until that time.

Chamberlain's reasons for selecting Kansas (aside from the cash) suggest the mind-set that would, in the fifties, begin sending African-American athletes to populate Midwestern campuses: one, he wanted out of Philadelphia and the East so he could have more personal autonomy and freedom from the pressure of being a hometown hero; two, he ruled out the West

Coast universities because, like most Easterners, he didn't respect their brand of ball; three, he wanted to go someplace with a heavy basketball reputation such as Michigan, Indiana, or, ultimately, Kansas, where Naismith taught and his protégé Phog Allen coached for a decade. Unfortunately for Wilt and, possibly, for college basketball history, Allen turned seventy before the 1957 season. That was the mandatory retirement age for a University of Kansas professor, so Allen's assistant, Dick Harp, was named Jayhawk coach.

Maybe Allen, a pioneering strategist, could have made college ball more fun for the Philly prodigy. Clearly, Harp didn't. Between the brutal rib-bashing by smaller centers, the slow-down tactics of opposing coaches, and the taunting—both about his height and race—from white Midwestern crowds, Chamberlain quit Kansas after his junior year. As he told Frank Deford about his first varsity year there, "Looking back, I don't remember feeling any pressure that season. All I can remember is getting bored so often."

Chamberlain's size so intimidated opposing coaches that, just as with George Mikan in the thirties, at least four NCAA rules were changed to cramp his style. Kansas could no longer throw the ball over the backboard to Chamberlain on the inbounds play. The offensive goaltending rule was now altered so Chamberlain (and other centers, too) could no longer steer in a teammate's shots while in the cone of the basket. Where once on foul shots each team lined a player up next to the hoop, now only the nonshooting team could place players there. Finally, fearing that Chamberlain would begin leaping from the foul line to stuff in foul shots, they ruled that players had to shoot from a stationary position behind the line.

The key contest of Chamberlain's college career was, like DuSable versus Mount Vernon, a style war that pitted him against one of the last great New York City ethnic squads. Following the 1951 betting scandal, New York's top scholastic players and coaches began moving to schools around the country. Coach Frank McGuire moved from St. John's to the University of North Carolina with the goal of recruiting New Yorkers—mostly Irish and Italian, as well as a few Jews, down to the Bible Belt to play ball. By 1957 these "Noo Yawk" Tarheels consisted of Pete Brennan and Joe Quigg from Brooklyn, Bob Cunningham from Manhattan, Tommy Kearns from New Jersey, and high scorer Lennie Rosenbluth from the Bronx. This quintet won the Atlantic Coast Conference title and made the finals by beating Michigan State, 84-80, in triple overtime. Kansas stomped the Russell-less San Francisco Dons, 80-56, to get their ticket to the last round.

The final game opened with a psychological gambit. The Tarheels sent the 5´11˝ Kearns to jump center against the Kansas center. That sideshow was the beginning of the longest game in championship history. Wilt was magnificent, scoring twenty-three points and grabbing fourteen rebounds. But no one else on Kansas shot well, while North Carolina had four men in double figures. Chamberlain's Jayhawk teammates had several opportunities to be heroes in overtime, but missed free throws, and blown passes kept the Tarheels alive in the first overtime.

Two plays at the end of the third overtime won the game for North Carolina. With thirty-one seconds left Kearns drove the lane and Chamberlain rejected his shot. But Quigg, trailing the play, grabbed the ball and was fouled. With six seconds left Quigg nailed two free throws to make the score 54-53. When Kansas inbounded, the Tarheels engulfed Chamberlain. Harp called for an alley-oop to their center. The ball came in low, Quigg batted it away, and the buzzer sounded.

In retrospect we can see this contest as historic for a number of reasons. Following this game it would be rare to see a team composed of predominantly white New Yorkers excel in national competition. (Thereafter, African-American New Yorkers would, with a few notable exceptions such as Billy Cunningham and Chris Mullin, be the Big Apple's most desired products.) McGuire's team also instigated a North Carolina basketball boom at colleges and the schoolboy level that decades later would produce a rich crop of local talent, including Brad Daugherty, James Worthy, and Michael Jordan.

After the game McGuire said forthrightly, "We had a better team. We played Kansas, not him. We beat Kansas, not him." Yet most reporters at that time put the blame on Chamberlain. "He came in the invincible giant, but when he went out, he carried with him some vague impression of defeat's being his destiny," wrote the eloquent Deford twenty years later. Coming off this defeat and a frustrating junior year Chamberlain escaped. "Basketball had become such drudgery at Kansas that I was afraid another year there might leave me so disillusioned with the game, I'd quit playing completely and never try the NBA," he wrote.

So it is easy to understand why Chamberlain found playing for the Trotters a blast. Earning a then unheard of $65,000, getting a chance to play backcourt, playing in the Magic Circle through Europe was, after the trials of Kansas, a paid vacation. The lack of competition didn't faze Chamberlain. For him the game was a showcase, a form of self-expression. At Kansas basketball wasn't fun, and with the Trotters it was. Eventually, the NBA would prove to be as frustrating as Kansas and as fulfilling as the Trotters. He'd be judged harshly for big-game losses. But Chamberlain was a great soloist who shouldn't be judged by the quality of his band mates but by the incredible music he made.

NAPTOWN MANCHILD

The tape comes in a brown video-cassette case. Typewritten on its label: "Silent Film, Final 1956 Basketball, Crispus Attucks vs. Jefferson-Lafayette." Lafayette is a white team in dark jerseys with a high-post, half-court offense that emphasized twenty-foot set shots and ten footers from its pivotmen. Once across half court its players rarely took more that two dribbles before passing, usually a chest pass around the perimeter or a bounce pass into the pivot. Fast breaks occurred only on steals off its decidedly passive man-to-man defense.

The team members of Crispus Attucks, Black boys in white uniforms, all look to be of equal height and exceptional agility. Even on made baskets Attucks pushes the tempo, especially in the first half, and as the game progresses its 2-3 zone gets increasingly active, harassing Lafayette guards thirty feet out. Attucks's attack is a free-lance festival—running hooks, length-of-the-court rushes, thirty-foot jumpers. Shooting percentage is clearly not an Attucks concern, and it doesn't have to be because whenever Attucks needs a key offensive rebound they get it. At the end of the first quarter Attucks leads, 20-11, and Lafayette, despite some exceptional long-range set shooting, never gets closer than eight. Their deliberate style makes a comeback difficult.

So does the presence of Crispus Attucks's number 43, a wide-shouldered, one-handed shooter who seems to have either no position or several. Early in the game he brings the ball up. In the third and fourth quarters he posts up low like a center or forward. At about the seven-minute mark of the fourth quarter two plays suggest his versatility. After a missed Lafayette lay-up the Attucks rebounder kicks the ball out to a man in the corner. He then spots number 43 with his arm up, breaking up-court near the sideline. Number 43 receives the pass two strides over half court and slows a second, letting the mass of running players not only catch him but pass by. Lafayette is back but not yet set. He senses this and, after putting a stutter step on one defender, dribbles crosscourt through traffic, cuts through the top of the key, low-dribbles by one would-be thief, and then guides in for a running hook.

A minute later number 43 sets up on the left side of the foul lane ten feet from the basket. There's a defender on his right hip. The entry pass is sloppy and, with his back still to the basket, he controls the ball near the foul line. Two defenders converge on him, but number 43 just turns in midair and with his large right hand pops it in. Though only a high schooler the kid looks and plays like a pro. In the game's last minutes he brings the ball up and flips in a string of twenty-, twenty-five-, maybe thirty-footers. Final score: Crispus Attucks 79, Lafayette 57.

The trophy presentations offer the tape's only close-ups. The Lafayette players, a collection of crew-cut, rawboned country boys, stand hands on hips with warm-up jackets draped over their shoulders as they receive second-place trophies. Laughing and hugging each other as they sit on the floor is the Crispus Attucks squad. In the center, encircled by Black coach Ray Crowe and his teammates, is a baby-faced seventeen-year-old named Oscar Palmer Robertson. It is Robertson's last game as a member of Crispus Attucks and both the beginning and the end of a fascinating tale of race in Indiana.

Back in the twenties Indiana was one of the most racist states outside the Deep South. The catalyst for this hate was the Ku Klux Klan, which wooed the state's mostly rural population by feeding fears of the Catholic Church, big-city dwellers, Darwinism, "demon rum," and African-Americans. The KKK humbly offered itself as the true guardian of Indiana's "pure" white heart. In 1925 the KKK, under the charismatic leadership of Grand Dragon David C. Stephenson, openly financed the successful campaign for governor Ed Jackson as well as pro-Klan judges, mayors, and state legislators. "Nigger, don't let the sun set on you here!" signs dotted the flat Indiana landscape. White robes and peaked hats were readily available at six dollars apiece.

Helping spark Klan mania was the wave of African-American migration North into East Chicago, Hammond, Gary, and Indianapolis. In 'Naptown, the city that was home base for the Indy 500 and for millionaire black-hair-care entrepreneur Madame C. J. Walker, the desire to create a separate Black high school grew among its white residents. In September 1927 Crispus Attucks High, named after the Revolutionary War hero, opened with 1,385 students, twice the number expected, as Blacks from all over Indianapolis were forced to attend Attucks. The KKK even had a parade to celebrate this blessed event.

Crispus Attucks was chronically overcrowded and under-budgeted. One look at the school's hand-me-down uniforms revealed that. Neither Attucks nor the state's other two large all-Black high schools, Gary's Roosevelt and Evansville's Lincoln, were allowed to compete against white public schools until 1942. Indiana's first Black high school star was Jumpin' John Wilson of Anderson, who, at 5'11" could dunk, an indication of the leaping ability that led his school to the 1946 state crown and a frightening harbinger of what might happen if too many Blacks were allowed to compete.

Those folks had reason to be fearful. In parks around the state young African-American men with Wilson's natural ability plus size and more all-around skills were developing their game. In Indianapolis the place to be was an asphalt playground located inside the Lockfield Gardens Housing Project that everybody called "the Dust Bowl." Lockfield was a short distance from Attucks, where in 1945 Ray Crowe, a mathematics instructor, ran an afternoon intramural basketball program. Short but stocky and strong-willed Crowe commanded the respect of Lockfield's kids. Though not initially versed in the nuances of basketball, Crowe had an enthusiasm that led Attucks's administration to name him assistant coach in 1950. Next season the head coach unexpectedly resigned and Crowe replaced him. Remarkably, Crowe almost took Attucks to the Indiana high school title that first year. Led by an agile jump shooter named Bailey "Flap" Robertson, Attucks made it to the semifinals.

Sadly, this success brought Crowe as much censure as praise. The principal was afraid the team's victories would make players and students too aggressive, something Black men certainly weren't supposed to be in 1951. City officials worried as well because after every Attucks win there were wild celebrations in the town's Black neighborhoods; it was as if Joe Louis had won whenever the local boys came out on top. The school's cheerleaders even created their own victory song, "C-R-A-Z-Y," to commemorate the season. Members of Crowe's early teams moved up the basketball ladder—Hallie Bryant was one of the first Black players enrolled at Indiana University, and Willie Gardner joined the Trotters out of high school.

But the best was yet to come at Attucks. Flap Robertson's younger brother, Oscar, had, as an eighth grader at P.S. 17, taken his school to the elementary school championship. "He could shoot well and had all those moves and fakes," but what really impressed Crowe was that "he just ran the game." At twelve years old Robertson was already a force on the court. "I kept my basketball with me all the time," Robertson recalled. "I was always being teased about it—about dribbling balls all over the neighborhood. I carried my basketball like a musician carries his trumpet with him all the time." For Robertson, "Playing was not a dream per se. It was the competition I was thinking about—whether I could actually compete and on what level."

The story goes that as a child Robertson was always trying to bogart his way into games with older guys but was usually thrown back to play with the kids. Then he spent one summer down with relatives in Tennessee. Between hormones, good country cooking, and old-fashioned manual labor Robertson came home a muscular 6′3″, ready and eager for revenge. "He was always challenging people," Bryant told Phillip Hoose. "He was big for his age, but had to gain the older guys' respect to get on the court. So he was always saying 'Get this, get this,' like 'See if you can block this,' even to guys with big reputations." From the start Robertson was a talker who verbally and physically challenged opponents (and later pro referees) to either raise their level of play or get out of his way.

As a sophomore in 1954 he played forward on an Attucks team that was overrun by the miraculous Milan High team that won the state title and, years later, was immortalized in the film *Hoosiers*. But in '55, with Robertson handling more back-court duties, Attucks went 21-1 in the regular season. Strangely, up until then Indianapolis, the state's biggest city, had never produced an Indiana basketball champion. The city fathers were both proud and fearful of Attucks's chances for the title. These were men only a generation or so removed from the Klan-dominated state government of the twenties. At one point Attucks's principal, Russell Lane, was summoned to City Hall, where he had to reassure a mayoral deputy and the board of education, as well as the fire and police chiefs, that an Attucks championship would not incite an antiwhite riot.

Ironically, the 1955 final was an all-Black affair. Pitted against Gary's Roosevelt High and star forward Dick Barnett, Attucks wasn't to be denied. They crushed Gary, 97-64, which was twenty-nine more points than any team had scored in Indiana tournament history. Oscar had thirty. The mayor and company, still uptight about Attucks's success, routed the school's celebratory motorcade away from the downtown business district and into Indianapolis's African-American precincts. Many, including Robertson, resented the slight. The next year, after Attucks marched to its second straight IHSAA title, there was finally a City Hall ceremony, but the bitter taste lingered. These back-to-back championships broadcast on television statewide were, according to Indiana historians, instrumental in integrating the city's schools. In basketball-mad Indiana whites feared, with some justification, the flow of all Indianapolis's Black students to one school could make them perennial champions. As a result, the city's schoolchildren were more fairly distributed.

As Indianapolis began to pull down the walls of legal segregation, Robertson moved on to build a monument to himself in Cincinnati, Ohio. Unlike his peer Barnett, who chose a predominantly Black college, Robertson decided to go to a white university. Aside from his athletic excellence Robertson had made the National Honor Society for his academic accomplishments, so his choice of schools was limitless.

He selected the University of Cincinnati because it was close to home, strong academically, and, while not an athletic power, had a schedule filled with top teams. The recruitment of any African-American player by a white college in the fifties was clearly a statement against segregation. But enrolling Robertson was more than a political gesture. As the first of his race to play for the Bearcats, Robertson, by his mere presence, would jumpstart its athletic program. Though they didn't win the NCAA championship during his three varsity years, Robertson's prominence greatly enhanced Cincinnati's recruiting efforts. With Robertson the Bearcats made the Final Four in 1959 and 1960. With the players he helped attract, the Bearcats made the Final Four in 1961. After he graduated, Cincinnati finally won the crown in 1962 and in 1963 lost in the finals.

From 1957 to 1960 Robertson matured physically, reaching his full 6'5" height, and grew in his knowledge of the game. At the Dust Bowl he had been a big boy among teens; in the NCAA's Division I he was a man among young men. Eleven games into his sophomore season Cincinnati played Seton Hall at Madison Square Garden. In front of the nation's biggest sportswriters Robertson forged his national reputation. "They knew right away, soon as the kid handled the ball," wrote New York columnist Jimmy Cannon. "It was the way he dribbled, crouching, shielding the ball with his body. There was the quickness of his hands, the agility of his body ... Not many were there either, but as Oscar Robertson's legend increases, the liars will put themselves in the Garden on the big night of Thursday, Jan. 9." With twenty-two field goals and twelve of twelve free throw shooting Robertson set a Garden scoring record with fifty-six points in a 118-54 shipwrecking of the Pirates. Three more times that sophomore year Robertson cracked fifty. Cincinnati listed him as a forward, but he often handled the ball against trapping teams while consistently topping the Bearcats in rebounding. As a collegian he quickly became a legend, loved by classroom-ball coaches like Joe Lapchick. James Thurber wrote a poem, "The Wonderful O," about him.

Viewed in the light of the contemporary game Robertson presents a challenge to our expectations of Black ballplayers. He was no leaper—on retirement he claimed never to have dunked in competition. Nor was he flashy. In fact, just the opposite. Almost everything about Robertson's game was textbook. He dribbled with both hands, used his strength to get inside positions for rebounds, passed with intelligence, and could shoot accurately from any spot thirty feet in. The musical equivalent of his game was Nat "King" Cole, a smooth, understated, yet swinging vocalist who blended the crooning big-band singing tradition with the slick blues he played as a pianist. Robertson did everything the classroom coaches loved; he just did all of it better than anyone else ever had.

Robertson fits the current mold in one important way: in his aggressive, in-your-face attitude. For a guard, he was relentlessly physical, using his muscular hips to push back players he couldn't go by quickly. Dick Barnett's famous observation about Robertson deserves repeating, since it illustrates the tough, intimidating edge of the Big O's style: "If you give 'O' a twelve-foot shot, he'll work on you until he's got a ten-foot shot. Give him a ten and he wants eight. Give him eight and he wants six. Give him six, he wants four, he wants two. Give him two, you know what he wants? That's right baby, he wants a lay-up." Bill Russell also felt Robertson's wrath: "I knew that whenever I guarded him on a switch, Oscar would be dribbling with one hand and trying to club me to death with the other. This was what we called Oscar's 'free foul' because referees would never call it on him ... Oscar's free foul was in keeping with his attitude toward the game. He'd gobble his way up your arm if he could. He always wanted something extra." The Big O proved that African-Americans could play the game any way necessary, yet always with a style as personalized as his one-handed jumper.

HANG TIME

Throughout the fifties the big cities of the East spawned an unprecedented wave of African-American basketball talent. Just as schools, housing, and business opened up to Blacks, new opportunities came to play at once all-white colleges—if you were a star high school player. At this juncture only truly exceptional players were being nurtured. Elgin Gay Baylor and

Cornelius "Connie" Hawkins are two artistic peers, but one almost slipped through the cracks, while the other became a tragic victim of his own innocence. Baylor, matching hard work with God-given skills, made his mark and introduced fans to the dynamics of hang time. Hawkins was a similar master of suspended animation but was for too long denied his rightful place in the basketball pantheon; his is a story of a man squeezed between naïveté and racism.

Baylor emerged out of the same city that Edwin B. Henderson made a basketball hotbed in the twenties. Today the nation's capital is a "chocolate city," noted for both its overwhelming African-American population and its controversial longtime (now former) mayor Marion Barry. Back in the fifties it was an extremely segregated city, a place where the white leaders of this country only saw Blacks when they shined their shoes or washed their clothes. Baylor recalled, "There was nothing there: the movies were closed to us. We couldn't go. We had what was supposed to be a public park but Blacks and minorities couldn't play there, so we spent our time entertaining ourselves by playing in the alleys, playing stickball, or maybe football if someone was fortunate enough to find a football. We never had a basketball or any place to play with it."

Family friend Clarence Haynesworth, who was attending Miami Teachers College, came home one summer with a basketball and asked Baylor, 6´2˝ while still an adolescent, to play with him at a recently integrated park. For two years, under Haynesworth's tutelage, Baylor grew to understand and love the game. One problem—he couldn't beat his teacher one-on-one. Finally, after two years, Baylor bested Haynesworth. Enthused by that win Baylor joined the local Boys Club team and the Springarm High junior varsity. When, as a sophomore, he didn't make the varsity, upset, he refused to return to the junior varsity. Instead, he competed in a recreational league composed of high school grads and ex-college players. Against these bigger, older men Baylor improved immensely. Not only did he go back and make Springarm's team, but he was named a high school all-American in his senior year.

Unfortunately, Baylor blossomed too late to attract many college recruiters. Most of his scholarship offers came from schools in the District or Maryland, and he desperately wanted to go out of town. A home boy attending the College of Idaho on a football scholarship told his coach about Baylor's great athletic skills and, apparently, talked him onto the football team. Luckily for Baylor it rained for two weeks when he first arrived in the Potato State, so the football team spent its time playing basketball. It didn't take long for folks to notice how much better Baylor was at shooting than carrying a ball. Soon he had a basketball scholarship and as a freshman tore up his junior college opposition. That spring he listened to the 1955 NCAA title game between Russell's Dons and LaSalle on the radio and began contemplating big-time college ball.

Happy away from the oppression of D.C., Baylor decided to go farther West, accepting a scholarship to Seattle University. The Northwest, which had few African-American residents at the time, was considered a relatively liberal region. After World War II the city hosted a vibrant jazz and r&b scene that nurtured Quincy Jones and Ray Charles, among others. In this relaxed environment Baylor thrived. In 1958 Seattle made the finals, and its lead guard (and second leading scorer and rebounder) was ex-DuSable Panther Charlie Brown, who was to Baylor's offense what K. C. Jones was to Russell's defense.

From the East Coast Baylor brought the shakes, fakes, and jazzy feints that marked Black street ball. But Baylor added something personal—the ability to walk on air. As a Seattle newsman wrote, "He has never really broken the law of gravity but he is awfully slow about obeying it." Watching film clips of Seattle's number 22 in his white Chieftains jersey one sees moves that are the commonplace of the NBA circa 1990: Baylor goes up, under the backboard, and lays the ball up on the other side; Baylor barrels down the left side of the court and then takes off, gliding forward to the hoop and then—suspended in flight—flips the ball in with his right hand. His release point on that drive is rim high, and his hips are at the same height as one earthbound defender's head.

In 1959 *Sports Illustrated* contained this wonderful description of prime-time Baylor: "For spectators probably the most pleasure yielding move this graceful young man makes comes when he brings the ball up court alone and, unable to spot a free teammate, decides to work his way toward pay dirt without help. He turns his back to his defensive man and begins a series of rhythmic dribbling feints from side to side, all the while sliding steps closer to the basket, protecting the ball with elbows and shoulders ... If the defensive man gets no help Baylor nearly always drives him with continuous feints to distraction and error, and slips in for a twisting lay-up. In this climactic move he hangs in mid-air seemingly for long seconds while he makes up his mind whether to shoot or pass off, so that to the very end the defense is mystified."

In today's jargon Baylor played "big." At 6′5″ Baylor jumped over and sailed past the era's lumbering centers and forwards with impunity. You could practice Baylor's moves, but the wings were all his.

Connie Hawkins, according to sundry eyewitnesses, could hang as high as Baylor when still in high school. "Ghetto ball puts a premium on style, spring, moves, grace and showmanship," wrote his biographer David Wolf. "Hawkins, even at age 17, had these in abundance. He was already stunning spectators with his hesitation hook. Connie would leap toward the basket, the ball raised above his head in one hand, then hang in the air—as though suspended by invisible wires."

Skinny to the point of looking undernourished, extremely poor even by the lower-working-class standards of his friends in Brooklyn's Bedford-Stuyvesant neighborhood, and shabbily educated by his teachers at Boys High, Hawkins could easily have become just another forgotten young brother. But his hang time made Hawkins a commodity and that, along with the changing personality of his school, was both his salvation and curse.

During the fifties Bed-Sty, a section of mid-Brooklyn dotted with beautiful brownstones, overcrowded tenements, and projects located in the center of New York's most populous borough, saw its population shift from white ethnics to African-American and Caribbean-American immigrants. When Hawkins enrolled in 1956 Boys was about 50 percent white. When he exited in 1960 brothers and sisters constituted 70 percent of the school population. This changing population led many white teachers to disrespect its now predominantly Black population. Hawkins, for example, was regularly referred to as an "idiot" by one so-called educator. Due to his real reading difficulties and tests that were culturally biased in a time before this was realized, Hawkins's IQ was found to be sixty-five, or that of a moron.

Instead of dealing with his educational inadequacies Boys' administration, like so many schools then and now, pimped him. The school's philosophy was that athletes should be allowed to play because their achievements bolstered school pride. This meant player-students weren't required, expected, or even be able to learn. It meant that the true message Boys' teachers communicated, to players and to the student body, was that athletics were more important than academics for poor Black folk. By holding up Boys' sports stars as the school's role models its white administration made academic

excellence seem a secondary goal. Academically, Hawkins, basketball legend, was a tragedy. At Boys, and at schools like it
around the nation, white teachers had contemptuously low
expectations of their Black charges. Robert Lipsyte captured
the idiocy of Hawkins's situation when he wrote, "The scouts
and college coaches who infest schoolboy basketball said
Hawkins would be a superstar in the NBA, that the only thing
he couldn't do was sign his name for autographs. It seemed
unnecessarily cruel at the time, but they were, of course, basically right."

While Hawkins floundered in the classroom (when he
showed up), he overwhelmed all competition on the court—
whether at the Rucker, at public school, or in games at Brooklyn's Riis Park. As a sophomore Hawkins watched from the
bench as Boys was upset by another Black athletic factory, the
Bronx's De Witt Clinton. Over the next two years, a time
when doo wop was the coolest sound on the city's streets, the
Hawk led Boys to titles in 1958 and 1959. June 29, 1960, was
a key day in Hawkins's life. That morning he received a general diploma from Boys High. That afternoon he was most valuable player of a high school all-star game in Jersey City despite
arriving late. As an extra-special bonus he dominated his longtime rival, Wingate's Roger Brown.

The seeds of Hawkins's tragedy were planted in the same
schoolyards that gave him an identity. At Rucker and Riis
Park, where the cream of the city's basketball crop congregat-
ed, so did older men playing the angles. Some were simply
recruiters seeking to steer kids to certain schools. Many others
were gamblers. The 1951 scandal had put a damper on local
sports betting, but it never disappeared. By the late fifties a
national network of college-sport gambling was once more a
profit center for organized crime. Enter Jack Molinas, a street-
wise Bronx baby, an honor student at Stuyvesant High, a 6'5"

forward who led Columbia to the Ivy League title in 1951 while, though no one knew it, he was shaving points. He was highly regarded by coaches and was, in fact, selected to play against the Trotters in a series of college all-star games. As a rookie with the Fort Wayne Pistons in 1953–1954 Molinas was thought to have rookie of the year potential as he averaged 12.1 per game the season's first half. But twenty-nine games was all the NBA ball he'd ever play. Caught betting on games through a Bronx bookie, Molinas was banned from the NBA for life by commissioner Maurice Podoloff. Once back in New York Molinas graduated from Brooklyn Law School, played and coached in the Eastern League, and gambled at night. Along with an older gambler named Joe Hacken, Molinas developed a network of players and referees in football and basketball who shaved points. In the summer of 1960 he met Hawkins at a ball court in Manhattan Beach, Brooklyn. All Hawkins knew was that Molinas was an attorney who once played in the NBA and was friendly with lots of young players. And that's all Molinas let him know. Loans of small cash and access to a car Molinas provided Hawkins were all part of a setup, but Molinas hadn't planned on approaching him about point shaving until Hawkins's sophomore year at whatever college he attended.

So Hawkins went off to the University of Iowa in the fall of 1961 ("They seemed like nice people, and they offered me the most money," he said), blind to Molinas's machinations. For eight months Hawkins stumbled through school. He wasn't just unprepared for classes, he, again like many other less celebrated Blacks, was socially uncomfortable in its virtually all-white atmosphere. When he destroyed junior forward and future Celtic star Don Nelson in varsity-junior varsity contests, the Iowa athletic department was ecstatic. Whether they could have kept Hawkins academically eligible for another three years is an unanswered question. We'll never know because at the end of that eighth month a New York detective traveled to Iowa to bring him home.

Ten years after the 1951 scandal D.A. Frank Hogan again cracked a college sports betting case, and the Hawk, whom Molinas had loaned $200 the summer before, was about to take a fall—at the time he didn't even understand what point shaving was.

For the next two weeks Hawkins was grilled by Hogan's staff and, ultimately, would not be one of the twenty-two players indicted with Molinas. But during that fateful two weeks Hogan told the press Hawkins and longtime rival Roger Brown had introduced Molinas to many other players, suggesting the pair were procuring for the gambler. When he arrived back in Iowa, athletic department officials, the same folks who'd planned to keep him eligible, informed Hawkins there was no way he could catch up in his studies. Now a public relations liability, no longer a valuable commodity, Iowa showed Hawkins the door. The 1961–1962 season was a magical one in NBA history. Chamberlain averaged 50.4 points a game (including 100 in one historic contest against the Knicks) for the Philadelphia Warriors. Baylor had a career-best average of 38.3, including a play-off record sixty-one against the Celtics. Oscar Robertson was the only player to average double figures in assists with 11.4. Overall league scoring reached 118.9 per team, a mark not attained again for another eighteen years. Yet it was Russell, knocking in a career-high 18.9 points himself, who led Boston to its third straight NBA crown with his defense. With Russell backstopping against opponents the Celtics gave up a league low of 111.9 per game and at 9.2 enjoyed the greatest margin between points scored and points allowed.

It was also the year Hawkins made his pro debut in a short-lived enterprise named the American Basketball League. The ABL was the brainchild of the Trotters' Abe Saperstein, who sought revenge for being denied the first NBA franchise on the West Coast. The ABL was historic in two important ways: it introduced the three-point shot, and John McLendon, who'd left Tennessee A&I, became the first African-American coach employed by a national pro league. Sadly for McLendon and Dick Barnett, who'd left the Lakers to play for his old coach, the team was owned by an overbearing shipbuilder named George Steinbrenner. The young Steinbrenner interfered with McLendon from day one, including coming down to sit on the bench during some games. The ABL started a lot of trends.

For Connie Hawkins 1962 began some long sad years of gypsydom. He was one of the game's greats, yet he spent most of his prime years playing in half-filled arenas for obscure teams pining away for NBA acceptance—an apt example of where most African-American players stood at the beginning of the sixties. Despite the presence of superstars on the pro and white college courts, quotas and racism kept the majority of African-America's most gifted b-ball artists playing their music away from the spotlight. Still, those breakthrough stars fed a fever of desire for the game in the young. To be fly, slick, clever, and cool was to be a ballplayer. Those with a practical bent saw basketball as H. B. Thompson did, a vehicle for young men to get to college and use that free education to set up the rest of their lives. Unfortunately, in the ten years to come basketball became more than a means to an end; it became the end itself.

CHANGING TIMES

n September 1964, ten years after the Tennessee National High School Athletic Association moved toward integration, forcing the NHSAA to move from its site on Tennessee A&I's campus to Alabama State in Montgomery. From 1954 to 1964 schools from Kentucky and Tennessee captured eight titles, and Nashville's Pearl High, located just a short school bus ride from Tennessee A&I, won four of them. The star of a couple of those victorious Pearl High teams was Perry Wallace, the player Fisk's H. B. Thompson couldn't reach, who, in 1965, enrolled at Vanderbilt and became the Southeastern Athletic Conference's first Black player. Appropriately, considering its history, the NHSAA's final victor was a school from Montgomery named after Booker T. Washington. For the twelfth time in the forty-two Black high school tournaments a school named after The Wizard of Tuskegee made the finals. Washington's philosophy of economic self-help and social accommodation had made him a symbolic leader of Blacks, even long after his death. But the forces that integrated high school basketball, and killed this tournament, introduced a new commonplace name for minority schools. For the rest of the decade and well into the future, public, middle, and high schools would be named not after Washington but after Dr. Martin Luther King, Jr.

■   ■   ■

The careers of many NHSAA grads reflect the way the cutting edge of Black athletics shifted from Black schools determined to maintain strong, self-sustaining activities to white coaches eager to pluck outstanding individual players. In 1963 Eddie "Man with the Golden Arm" Miles was the Detroit Pistons' number-one draft choice after a college career at Seattle University, where he had challenged Elgin Baylor's scoring records. In that same year Victor Rouse and Leslie Hunter were crucial cogs of the NCAA champion Loyola of Chicago squad. The first national platform Miles, Rouse, and Hunter performed on was the NHSAA's Black high school tournament. Back in '59, as a senior at Arkansas's Scipio Jones High, Miles knocked in forty-five points in a 76-72 defeat by Nashville's Pearl High in the title game. (Pearl's leading scorer that year, Ronnie Lawson, received a scholarship to UCLA.)

In 1960 6´6˝ Rouse and 6´7˝ Hunter, both of Pearl, made the all-NHSAA tournament team and were spotted by Loyola coach George Ireland as they led the Nashville school to its third straight title. Ireland later noted, "I was the only coach in the stands at the tournament at Tennessee A&I in Nashville when Hunter and Rouse were seniors in high school. The year after we won the NCAA championship there were so many coaches there that you couldn't get tickets."

The recruitment of Black athletes begun in the fifties on a piecemeal basis with the recruitment of Robertson and Chamberlain was now in full swing. For the first time Black males were a prominent presence on white campuses and its students and alumni were confronted with having to root for their success if their alma mater was to prosper athletically. More significant, in pursuit of victory ambitious coaches took a stand and abandoned the "two Blacks on court at home, three on the road, and four when behind" formula.

Two historic midsixties NCAA champions, Loyola in 1963 and Texas Western in 1966, shattered the limits on Black participation. George Ireland, a pioneer in seeking out Black talent, with Rouse and Hunter in his starting lineup, went further in 1963 by starting four Blacks. Along with forward Rouse and center Hunter, guards Ron Miller and all-American Jerry Harkness were introduced to the crowd at the start of Loyola games. Back in 1963, even up North, this was considered a radical move. The Ramblers were probably one of the first integrated teams in NCAA Division I actually to start its best five players, regardless of color. Ireland's enlightened self-interest paid major dividends, for not only did Loyola win, but it won with flair. New Yorker Harkness, a high school track star, had blazing speed that gave him easy hoops and a 21.4 per game average. With Harkness setting the tempo the Ramblers scored an average of 91.8 points a game and gave up only 68.1. No surprise then that Ireland's team won twenty-nine of thirty-one contests.

In this transitional time in American society every blow against segregation had heightened significance. When his team was denied room service in New Orleans and Houston,

Ireland used the accompanying furor to speak out against prejudice and gain national notoriety. Loyola's most racially sensitive game in 1966 came during the NCAA tournament. After smashing Tennessee Tech, 111-42, in the first round, the Ramblers were pitted against Southeastern Conference champ Mississippi State. In the past the Bulldogs, respecting the state's segregationist policy, had bypassed the NCAA to avoid the possibility of playing against Blacks.

But even at Ole Miss times were changing. Coach Babe McCarthy displayed courage by sneaking his team off campus to the NCAA site before a Mississippi court order arrived prohibiting his all-white squad from playing in the NCAA tournament for fear of on-court race mixing. McCarthy decided it was a civil rights issue: the rights of his players to compete were being denied by state officials. So his bold move can be seen as a response to the civil rights movement. Besides, McCarthy thought, if the Bulldogs played their usual slow-tempo game, they might upset the Ramblers and win a smashing victory for the state. It almost worked, as Loyola won in a tight contest, 61-51.

In the NCAA final Loyola was matched against a well-integrated Cincinnati club that had won two straight titles. The championship game was Loyola's first national television exposure of the year, so the sight of all those brothers on court at one time shocked many viewers. Cincinnati was rightfully favored, but in overtime Rouse, product of Black schools and the NHSAA, grabbed an offensive rebound and laid it in to win the title for Loyola, 60-58.

Three years later, the inevitable happened. An all-Black starting five made the finals in a game that summed up basketball's altered sociology. Texas Western's (now Texas at El Paso) starting five of Bobby Joe Hill, Orsten Artis, David "Big Daddy" Lattin, Harry Flournoy, and Willie Cager amassed a

23-1 record in the 1965–1966 season (the team's other five were seldom-used whites). But since Texas Western didn't play any top teams, was based in the Southwest away from the basketball press, and was an independent, their quality was questioned. Moreover, Don Haskins's reliance on so many Blacks and their free-lance offensive system led many to label them "uncoachable, if not incorrigible," according to sportswriter Joe Gergen. Both attributions, like the popular urban crime term, "law and order," were used in the sixties as code words for racist assumptions. Those who hadn't seen the Miners before didn't know that the team's foot speed and leaping ability, certainly useful on offense, could be devastating on defense. Playing a gambling, go-for-the-steal style, Haskins effectively exploited the Miners' quickness as a weapon. They were a step or two swifter than most opponents, and over the course of a game that difference, plus intensity, resulted in easy lay-ups and created turnovers. Blinded by bigotry, many claimed the Miners won only with raw talent, and didn't play intelligently. But the pressure game, applied by 5'6" jumping jack Willie Worsley as well as 6'7" Lattin, was a system that suited Haskins's aggregation.

Quite appropriately, the coach confronting Texas Western's Black aesthetic style was the reigning granddaddy of classroom ball, Kentucky's crusty Adolph Rupp. At sixty-four the Baron had already won two NCAA titles, and that year's Wildcats—labeled Rupp's Runts because no player measured over 6'5"—seemed poised to exploit the "helter-skelter" Miners. It's interesting that in the midsixties, UCLA, with titles in 1964 and 1965, and this Kentucky team made the NCAA finals with no players over 6'5". All three teams emphasized quickness, passing, and solid coaching. The difference was that while UCLA mixed white and Black players, Kentucky remained a symbol of segregation with a team as lily-white as their jerseys. The stars of the Wildcats were two long-range shooters, forward Pat Riley and guard Louie Dampier.

Rupp was, to many Blacks, the basketball version of Birmingham police chief Bull Connor and the embodiment of segregation's lingering hold on the South. His Runts were a quick, smart club, but on March 19, 1966, at College Park, Maryland, it became apparent early on that Riley and company weren't swift enough. Midway through the first half, on consecutive Kentucky trips up-court, Bobby Joe Hill stole the ball from the Wildcats and drove in for lay-ups that pushed the score from 10-9 to 14-9. This application of Texas Western "D" was the game's turning point. Kentucky got as close as one point in the second half, but the "uncoachable" Miners kept their poise and knocked down twenty-eight of thirty-four free throws. Final score: Texas Western 71, Kentucky 65. In a close game the African-American players rose to Kentucky's challenge, and that extra step had been the difference. For liberals who sought social symbolism in sport the 1966 NCAA title contest was perfection.

For Don Haskins, however, it just opened a can of worms. Winning the title focused national attention on the school, and what was discovered embarrassed Haskins. Most of the Texas Western players were either failing academically, or worse, being carried by the school to keep them eligible. Haskins was publicly accused of exploiting his Black recruits for his own glory. For the first time the question of the intellectual cost of athletic integration was being raised. Yes, a basketball scholarship got these brothers into college. But what good did it do them if they made no progress toward a degree? Or if their basketball training didn't result in a long, lucrative pro career? Over time many of the Texas Western starters did earn their degrees, but their athletic pimping revealed the dark side of the Black player + white school equation. It was one triumph for Blacks to gain entry to these august institutions. It was another for Blacks to truly benefit from the academic opportunities.

In addition, the acceptance of Black players led optimistic Blacks and well-intentioned whites to concoct a grossly unrealistic and romantic notion of what the celebration of a few jocks meant about the perception of all Blacks. Sure, it was all right for a brown-skinned man to score two points for the alma mater or for white students to cheer his feats in the anonymity of a crowded stadium; it was quite another for him to move next door, date a white man's daughter, question the circumstances of his employment, or make millions while wearing shorts.

Throughout the sixties and into the next decade Black players began committing all these taboo acts. An antagonism between these players and their fans, unfailingly pointed out and often exploited by the sports media, built into a long, ongoing war of words. Phrases like "discipline problems," "schoolyard style," and "poor work habits" appeared on sports pages. They were supposed to be "informed" judgments, when actually they were merely coded terms for deeper conflicts over values, politics, and money that were causing turmoil in the entire nation, not just the sheltered dreamland of sports.

The era's cultural struggles spilled onto the playing field and into the locker room. The wearing of an Afro hairstyle, an interest in the Black Panthers, or the playing of James Brown's "Say It Loud—I'm Black and I'm Proud" on an eight-track tape player on the team bus could be perceived as a break with acceptable athletic protocol. Just as civil rights gave birth to Black militants, pioneering ballplayers gave way to less complacent athletes. The brilliant center fielder Willie Mays, a humble Southerner always eager to play and ready with the innocuous quote, was considered a "good Negro" role model not only because he played the game like a God but because he sported a "just-happy-to-be-here" attitude.

The designation of certain African-Americans as "role models" and "credits to their race" was a staple of speechmakers and sportswriters of the period. But the role-model notion was nothing more than a placebo that clouded the general failings of the government in aiding its darker citizens. "If this gifted jock can make it, what's the matter with the rest of you Negroes?" the role model's presence implied.

DYNASTY BUILDERS

Still, many in the nation were seized with a genuine desire for brotherhood. And coaches at major universities, quite legitimately, sought ways to accommodate Blacks "because it was the right thing to do." That it meant wins that generated revenue for the franchise or university didn't hurt one bit. At the height of the civil rights movement two European-American coaches devised systems that made Black style integral parts of their teams' personas. The result? The longest-running dynasties in basketball history and the introduction of a formula for victory that would soon dominate the game. The architects, Boston Celtic coach-general manager Arnold "Red" Auerbach and UCLA coach John Wooden, couldn't have differed more. Auerbach, the son of Russian immigrants, was born in Brooklyn, learned the game in the era of the Original Celtics, and coached with several pro clubs before coming to Boston. Red was a volatile, passionate, cigar-smoking, loud-talking, big-city kid. He cursed referees, screamed at players, and was constantly scheming up ways to bedevil opponents. That the opposing team's locker room at Boston Garden is often heat-wave hot, the showers icy-cold, and the stalls unnecessarily small testify to his gamesmanship.

Wooden, a devout Christian from the small Indiana town of Martinsville, was an outstanding guard at Purdue before coaching for many years in the Midwest. Wooden never swore, wrote bits of optimistic poetry, and believed in a pyramid of success he used as a guideline for living. According to his pyramid, "Success is a peace of mind which is a direct result of self-satisfaction in knowing you did your best to become the best that you are capable of becoming." If Auerbach's demeanor suggested a Lower East Side retailer, Wooden looked and talked like a genial high school history professor.

Yet their coaching environments conspired to make them kindred spirits. Celtic owner Walter Brown had been the first to draft an African-American and, with the acquisition of Bill Russell, the first to allow his coach to build their club around one. Brown's liberalism allowed Auerbach to steadily challenge the league's quota system until, in 1964 Boston—in the eighties chastised for its abundance of white players—had the NBA's first all-Black starting lineup. Though sixth man John Havlicek was a key player, Russell, K. C. and Sam Jones, Tom "Satch" Sanders, and Willie Naulls opened most contests.

Naulls, also known as "Willie the Whale," played at UCLA under Wooden and was part of a long African-American sports tradition at that Southern California school. Nobel Prize–winning diplomat Ralph Bunche, Olympic track stars Ralph Metcalfe and Rafer Johnson, and, of course, Jackie Robinson were all celebrated and well treated there. The progressive environment of the Westwood campus, complemented by Wooden's own intolerance of bigotry, made it easy for the school to attract Black stars.

Auerbach and Wooden, products of two different but venerable basketball atmospheres, came to the same conclusion—the jumping ability and quickness African-Americans brought to the game demanded systems that capitalized on these gifts. The Celtics and the Bruins dominated the sixties because Auerbach and Wooden understood how to utilize Black talent more intelligently than their peers.

WALT AND THEN LEW

The UCLA Bruins won the NCAA championship in 1964, 1965, 1967, 1968, and 1969 (and then took five of the first six titles in the seventies). Teams covering a ten-year span tend to vary based on individual strengths and weaknesses. But the Black aesthetic thread running through them is clear, and it starts with Walt Hazzard, who in '64 was a 6′2″ senior point guard with a mixed reputation. A *Sports Illustrated* preseason preview commented, "Flashy Walt Hazzard still leads the Bruins," then added, "He is one of the best offensive players in the nation and one of the worst defensive players on the coast. As he goes, so go the team's chances." Hazzard was a product of Overbrook High, which aside from Wilt Chamberlain spawned NBA stars Wali Jones and Wayne Embry, and was viewed negatively by some because he was a behind-the-back, through-the-legs smoothie whose instincts often ran counter to Wooden's conviction that you don't embarrass an opponent. At one point in 1961 Hazzard had considered quitting UCLA after a Wooden benching. Only a strong reprimand from his minister father kept him on the Coast.

Hazzard has his own view of those prechampionship UCLA years. "There was an article in the L.A. *Times* celebrating the twenty-fifth anniversary of our championship team in which he [Wooden] said I had a lot of 'hot dog,'" he says. "Well, that was a bunch of bullshit," Hazzard says. "I made passes that were not in the textbook, but the passes were on the money. If I made a behind-the-back pass or did something beyond the norm it was because the situation was created and I was just capitalizing on it. That was something he had to learn. The implication of the quote was that he had to give me discipline. I had discipline all my life. My father was a minister. Shit, I can talk about discipline. I was no street kid. My father had a Ph.D. since nineteen fifty-two from Temple University. So, no, he didn't have to tame me: I was never in gangs, I was never in trouble. I was a kid who loved to play ball.

"Those kind of comments reflect that whole stereotype that all Black kids are the same. It's like people who criticize 'The Cosby Show,' saying it isn't realistic because we have all types of families in our communities. We have poor, middle-class, we have rich. We have zillionaires and have always had them. I resent that general imagery.

"I went to UCLA because it had a tradition that dated back to the twenties of having Black athletes. When a Saturday football Game of the Week came on that had Ole Miss or Alabama, we'd turn the TV off rather than watch that crap. But when UCLA or USC came on there were Black players out there. UCLA had Jackie Robinson, Ralph Bunche, Willie Naulls, Willie Strode, Tom Bradley. Willie Naulls recommended me to John Wooden. I was the high school player of the year in Philadelphia and Willie saw me play in the preliminary game of a Philadelphia Warriors game when they were still in Philadelphia."

Wooden knew Hazzard's exceptional speed and quick decision making could lead to a title. But changes, not just in Hazzard's game but in Wooden's approach, were necessary. Bruin assistant coach Jerry Norman later recalled: "We knew Walt was fantastic on the run, especially if we spread the court. The question we asked ourselves was, 'How do we create it?' The answer was by forcing the tempo more to our liking. We needed to create more full-court and spread-court situations, to take advantage of all our quickness."

Wooden went back to his years as a coach in Indiana for the answer. By utilizing a 2-2-1 zone press, UCLA forced turnovers and bad shots, which led in turn to Bruin fast breaks. Though no starter was taller than 6'5", the Bruins' attacking style left them undefeated in thirty games. As UCLA coaches had anticipated, Hazzard thrived in a system tailored to his talents, going on to average 18.6 per game.

After they beat Duke for the title, 98-83, Hazzard was named consensus all-American, college player of the year, and the NCAA tournament's outstanding player. But Hazzard did more than help UCLA win one title. His play established a tradition of quick, sharp-shooting African-American point guards that spanned their dynasty: Lucius Allen and Mike Warren in 1967 and 1968 (both years they were second and third leading scorer); Henry Bibby in 1970, 1971, and 1972; Larry Hollyfield and Tommy Curtis in 1973; and Andre McCarter in 1975.

Speed in the frontcourt was the hallmark of the 1964 champs and, subsequently, of Bruin basketball. Wooden disdained lumbering big men for players modeled after 6'5", 230-pound starting center Fred Slaughter, 6'3" reserve forward Kenny Washington, who starred in the 1964 and 1965 title games, and white leaper Keith Erickson. Taller, but in the same quick unselfish mold, would be dynasty upholders like Curtis Rowe, Sidney Wicks, Keith (later Jamal) Wilkes, and Marques Johnson. And Lew Alcindor was no one's idea of the immobile big man. Like Bill Russell and Wilt Chamberlain, this young man would redefine the center position. Equally important, this New Yorker would help introduce the nation to a new, more complicated vision of the African-American athlete.

Alcindor chose UCLA because of California's natural beauty,

the construction of a new arena called Pauley Pavilion, the Bruins' recent on-court success, and the fact that Wooden was "a well-read, genuinely caring man." When Alcindor announced he would attend UCLA in 1965 Wooden was confronted with a challenge that had overwhelmed Dick Harp at Kansas a decade before: how to turn a gifted seven-footer's skills into titles.

Previously, Wooden had successfully employed a high post offense that had his center stationed at the top of the key. This, for example, put Slaughter in position to set picks for jump shooters and left the middle open for UCLA cutters. It was an offense well suited to a quick team, most of whose scoring was generated by smaller players. Alcindor's recruitment led Wooden to scrap his highly successful high post offense for "a complete low post offense [that] placed the center deep, near the basket and well inside the free throw line." Never before, in over two decades of coaching, had Wooden employed a single low post, but "to take full advantage of his height, I wanted Lewis Alcindor no farther from the offensive basket than he could reach ... no more than eight feet away."

The bespectacled educator also made radical changes in his defensive system. Before, his forwards were forbidden to allow opponents any access to the baseline. Now, with Alcindor patroling the area under the basket, "We wanted our forwards to free-lance more on defense, gamble more, take more chances." With Alcindor anchored in the middle Wooden turned away from a formula that won titles in 1964 and 1965, feeling that "we were so strong with both our set offense and set defense that I decided not to make the press a basis of our defense and to fast-break only when Lewis could outlet the ball for a definite and obvious advantage."

Wooden's flexibility, based on a desire not to mold Alcindor in his image but to capitalize on his players' strengths, produced an eighty-eight and two record, including three NCAA crowns from 1966 to 1969. Before Alcindor's junior year his dominance led the NCAA rules committee to make dunking a violation. Though Alcindor was its chief target the savvy New Yorker saw the rule change in broader terms. "The dunk is one of basketball's great crowd pleasers," he said, "and there is no good reason to give it up except that this and other niggers were running away with the sport." This ridiculous barrier to basket bashing—rescinded ten years later—ironically had a profoundly positive effect on Alcindor's game. Denied the dunk's ease, he developed a variety of shots, including an embryonic skyhook, giving his game a dimension no seven-footer, including Wilt Chamberlain, ever possessed.

"It often seemed unfair that he should be on the same court with those little white boys who were trying to shoot over his head or drag him down by his underarm hair," wrote *New York Times* columnist Robert Lipsyte of the collegian Alcindor. "He was so tall, so mobile. He sometimes looked goofy on court, mouth open, ropy arms dangling as he loped along or just stood loafing in a corner, but in the moment of scoring or rebounding everything worked so efficiently; there was no scramble or tussle or herky-jerk about Alcindor. He seemed to know exactly where he was going and how to get there without knocking anyone down or using force of any kind."

Alcindor's nature, as player and man, during his UCLA years is suggested by his attitude toward the two games that involved him in an intraracial style war. Throughout his long career Alcindor's primary challenges came not from other competing seven-footers but from small, quick, jump-shooting centers. Elvin Hayes, a dirt-poor Louisiana kid, was the first. Driven by the philosophy, "I take the floor for every game confident I can beat my man and determined to do it," as a high school senior Hayes led Eulah Britton of little Rayville, Louisiana, to a state title. In 1964 his school was undefeated in fifty-four games that championship year as the 6´10˝ center averaged thirty-five points per game. In the midsixties, a time when athletic integration was outpacing integration in the student population at Southern schools, Hayes and guard Don Chaney became the first African-American players at the University of Houston. Yet Hayes felt underappreciated, particularly in comparison to Alcindor, who, playing at New York's Power Memorial High, had been the subject of national publicity since puberty. Hayes's envy led him to bad-mouth Alcindor following a UCLA win over Houston in the 1967 semifinals.

While country boy Hayes dogged Alcindor in the press with a vehemence usually associated with inner-city macho, Alcindor was unwilling to respond. He didn't buy into verbal bravado. The product of a dignified, staunchly Catholic, middle-class Trinidadian family—his father was a frustrated concert conductor forced by discrimination to work as a transit authority cop—Alcindor had a reserved, bookish demeanor that to Houston's center clearly meant "soft." By playing Cassius Clay to Alcindor's Sonny Liston or Floyd Patterson, Hayes sought to psyche out his taller opponent.

Hayes's rhetoric and the undefeated records of the two schools made UCLA's January 20, 1968, visit to Houston a national event. Attendance at the recently opened Astrodome was 52,693, including 4,000 standing-room tickets. In the era before network contracts to cover college ball, 150 independent stations organized to broadcast the game. It was so rare to have basketball at the huge indoor arena that Astrodome officials had to ship in the court itself from the Los Angeles Sports Arena. Enhancing the drama was an accident that happened eight days before the showdown: Alcindor had an eye scratched in a game against California. That injury resulted in Alcindor's shooting a pitiful four of eighteen in the showdown. Hayes's fired-up play, including twenty-nine points in the first half,

lifted the Cougars to a 71-69 victory as 50,000-plus Houstoni-
ans chanted, "E! E! E! E!" On the cover of *Sports Illustrated* the
next week was a photograph of Hayes shooting over Alcindor.

Sophisticated enough to know that any sign of bitterness
toward Hayes would become an instant headliner, Alcindor
played it cool. But inside his locker the *Sports Illustrated* cover
was taped up. The teams met again in the 1968 NCAA semifinals in Los Angeles with Hayes's hard-core mentality and
Alcindor's intense, yet introverted, competitiveness apparent in
this passage from Alcindor's autobiography, *Giant Steps:* "The
first or second time down the floor on offense, as I posted low
and looked for the ball, I felt Elvin lean on me and heard him
threaten, 'We're gonna beat you. We're gonna beat you bad!' I
didn't answer, I was too busy." Using a revamped defense that
held Hayes to ten points the Bruins smashed Houston, 101-69.
For Alcindor, who scored nineteen points and grabbed eighteen
rebounds against Hayes and company, the next day's finals victory over North Carolina was anticlimactic.

Alcindor could stay so detached from the boasting so integral to Black jock style because his perspective had grown
wider than the court. Unlike so many players whose self-
images were wrapped up in stardom, Alcindor spent his college years engaged in a spiritual quest. He'd say later, "All
sophomore and junior years I'd been looking for something to
believe in." Under the spell of Malcolm X's autobiography, the
saga of the slain leader's evolution from the pimp Detroit Red
to Black Muslim spokesman to Islamic convert, Alcindor
embarked on his own internal odyssey. After much reading
and reflection he found a home in the Sunni sect of Islam during the summer of 1968. Though not yet announcing it publicly he changed his name from Lewis Alcindor to Kareem
("noble and generous"), Abdul ("servant"), and finally Jabbar
("powerful"). It was this new consciousness that helped inform

his decision not to join the U.S. Olympic team.

The call for a Black boycott of the summer games in Mexico City had been instigated by activist-educator Harry Edwards. Edwards's argument was simple: African-Americans could use the boycott to dramatize American racism on an international stage. The pressure on young Black athletes to play was tremendous, but Jabbar, political and pragmatic, said simply that he "had better things to do. Playing the Olympics would have meant losing a full quarter's worth of classes and not graduate from UCLA on time, and I had no intention of disrupting my education so that a country that was abusing my people could be made to shine for the world."

He was deluged with hate mail, booed at away games, and taunted in the press—nothing new for seven-foot Black men unfortunately—but now it was all with a new vicious edge. That hate grew when his name change and adoption of a non-Christian religion was revealed in 1971. In the sentimental glow of his retirement in 1990 it's easy to forget that during his college and early professional career Jabbar was, to many Americans, an uppity, unpatriotic freak who, like Muhammad Ali, Olympic protesters John Carlos and Tommy Smith, and football-hero-turned-actor Jim Brown, was challenging the complacent platitudes white fans got from the previous generation of Black athletes.

THE HUNTER REVISITED

In 1968 another center who would have made that list of most unpopular jocks played in his last NBA campaign. During an election in which George Wallace and future President Richard Nixon were exploiting white fear of Black gains, Bill Russell was "disenchanted with the civil rights movements," too. His reasons, however, would have made Wallace and Nixon cringe. "I do not believe there should be more compromises," he wrote in *Go Up for Glory*. "I know it is not practical, but I still believe there should not be ... Civil rights today tranquil, too filled with compromise. A few years back it was superb. ... But, you see, this one time—the first time—when Negroes should have stood together alone, representing all Negroes. Then, they might have done more with the power block. Instead, they began in a situation which led to compromise. And they began feuding among themselves, fighting for power. Any organization such as that can be defeated. Is defeated."

"Militant" comments like these freaked out the sports establishment in general and Boston sportswriters in particular. Anything he said regarding race relations, and Russell rarely bit his tongue on the subject, was open to misinterpretation. In 1959, after traveling to Liberia, he spoke of the deep yearning all Blacks have to visit Africa. In an offhand remark he told a writer, "Yeah, I'm moving to Liberia. Maybe I will. I'll get away from *you* anyway." The reporter left out that last sentence and reported that Russell was planning a move to Liberia. He was labeled, without a smile, "Felton X" (Felton being Russell's middle name) by some in the media. Even Russell's goatee, a hip, bebop-inspired look, was viewed by some Beantowners as evidence of subversion.

Despite these breaches of athletic decorum, criticism of number 6 could only go so far. From 1956 to his retirement in 1969 he led the Boston Celtics to eleven championships, a record of excellence unmatched in the history of the sport at any level. The key was defense—Russell's defense. Auerbach built a defensive system around his center just as Wooden did around his. But considering how long it worked and the competition it was employed against, the Celtic success must be viewed as the greater achievement. As teammate Tom Heinsohn has said, "Prior to Russell, everyone was involved essentially with guarding his own man. But then Russell introduced us to what he called 'help defense,' or what some of our guys began calling the 'funnel defense,' in which everyone was free to gamble a bit, to overplay his man on the outside, driving all of that traffic inside or down the middle, where Russell had set up a roadblock."

Russell was so quick and his presence so dominating he literally ran guys out of the league. Both Heinsohn and Bob Cousy cited Neil Johnston as a victim of Russell's wrath. "Neil was a 6–8 center from Ohio State," Cousy said. "He had a square jaw and a funny half-hook, half-runner shot that was accurate enough to make him the league's leading scorer for three consecutive seasons. By the time Russ came along Johnston was a little past his prime, but the Philadelphia Warriors weren't in the market for a replacement. Neil Johnston was still a respected player in the league ... Right from the start, Russ didn't even have to jump to block Johnston's shot. He would be there quicker and poor Neil went from being scoring champion to being out of the league. In short order. It wasn't just Russell; Neil Johnston couldn't play against anybody. It was incredible the effect Bill Russell had on a man who had been such a scoring machine."

Once Russell had either blocked a shot or intimidated opponents into a miss, the second phase of his skill, and the Celtic game plan, went into effect. "Russell had an effective rebounding range of eighteen feet," Heinsohn said. "If he was nine feet off to one side of the basket, he could race over to pull down a rebound nine feet off to the other side! I saw him do it many times. That's the kind of athletic ability he had. So now all I had to do on defense was check my man, just hold him off until he was in no position to challenge for the rebound, then release him and take off ... In effect Russell was making me play faster than I really was, and he was doing the same thing for Loscy [Jim Loscutoff] and the others. Energies we once had to expend on defense were now almost totally concentrated on offense. We began crashing the offensive boards with abandon, which meant we were now taking more shots than ever, and our fast break became truly devastating." Not only did Russell scoop the ball off the defensive glass, he also threw long accurate downcourt passes to breaking teammates.

At the start of his Celtic career Russell's best offensive move was to beat the opposing center downcourt for lay-ups. In a half-court offensive Russell was a poor dribbler and didn't have the one or two automatic shots every scorer needs. But over time he developed a solid jump hook and a fifteen-foot jumper. By the early sixties, especially against a slow-footed center, Russell was a genuine scoring threat, though he'd never average more than eighteen points per game. But in Auerbach's system it wasn't necessary.

The modern idea of the role player—the power forward, point and shooting guard, the sixth man—were Auerbach-inspired innovations. With Russell the defensive hub and occasional scorer, Auerbach constructed teams that, whether by design or not, featured whites as scorers and African-Americans as defenders. During Russell's thirteen seasons the Celtics' leading scorer was white eight times and first and second leading scorer six times. The Celtics sought points from Sam Jones, Cousy's replacement at lead guard spot, or whoever played the small or shooting forward. Whether it was shooters like Heinsohn or Bailey Howell or swingmen/sixth men like Frank Ramsey and John Havlicek, the players in these positions put up the most shots per game. With the exception of Sam Jones, the African-American Celtics performed in Russell's defensive mode. The crucial characters were Russell's longtime running mate K. C. Jones and New York University's star forward Tom

"Satch" Sanders. During his nine years as a Celtic K.C. never averaged in double figures and Sanders, in thirteen seasons, never averaged over 12.6 points. Jones's job was to handle the ball, feed the shooters, and harass the Oscar Robertsons and Jerry Wests of the NBA into poor shots and frustration. Up front Sanders covered Elgin Baylor, Chet Walker, and every other high-scoring forward in the league. While K.C. had been a defensive specialist in college, Sanders had been the scoring star of an upstart New York University squad that crashed the Final Four in 1960. Auerbach saw in Sanders's ability to rebound and his unusually long arms the perfect complement to Russell, and he was. John Thompson, a Washington, D.C., native who played at Providence, Russell's backup from 1964 to 1966 and Wayne Embry, who played behind Russell from 1966 to 1968, were rugged, big-bodied men assigned to get rebounds and pound the opposition when Russell rested. It's significant that during the Russell era, a time when the Black aesthetic was altering the game, Auerbach's Blacks played very straight. Sam Jones, a man whose use of the bank as an offensive weapon was "revolutionary" according to Auerbach, was the closest Boston came to flamboyance. Jones, however, was a quiet, soft-spoken man who never encouraged press coverage or attempted to dominate games. Yet he seemed to be able to do it when he wanted to. Russell asked him about it at one point and recalls him saying, "I don't want the responsibility of having to play like that every night," a decision that perplexed Russell and reflects what made Sam Jones a key to, but not the star of, the Boston Celtics.

When you look at Russell and the Celtics it's hard not to think of their great antagonist, Wilt Chamberlain. He faced the Celtics in playoff competition as a member of three teams in three cities—the Philadelphia 76ers, Los Angeles Lakers, and Philadelphia (later San Francisco) Warriors. It was these confrontations with Boston that earned Wilt "the loser" label and years later won Russell the award "Greatest Player in the History of the NBA." Russell truly deserved that award over Chamberlain only if it said "Greatest Winner." Chamberlain's statistical mastery is immense. Even Jabbar, who broke many of Chamberlain's records, did them in longer seasons and in more years; his stats should be viewed with the same skepticism Jim Brown has for Walter Payton's "breaking" his NFL rushing mark over many more games and seasons than it took to create the record.

Alas, the bottom line is that Chamberlain himself could have won several of the games that earned his loser rep. In four seventh-game playoff losses to the Celtics (1962, 1965, 1968, and 1969), the Celtics triumphed by a total of nine points. In those four losses Chamberlain missed twenty-four free throws. Quite clearly Wilt Chamberlain was master of his fate.

One of the ironies of the Russell as "winner," Chamberlain as "loser" dichotomy is that, politically speaking, Chamberlain should have been a press darling. Sportswriters of the sixties constituted some of the most conservative elements of the media. Men like the Daily News's nationally syndicated Dick Young were openly hostile to the sixties social upheaval. The politics of Jabbar and Russell offended their patriotic souls. Yet Chamberlain was a practicing Republican who served as a Nixon delegate to the 1968 convention. After Nixon's election Chamberlain was a leading advocate of "black capitalism," a White House slogan for encouraging Black businessmen even as the administration began the long, successful process of dismantling the Kennedy/Johnson Great Society social programs. If Chamberlain had hit a few more foul shots his liaison with Nixon might have won him better press.

Bill Russell's last game was May 5, 1969, when an aging, gutsy bunch of Celtics scrambled to a two-point win over the

Los Angeles Lakers in the NBA final. This was Russell's last title as player but his second as Celtic coach. Acknowledging Russell's team leadership Auerbach gave the reins to his center in 1966, making him the first Black head coach in a major professional league. Considering the Celtics' personnel and Russell's personality it wasn't a surprising move, which says a lot about what Blacks had accomplished in basketball. Imagine similar scenarios in baseball or football at the time. Willie Mays managing the San Francisco Giants? Jim Brown coaching the Cleveland Browns? No way. But the integral role of Blacks in basketball was now so firmly established few batted an eye, even when the coach was a man whites thought self-righteous.

WEARING STRIPES

Russell's impact on the NBA in the sixties didn't end with defense, championships, and coaching. Through a recommendation the Celtic great facilitated the hiring of the league's first regular African-American referee. Ken Hudson was working for Gulf Oil in Boston when he met Russell through his friend Sam Jones. Hudson, born in Pittsburgh, had attended Black Central State University in Ohio, where, as manager of the basketball team, he refereed at practices. Hudson befriended Jones when the Celtics played a regular-season game in Pittsburgh during 1961 and renewed the relationship in Boston. Hudson became well known around the city for refereeing in summer leagues. The result of all this was a summer 1966 conversation between Russell and Hudson outside the center's Boston restaurant. Hudson recalls, "I said to him, 'You know something? I would like to referee an NBA game!' He said, 'Oh. I guess you could be as bad as anyone else in there. Let's go for a ride.'" They traveled out to the Celtics' training facility, where

Russell introduced him to Auerbach. Soon, along with handling high school ball, Hudson began refereeing Celtic practices and then working at basketball camps held by Sam Jones, Alex Hannum, and others. "I went to all the camps to get as much experience as I could because refereeing, no matter what level, it's all the same game," Hudson says. "Obviously the higher you go, you become more sophisticated and technical. But it's like playing sports and learning math—if you learn the basics, the other things fall into place." During 1966, Russell's first year as Celtic coach, the club asked him to handle a series of intrasquad exhibitions being held in Hartford, Connecticut, and upstate New York. "Then the league invited me to the Knicks game at McGuire Air Force Base. It was Walt Frazier's first year. Red Auerbach recommended me along with Russell and Wayne Embry. I was there three days. Nothing materialized for a while, but I stayed in the game, doing camps and high schools.

"I was getting semipro money. Ten to four dollars per game. I was working with Gulf Oil, so I was getting free gas and had a company car. I remember one night I was on assignment in Portland, Maine, for Gulf Oil. It was two hours from Boston. I drove down to referee for ten dollars and drove back because I was into it. I kept sending letters to the NBA. Then I received a call and a letter. They said they'd let me referee three exhibition games. Three games. You really can't tell what a person can do that way. It normally takes about five games just to get going.

"When I got the letter I panicked. My first game was in Toledo, Ohio. It was Cincinnati and Detroit. The players treated me like a rookie, but nothing really happened. All three games had the Royals. The next two games were against Boston in Columbus and Indiana. It was a league rule that if you were refereeing a game and you have that same team and they are traveling by bus, get a ride with them. So I sat next to Oscar [Robertson] on the bus and it was fascinating. He wanted to know about my background. One of the things that created a problem for me later was that guys wanted me to do well. That almost created a problem for me without them really knowing it. He said, 'Hang in there and work hard. People are going to talk about you anyway. If you believe what you see, call it. Be on top of it. Stick to it. We're going to give you hell anyway, but we want to see you succeed.'

"I worked with Norm Drucker. It's interesting because those three games I worked with John Bank, Drucker, and Joe Gushue. Later I became very good friends with all three. They were all supportive. There were only one or two white referees I felt uncomfortable with, but basically they were very support-ive. Anyway, the game was going on and Oscar jumps and my first call was on him. He looked at me and said, 'Shit.' So I called a technical foul on him. It was funny, because I wanted to see how everyone reacted, especially the Celtics. They were saying, 'Well, O.K., this guy is all right!' So I did those three games and then I heard on the radio one morning, 'Bostonian chosen referee for the NBA!' They were paying ninety dollars per game plus expenses. This was squeezed in around my regu-lar job."

Hudson's first league game was a 1968 Chicago Bull visit to Philadelphia. He remembers: "I get there maybe three P.M. I checked in and told the desk I wanted a six P.M. wake-up. I kept doubting whether I wanted to do it. Then the cab turned the corner and there was the Spectrum. I figured it was too late to change your mind now. The interesting thing was that Hal Greer's wife and I were college classmates at Central State and Chet Walker and I were also pretty good friends. They didn't know I was refereeing this game. I walked out on the court and Hal Greer is warming up. He looked up and said, 'I'll be damned. Look who's here?' The game was competitive. That Philly crowd just compounded everything. Then I looked at the schedule. This was Saturday and the next game was Wednesday night in Atlanta working with Earl Strom. That was the night Willis Reed decided that he was going to wipe out four or five guys. There was war. This was one of two times in his career Willis just went wild.

"Guys started tackling each other and he'd had enough and told them he'd had enough. See when a team like the Bullets or the Knicks or the Hawks are playing, the referee is hoping the ball will go in the basket. If it didn't guys would crash the boards, knock each other down, pull each other down. As a referee you would have to make a decision as to what happened. Normally, the last one standing was the one who committed the foul. For two hours this was going on, then Willis turned to somebody and said, 'Where I come from the guy who is holding you is who you knock out first, so you better get away from me.' Guys would make a run for the basket and someone would just haul off and hit them. I remember saying to Earl Strom, 'Do I really want to do this?' He said, 'Welcome to the league.' I was so nervous because I felt Walter Kennedy [NBA Commissioner] was watching this and I felt I would last two days in the game.

"The first year was a mixture of highs and lows. I ended up doing about fifty-five or sixty games. I was only supposed to do forty. It turned out well. That year the guys jumped to the ABA—Ed Rush, Earl Strom, Norm Drucker, etcetera. In the meantime it opened up some opportunities for me. The drawback I had working against me was that in refereeing you can't be a nice guy. I basically got along with people. I knew the guys on a first-name basis. I remember the first year I received a letter saying they [the NBA] were pleased and we would like to hire you for a full schedule of forty-eight games. I felt good about that because I was the only Black guy out there. The players, especially the superstars, were very supportive. I couldn't say enough about guys like Wilt, Jerry West, Oscar, Havlicek. After you reach a certain level referees don't affect how you play for the most part."

Ask Hudson about his career, and images from his first campaign fill his mind: "In Detroit Dave Bing came through and made some move to the basket. He must have done twelve twists and flips. I was in awe. Eddie Miles [of Detroit], who was on the court at the time, said, 'The next time you want to watch, why don't you buy a ticket?' He started laughing because it was an incredible move. To see these guys up close was intriguing. Lenny Wilkens. People always said, 'He couldn't go to his right.' But he really could if he had to. He would go all the way over to the right side of the floor and would drive to his left. No one could stop him. He didn't have a jump shot—at least nothing I would call a jump shot. But he always played the game like a scientist. When he played defense, Lenny was like a fighter. Stick and move. Lenny would guard you and shake his shoulders at you and get you out of your rhythm. You'd look at him, and he would shake again. The next thing you know he had the ball and was going the other way and you are still trying to figure out what was going on. You had guys like Oscar, who was so professional as he cut up the other team. You would be in the dressing room after the game and would hear the stats; Oscar Robertson thirty points, fifteen assists, and eleven rebounds and you would say, 'What game was I watching?'

"That first year I was the first Black to referee a game on national TV. I flew in from Los Angeles because I had worked Friday night in L.A. It was a pretty good game against Philly. When I got into Boston it started to snow in unreal quantities. Mindy Rudolph and Jack Madden were supposed to work.

Mindy said, 'You're in today. I can't get there.' I said, 'O.K. Really. O.K.' I get there, except for people in the league, no one knew I was doing this such as my family, etcetera. It was a hell of a game. It went into overtime, and it was a smoker. It was the kind of game you want to do. I'll never forget, 122-117, Celtics. On the last play Russell blocked a shot by Hal Greer. Damn, when I got home the phone never stopped ringing from people I never told I was refereeing in the NBA. People in school. Folks from all over called, 'What are you doing?' The experiences were some things I'll always remember. I met people that have made my life much better; except for a few negative aspects, I would do it all over again.

"In some cases you know the guys are going to try to use you for a scapegoat wherever they could. They tell me he's a decent guy, but Paul Seymour who used to coach Syracuse made some ethnic remarks that I just found very distasteful. For the most part the coaches would yell and scream. I remember one night announcer Chick Hearn interviewed me back in L.A., and he said for a young guy they were pleasantly surprised. That when they were on the road they felt comfortable that I would hang in there. You never know how they feel about you: one day you are liked and the next day they can't stand you.

"There were two real low points: one, we were out in Phoenix and got caught in a situation where we ended up putting the wrong guy on the line. I tried to get the guy who was the lead referee to correct it, but he didn't want to do it, so there was a mess about that. Then Jake O'Donnell came in the following game and he called, saying 'I heard what happened in Phoenix and I heard you had made the correct decision, but the guy you were working with didn't want to listen.' That doesn't go back to the league. The report given was that we screwed the game up, and that was a low point.

"It was a low point after my third year when, after looking

at evaluations, the league decided they were not going to hire me for the fourth year. They never said to me during the course of the year what I needed to work on. All of a sudden the ratings came out and, 'We rated you eighteen out of twenty.' I acted in a very defensive manner: 'If this is the case, why didn't you tell me that?' So I called Walter Kennedy and wondered how he could go from sending me a letter telling me how pleased you were with my work and then you tell me I've gone backwards without saying anything."

Hudson fought his dismissal and ended up working a full schedule of games in his fourth season, "but I knew they were trying to force me out." What kind of referee was he? Those who remember feel he was "decent," neither outstanding nor a dog. The general consensus was that white referees of similar ability have had long careers in the league. During that final year he spoke with Russell, his original sponsor: "He said, 'You already proved that you could do this. You don't have to prove anything to those guys. Move on, unless there is nothing else you do in your life.' That was a low point." That Hudson was Boston-based and made his initial entry into refereeing via the Celtics played a part in his troubles: "They were concerned about me living in Boston—I couldn't referee in Boston, which I felt was crazy. They believed if you lived in Philly you couldn't referee there or if you lived in New York you couldn't referee Knick games, etcetera. That was the excuse they had.

"I came to understand that, at first if you think about it, I didn't fail because I opened doors for other people. Lee Jones came in nineteen seventy. John Parker was in for a while. Lee is still at it. Now you see Black referees Hugh Evans, Jimmy Capers, Hugh Holland, and guys like that doing a tremendous job, and it makes it all worthwhile. Last year in the play-offs [1988], Hawks and Celtics, Hugh Holland and Hugh Evans did the game. Hugh Evans called me: 'Can you believe this?

Two brothers in the South in the play-offs and nobody is paying any attention. And you have K.C. coaching one of the teams."'

In 1990, after spending many years as an executive with Coca-Cola, Hudson moved back to Boston to run the Celtics' community affairs office.

AFROS AND ISLAM

"The Negro could not ever become white and that was his strength; at some point always he could not participate in the dominant tenor of the white man's culture. It was at this juncture that he had to make use of other resources, whether African, subcultural or hermetic. And it was this boundary, this no man's land, that provided the logic and beauty of his music."

— LEROI JONES,
Blues People, c. 1963

In the late 1960s this nation's African-American residents underwent an identity crisis of enormous proportions. The civil rights success of the postwar era had knocked down some of the most noisome symbols of Jim Crow. White separatists, it seemed, were on the defensive, desperate to turn the clock back, as the emergence of George Wallace as presidential candidate suggested. The progress appeared, not just righteous, but irreversible. But a younger generation, emboldened by legal and legislative victories, hungered for more and faster advancement. Signs of the new view were everywhere. "Negro" and "colored" were rejected in favor of "Black" and Dr. Martin

Luther King, Jr., was still the race's chief spokesman, but now there were angrier voices like the Black Panthers and Stokely Carmichael. Integration was viewed by many as accommodation to racism, and a strong desire for cultural nationalism flourished. The proud, optimistic, vaguely masochistic "We Shall Overcome" was giving way to "Black Power," a cry of assertion, bravado, and implicit violence.

These shifts in ideology and attitude caused explosions still incredible to recall. Looking back, we see that deep-seated Northern geographical and economic segregation ignited riots that, in the long run, only created a class of bureaucratic gigs for Blacks in America's big cities and no basic changes in America's socioeconomic structure. Homes and businesses were burned in Newark, Detroit, Watts, and elsewhere, and, decades later, they remain lonely shells untouched by time or renovation; other buildings anxiously await the gentrification of once working-class black neighborhoods.

Christianity received its first serious challenge among African-Americans in this epoch because it was so identified with peaceful integration. Along with seeking new empowering strategies, Black people sought a darker God (or at least a non-Western one) who meshed better with their "Black Is Beautiful" slogans, dashikis, and subscriptions to the Panther paper.

In the sports world this new Islamic religiosity caused name changes that rocked the American mainstream. Muhammad Ali had, of course, started it when, in 1964, under the tutelage of minister Malcolm X, the heavyweight champ embraced the Nation of Islam. In 1971 Lew Alcindor became known by his Sunni Moslem name Kareem Abdul-Jabaar. Other basketball players, such as Walt Hazzard (Mahdi Abdul-Rahmad), Wally Jones (Wali Jones), Don Smith (Zaid Abdul-Aziz), and Warren Armstrong (Warren Jabali) made the move from Christianity to some branch of Islam. Though these new names didn't always suggest deep militancy—only a new embrace of spirituality—they still irritated the hell out of people. Bobby Moore, a gifted, mild-mannered wide receiver on the St. Louis Cardinals, got a rough reception when, after much meditation, he decided to become Ahmad Rashad. Running onto the field in his first game after the name change, he remembers, "A cascade of boos drowned out the PA, an avalanche of bad noise aimed at me. I loped out there into this awful outpouring of disapproval, and it echoed in my helmet all the way down the field. When I got to my teammates, there were no high fives or claps on the pads—they were all looking the other way, like they were waiting on a bus or something. They hadn't even left me a place to stand in line."

His coach's attitude was no more enlightened: "He [Coryell] couldn't get my name right—he was always calling me 'Ramada' or 'Armada' or something. One day, I took two pieces of adhesive tape and put them on the front and the back of my helmet. I wrote my name on the tape. I went up to Coryell and told him, 'If you forget my name, just look here and read it off.' I turned around. 'And it's back here too, just in case I'm facing the other way.'"

Of course, rebellion in sport wasn't just a matter of religion. Brothers were sporting huge H-bomb Afros, bell-bottom pants, and gold medallions. They were reading Eldridge Cleaver's *Soul on Ice,* listening to the Last Poets, and smoking marijuana instead of drinking beer. And that was just what they were doing in their spare time. On the court, brothers once wore canvas Converses with plain white sweat socks like everybody else. But along with Afros came head bands like those popularized by musicians Jimi Hendrix and Sly Stone and wrist bands that came in solid colors, or patriotic red, white, and blue, or even groovier nationalistic red, black, and green for the full "Right on!" vibe. In any color combination sporting sweatbands was much hipper than wiping away sweat with your jersey. Knee-high socks, originally popularized by "The Dip" (aka Wilt Chamberlain) in Philly, became the official b-ball look, and in schoolyards nationwide brothers now took pride in wearing two or three pairs of socks, each decorated with colorful strips to match uniforms and/or wrist bands. And slowly, leather sneakers, low and high-top, would begin to overwhelm canvas sneakers.

With this funky new look came the latest turn in Black athletic aesthetic. The star players of the 1950s and early 1960s, along with a number of key teams, had opened eyes to the Black game's verticality, intensity, and panache. But just as a new breed of leaders was moving the community, the next generation of Black players was entering the spotlight. The brothers who followed the Big O, Russell, Wilt, the Hawk, and Elgin would take Black playing style to, literally, new heights while assaulting the game's protocol with a revolutionary's zeal. Marques Haynes had made shifty dribbling the bench mark for one era. Now another backcourt man, as surely as Afros, Islam, and "Black," signaled the start of the new phase. At one point in his life this b-ball legend questioned Christianity, but everyone nodded when fans labeled him Black Jesus.

THE PEARL

"A player," in record-biz parlance, is an entrepreneur who, because he controls one or more major hit makers, can negotiate lucrative deals with any of the multinational labels that dominate the industry. By those standards Earl Monroe is not yet a player. His Pretty Pearl Records, located in a neat but unimposing Manhattan office building, has had a few moments of glory in its existence—in the mideighties a singer named Curtis Hairston showed promise, and Pretty Pearl had a distribution deal with the mammoth WEA distribution network. But Monroe, who got involved with record promotion while with the Knicks in the seventies, loves the music business and plans to continue on until all his dues are paid. It's most appropriate he's involved in music since, in basketball, he popularized rhythms that have become essential to the game's more complicated compositions: the hesitation dribble, the spin move utilized in open court and, most rhythmically, a variety of double and triple pumps that left opponents in a trance and fans screaming any of his nicknames: "Black Jesus!," "Magic!," or "The Pearl!"

Monroe's songs were noted for an extravagance that made every herky-jerky arrangement seem loaded with significance. Few have used contact with opposing players, in Monroe's case bumping his opponent with his ass, so effectively. By creating a pattern of contact as he went downcourt Monroe set his own shooting rhythm. The more physical the man guarding Monroe, the more easily Monroe "read" him. Many players utilize this technique—Adrian Dantley is a master—but doing it in the middle of the court, employing tempo changes only Thelonious Monk would understand, made him unusually dangerous. Overplay him to either side and Monroe would feel the shift, spin away, and go up, though not too far. You'll find no photos of Monroe dunking. Look close, however, and you'll see him hovering at some weird angle, even sideways, with a defender waving at him. You'll wonder how he ever scored like that, and then you'll notice that his wrist placement, in whatever photo you see, is always as correct as an Oxford English professor's diction.

As a young man Earl Monroe, Sr., toured as a vocalist with a traveling revue built around blues diva (and sometime-Philadelphia native) Bessie Smith. It wasn't unusual for the elder Monroe to break into song at the slightest instigation and then tell tales of life with the Empress of the Blues. So he introduced show business, as a form of self-expression as well as a way to make a living, to his son early on.

Monroe, Jr., was introduced to basketball at fourteen. Until then baseball and soccer had been his main athletic interests. Then, one day, a junior high school coach noticed there was a 6'3", fourteen-year-old in school not on the basketball team. Quick as the coach could ask, "Can you play basketball?" Monroe was on the Audenried junior high squad as a gawky, too-young-for-his-body center. Though he only grew another inch and a half the rest of his life, that early introduction to the pivot would be an asset. From fourteen to sixteen Monroe learned the game with very little formal coaching. "All of my style came from the Philadelphia schoolyards, primarily because I never had anyone say, 'Earl do this or that.' All the things I was doing I found through experimenting. That's how I found my niche," he says about those years. He began haunting Philadelphia's version of the Rucker tournament, the Baker League, studying the brilliant batch of backcourt men emerging from Philly. Looking back, Monroe cites Villanova star and longtime pro Guy Rodgers as a significant influence. He says, "Guy wasn't a real behind-the-back type of player. He was very methodical. But he could pass his ass off. He was a very disciplined player. He would not take shots outside of his range, and he could find you on the court. He knew what to do and knew how to play the game. I played against all the older guys like Guy when I was coming up. When they did moves on us or so-called taking us to school, they called it 'the thirty-year move.' The guys I came up with, John Chaney, Sonny Hill, Guy, all kind of molded our games."

As a high schooler at John Bartram High, Monroe got a chance to play both forward and guard, as well as center, and develop his jumper. He'd already noticed that his peers were still growing, that he wasn't, and, that even in 1962, the demand for 6'2" college centers was decreasing. After high school Monroe felt so confident about his game that he wanted to sign with the American Basketball League after graduation, but the ABL disappeared before he could enter it:

"So I was off to Temple Prep. At that time a friend of mine, Leon Whitely, who went to Winston-Salem, approached me if I would come to Winston-Salem. I thought and decided I did not want to go down South. I had never been past Baltimore, so I did not want to experience it. A year went by and he came back and I was working, so I said, 'I will go down.'"

For this big-city kid, going to Winston-Salem marked a coming maturity in his worldview as well as his game. Coach Clarence "Big House" Gaines was a big part of that maturation process. Monroe and pal Steve Smith took the train down to North Carolina. "Between us we had one overcoat. It was so cold on the train we huddled up in a corner under this one overcoat. That's where the coach found us. That's the first time either one of us saw him. He was a very impressive guy, about 6'4", 290 pounds, and didn't take too much mess. Not only was he a very strong disciplinarian, but he was a father figure to you. Being so far away from home, it was very comforting to know that there was someone that you could always go to. Of course, it didn't start off like that. I didn't start my freshman year there and thought I should, so every time I would get angry he would call my mother. That would straighten me right out. It was a strange type of beginning for us, but once you found out what he was doing, you could not help but love him."

Gaines, who in 1990 became the second coach to win 800 collegiate games, told *Philly Sport,* "Earl was quick on the trigger and I'm not talking about his shooting. He had some arrogance about him, a temper ... He didn't like me getting on him for that spin move. Hell, guys were stealing it right and left." But as Earl settled down so did Gaines's criticism.

Off court, Monroe was as experimental as he was on. "Coming up in the sixties I was one of the original flower children," he says, "so my thoughts were a little beyond basketball. When Dr. King got killed I wore a black band that whole year. Nobody knew why. But then nobody needed to know why you are doing things sometimes. I did it because this was something I believed in. I studied the Koran. It was a fad, when you really look at it. Certain things changed my mind about it. Certainly when Malcolm was executed that took me to another head. I attended the rallies—I'd go and see Stokely Carmichael. But the thing that twisted me around was that we were rallying and talking about unity, but after the meetings they would go off with the white girls. That messed me up. So I turned to my own religion. I came back to Christianity. There is knowledge in the Koran and there's knowledge in the other books, but it's all how you implement it."

In Monroe's senior year, 1966–1967, Winston-Salem became the first Black school to win a NCAA Division II title. By then the spin move was perfected, the jumper deadly, and his main nickname in place. "In my first seven games in my senior year I was averaging fifty-three points a game. Some sportswriter [Louis Overby of the Winston-Salem *Sentinel*] listed the total points in the newspaper with the words, 'These are Earl's Pearls.'" North Carolinians picked up on it, shouting "Earl the Pearl!" when he handled the ball. He cooled down after the hot start to average *only* 41.5 for the year.

"Our team went thirty-two and one—we lost one game to the University in Greensboro," he recalls. "We were ranked number one for most of the season. We were very arrogant, and in our huddles we'd say our prayers and would end them with 'Kill! Kill! Kill!' We would go to campuses and just look around for a reason to beat these guys. This helped to make us champions. Nice guys are not champions. That is a myth. You have to have a certain amount of arrogance and ego to want to achieve it. That team that year had all the ego you could want."

Monroe was selected the number-one draft choice of the Baltimore Bullets in 1967, a sign of the changed times. No longer were all Black schools ignored by white scouts or their accomplishments dismissed. In the time from Sam Jones's arrival in the NBA in the midfifties to Monroe's rookie year a slew of quality players had successfully made the leap, including guard Al Attles of North Carolina A&T, Dick Barnett and John Barnhill of Tennessee State, Charlie Hardnett, Bob Hopkins, and Willis Reed of Grambling, and Woody Sauldsberry of Texas Southern.

Despite Monroe's undeniable brilliance, however, the story of Cleo Hill haunted him and Coach Gaines. According to those who played against him Hill was a shifty, shake-and-bake artist whose playing style wasn't very different from Monroe's. At Winston-Salem he set scoring records and was drafted in 1961 by the St. Louis Hawks. The Hawks had a rep for racism, not just from their Southern fans but among many of the team's stars, too. Hill's flamboyance not only didn't mesh with his teammates, it was openly disdained by some. Hill played in fifty-eight of St. Louis's games that season, averaging 5.6 points, shooting only .348 from the field but a nice (for the era) .774 from the free throw line. Hill was a shooter, but the Hawks already had a young African-American guard, Lenny Wilkens, as chief handler. St. Louis simply wasn't ready for an all-Black backcourt in 1962—the kind of backward thinking that would stifle the franchise's development until its move to Atlanta in 1968. Ironically, by then the Hawks featured an all-

Black starting five that included Walt Hazzard at point guard.

After that '61–'62 campaign Hill didn't play another NBA game and, in large part because of his bitterness over that fact, Gaines often told Monroe Hill's story. Monroe recalls, "I was ready for the NBA. I had geared myself toward it for quite some time. But a kid by the name of Cleo Hill had come through with tremendous talent and backed off from the NBA. The coach always drummed into me that I had to be a certain type of person in order to be successful in the professional ranks. Coach Gaines knew I was very opinionated, and he told me that sometimes you have to hold your opinions back until you get to where you want to get and then you can voice them. That was the important advice he gave me at that time."

Though he was the second player chosen that year (Detroit's Jimmy Walker was number one), Monroe was disappointed in the money offered. He says, "I had envisioned about $110 thousand or something like that, but I didn't get that kind of money. I signed the contract—I didn't have an agent at the time—and I thought my coach had seen it. So when the coach came in he said, 'Son, what have you done?' I said, 'Well, I made a mistake, and if I did I will pay for it.' That's one of my traits. So I lived two years with that contract."

Until Monroe's arrival the Bullets had suffered through a brief, yet awful history. The team was born as the Chicago Zephyrs in 1961. After two last-place finishes and little local support the franchise shifted to Baltimore's spanking-new Civic Arena. Led by journeyman pros Walt Bellamy and Bailey Howell, the Bullets rose to mediocrity for a season or two. But by 1967 they were back in the cellar. Monroe remembers being warned by ex-Tennessee A&T star and then Bullet Ben Walley, "Man, don't take the ball out of bounds. So in exhibition games the ball would go through the hoop and there would be four guys standing around the ball waiting to see who was going to take it out of bounds because once you did you didn't see it anymore."

Yet within two years the Bullets were NBA terrors. Their top pick in 1968 was Louisville center Wes Unseld, who at 6´7˝, 245 pounds played the middle like a shorter, wider Russell. In fact, as a fast-break outlet passer Unseld had few peers. At his side was Gus Johnson, a 6´6˝, 235-pound tower of strength. Today Johnson is best known for shattering backboards with resounding slam dunks. But Johnson was more than Darryl Dawkins's godfather. As Monroe testifies, "Gus Johnson created the new power forward position, where the guy comes in and jams way over guys. He placed his hands on your hip and moved you around on the court. When the guards got out of hand he knocked down guards, forwards, and he played the centers, too."

Monroe, Unseld, and Johnson, along with small forward Jack Marin and guard Kevin Loughery, backup center Ray Scott, and guard Fred "Mad Dog" Carter, were the core of a highly successful Baltimore squad for the next four and a half years. Of course, it was the Pearl who shone the brightest. During those four seasons Monroe averaged 24.9, 25.8, 23.4, and 21.4 points. Equally impressive were the adjectives used to describe his game. In a *Sport* magazine article Woody Allen wrote, "What makes Monroe different is the indescribable heat of genius that burns deep inside him. Some kind of diabolical intensity comes across his face when he has the ball … and yet he has enough wit in his style to bring off funny ideas when he wants to." In his autobiography, *Life on the Run,* future teammate Bill Bradley wrote that Monroe "plays like a man whose body was assembled through a mail order catalogue; each part seems to move independently yet is controlled from a single command center." *Philly Sport* said of Monroe during his Bullets days that "in a flash of a moment, with his instinctive command center controlling events already in motion, he would take it to the hole, spin a 360 in traffic and soar to the hoop, jackknifing in midair and lofting a soft shot from the hip, just over the outstretched hand of Chamberlain or Russell or Jabbar. The ball somehow found the hole."

Probably the best description of Monroe's style—and that style's impact on younger players—was written by black journalist Clayton Riley in the *Village Voice:* "With the Bullets, Monroe had remained, by inclination and temperament, a shooter, the player with points in his eyes and heart. He established several spinning moves to the hoop that have always invited walking or carrying calls from the referees. He made one-on-one into an attitude, the assertion of personal grandeur. Basketball purists were at first amused by what they regarded as the exotic quality of Monroe's passion for solos, which many regard as a childish—and even more important, a temporary—intrusion into a game made important by Bob Cousy and George Mikan. Just as a thousand reedmen had followed Charlie Parker's phenomenal dream, at least that many schoolboy hoopsters were to follow Earl Monroe into basketball's New World. One-on-one institutionalized itself and refused to disappear. Bebop came to basketball."

The Bullets' turnaround was part of a remarkable period in that city's sports history. In 1969 the Colts, led by backup quarterback Earl Morrall, compiled an amazing 13-1 record and entered Super Bowl III as heavy favorites. The Orioles, managed by the fiery pepper pot Earl Weaver, were about to become one of baseball's greatest dynasties, anchored by a versatile pitching staff and two Hall of Fame Robinsons, third baseman Brooks and outfielder Frank. For this then decaying Northern harbor town it should have been sports heaven, but Baltimore's revelry was dampened by the unexpected accomplishments of New York teams. Super Bowl III was dominated by Jets quarterback Joe Namath, fullback Matt Snell, and the mistakes of golden boy Morrall. In the 1969 World Series Weaver's Orioles were victimized by catches and hitting that were amazin', as in Mets. But just as galling as those one-shot failures was the annual whipping the Bullets received from the New York Knicks every spring—in 1968–1969 the Bullets lost four to one; in 1969–1970 they lost four to three; in 1970–1971 they beat New York four to three; lost again four to two in 1971–1972; in 1972–1973 they lost four to one; in 1973–1974 four to three. From 1968 to 1974 the Bullets lost five of six play-off series to the Knicks.

But the resentment Monroe, the Bullets, and the rest of the league felt toward the Knicks was about more than wins than losses. "This was sort of a golden age for the league because all of a sudden New York had a winning team," Monroe says. "This was the first team they made personalities out of. That particular team kind of imposed itself on the community because the team had someone in the community you could identify with. You had [Bill] Bradley from Princeton. You had your hardworking types with [Dave] DeBusschere. Willis [Reed] just became the all-American hero. Clyde [Walt Frazier], they called him Mr. Cool. Dick [Barnett] was a good player, but he couldn't compete with all the rest of that stuff."

Boston dominated pro basketball for more than ten years. Yet in the 1969–1970 season alone the Knicks may have generated more national press coverage and endorsements for their players than the Celtics enjoyed in a decade. Monroe notes that "people on the other squads didn't like New York because no matter what you were doing everything focused around what New York was doing. When you came to the Garden, you'd see Woody Allen and the other celebrities; when you came to the Garden it was like the L.A. Forum [in the eighties]." Books like Pete Axthelm's *The City Game* celebrated Walt Frazier's flashy wardrobe, Bradley's Rhodes Scholarship, DeBusschere's beer drinking, and Reed's leadership, as if one season of outstanding basketball made them all-time greats. Knick team slogans—"Find the open man!" and "See the ball!"—were intoned with amazing reverence by fans and sportscasters. The Knicks' rise solidified the NBA's national television contract with ABC and led folks to hype basketball as "the game of the seventies."

In actuality, this much-heralded championship five won only one NBA title and would last as a unit only another season and a half. This is not to say the Knicks weren't gifted—it's just that in the great flow of basketball history, they never exerted dynastic control of their era, as the Celtics had and the Lakers would. But if Monroe, like many of his peers, was bothered by the league's Knickitis, it didn't stop him from enjoying the confrontations: "I remember my second year, we went from last to first, and then we lost four straight to the Knicks in the play-offs, and then the next year we were very close to winning the division, but we lost to the Knicks in seven games. In order to get to the Garden for that game seven, we had to beat them in Baltimore in game six. That night I came ready for business. I came dressed in all black: black three-piece suit and black shirt—the only thing I had on red was the band around my hat. The guys said, 'Damn, Earl.' I said, 'I came here for business.' Black means business, it determines how someone is perceived. It was about that same aura. Coming up I was always perceived to be evil, a bad guy, because I was dark. Even today if I have a hat pulled down over my head they say, 'Uh-oh.' So I turned it into a positive. My game expressed a different type of thought and opinion than the normal game that was being played at the time."

Just as Monroe's scoring solos and moves are bench marks in the Black athletic aesthetic, so his relationship with the

Bullets' management foreshadowed the battles over money and pride that would scar basketball in the seventies. The terms of his rookie contract had left him with residual bitterness toward the team. Then, before the 1972 season, Monroe felt humiliated by management. "Management had promised that they would trade me after the end of the season," he remembers. "But it wasn't so much the salary, because I enjoyed being at Baltimore and I enjoyed the players. But management made a statement that they gave me ten thousand dollars to put as down payment on a house for my mother. I thought that was something that was supposed to be between us, so I was very offended by it. I never had been one of those people who took my problems to the papers. I felt that was a stab in the back. I decided I was going to leave. I had gone to Indiana in hopes of playing for the Pacers, which were then an ABA team, and they showed me a nice time, but it wasn't for me at that point, so when the trade occurred I decided to come to New York."

Immediately, the New York press, which had hyped the Knicks as the ultimate team, questioned whether Monroe could fit in. It was as if a deadly germ were being injected into a beautiful body. In reality, the Knicks were aging and ailing. Reed's knee, injured during the 1970 finals, had never fully recovered. During the 1971–1972 campaign Reed's career was in such jeopardy New York traded for all-star center-forward Jerry Lucas. Barnett was thirty-five and slowing down. Both Bradley and DeBusschere, while still effective, were finding it more difficult to get good shots now that the team's rhythms were off. Only Frazier, Monroe's great antagonist, was still playing at his peak. The speculation that The Pearl couldn't fit still rankles the Hall of Famer years later.

"You have people speculating on what the game is about, and they write these clichés for the unknowing public. They read them, and they believe it must be true," Monroe remembers. "But look back and see Earl scored a lot of points, but Earl is winning. We went from last place to first place in Baltimore. I had to be somewhat part of that, as well as in college playing on a team, whereas I led the nation in scoring and we won the championship, and the other guys on the team were happy as well."

Hampered by his own sore knees and the adjustment to the Knicks, Monroe averaged only 11.4 and 15.5 his first two years with the club. Toward the end of the 1972–1973 season Monroe says coach Red Holzman changed the offense: "When there were only seconds left on the shot clock and nothing was getting done, Holzman would yell, 'Give Earl the ball.' He knew I could go get it any time I wanted. Then I would give the Garden crowd something to let them know there was still a little of the old me."

During the 1973 play-offs Monroe was crucial to the Knicks' second title drive. On April 1, against his old friends on the Bullets, Monroe scored thirty-two points, his Knick career high, including a sizzling four straight baskets in a fourth-quarter sequence that won the game. On May 10, with the Knicks leading the Lakers three to one in the finals, Monroe burned the tenacious Gail Goodrich for twenty-three points to earn his only championship ring.

After that 1973 title the Knick franchise went downhill as Barnett, Reed, DeBusschere, and Bradley retired and Frazier was traded to Cleveland. Monroe, the dark God of one-on-one, the villain from Baltimore, became the last link between the Knicks' glory days and the 'Niggerbockers,' as some New Yorkers labeled the predominantly Black Knicks of the late seventies. On a more profound note Monroe ushered in a jazzy, exciting, demonstrative approach that old-school NBA observers hated.

But the revolution would be televised and, eventually, it would overrun the NBA. In fact, in 1967, Monroe's rookie season in Baltimore, a new basketball league began that blasted open financial, employment, and artistic opportunities for African-Americans. While Monroe made basketball's floor game fresh, in the American Basketball Association the game soared above the rim.

AIR BALL

"Tear the roof off the mutha sucker/Roof off the mutha
sucka/Tear the roof off the sucka."
—"TEAR THE ROOF OFF THE SUCKER,"
a hit for Parliament in 1978

Nineteen sixty-seven. The Vietnam War was the key issue in the upcoming presidential campaign. The American League saw one of the closest pennant races in history. Tammi Terrell and Marvin Gaye recorded a magnificent series of duets ("Ain't No Mountain High Enough," "Your Precious Love," "If This World Were Mine").

One seemingly minor event was the inauguration of the American Basketball Association. Enticed by the National Football League–American Football League merger, a group of ambitious businessmen thought they could crash the NBA with a similar buy-and-bust-in strategy. If they could sustain the heavy initial losses these money men felt with talent raids and a possible network contract they would force their way into the NBA. In 1961 Abe Saperstein's American Basketball League had been motivated by the Trotters' founder's spite at being denied a West Coast NBA franchise. The ABA had no particular bone to pick: the owners just wanted to make money.

Unfortunately, the ABA's initial roster of owners found their dreams were bigger than their bankbooks. Right up to the day in 1976 the NBA-ABA merger was signed and four teams (the New York Nets, San Antonio Spurs, Denver Rockets, and Indiana Pacers) joined the big boys, much about the ABA was cheap, corny, and definitely minor-league. The league never got the kind of network television support that, for example, the AFL got from NBC.

But for African-American athletes the ABA was an incredible success. First and foremost it meant jobs. The ABA started with eleven teams—Pittsburgh, Minneapolis, Indiana, Kentucky, Oakland, New Jersey, Anaheim, Houston, Denver, Dallas, and New Orleans. That same year, 1967, in response to the ABA challenge, the NBA added clubs in Seattle and San Diego. In sum, the new league produced thirteen new pro teams in one season, and most of these roster spots went to Black men.

The ABA-NBA competition led to a salary explosion unmatched in any team sport. The idea of riding the ghetto-to-millionairedom express with a brief stop at a university, became central to the sports industry and it was fueled by the pro basketball experience. By the 1970–1971 season forty-four athletes had average yearly incomes of $100,000, twenty-nine in the NBA, fifteen in the ABA. Every NBA team and all but three ABA squads had at least one $100,000 man. The Knicks, then the game's most profitable franchise, had five, and the Indiana Pacers, the ABA's most stable entity, had four. Of the forty-four blessed with this money, thirty-three were Black. Where once Wilt Chamberlain and Bill Russell alone commanded six figures, now college underclassmen and eventually high school seniors would negotiate six- and, remarkably, seven-figure deals during these hectic years. Today's multimillion-dollar pacts, not just in basketball but in all professional sports, have their roots in the bidding war sparked by the ABA, a league dominated by the Black athletic aesthetic.

But the breakthroughs weren't just financial. "Throughout sports, and particular in basketball, speed became the most important factor for a player. That's what the ABA emphasized," wrote Walt Frazier. "Running and jumping and getting the ball upcourt quickly and then putting on the moves. I think the NBA was ripe for some changes and ready for what the ABA represented. Right around that time Golden State won the NBA championship using the whole bench and running the court all the time. Then the ABA came in and the transition to a speed, showtime type game really took off."

Key to the ABA style during the league's nine-year history was its domination by forwards. With no Wilt-Russell-Unseld–caliber centers clogging the lane and three-point shots spreading the court, forwards found more room to maneuver outside and less opposition when they drove inside. While Rick Barry, a white forward with a polished array of basketball skills, was an ABA force during his years with Oakland, Washington, and the Nets, it was airborne brothers who defined ABA ball. In 1967–1968, Connie Hawkins, though by then underweight and cynical, was still capable of cradling the ABA's red, white, and blue ball in his huge mitts for acrobatic dunks. The Hawk led the baby league in scoring (26.8), free throws made and attempted (603 of 789), and average minutes per game (45), and he took the short-lived Pittsburgh Pipers to the first ABA title.

Spencer Haywood, a University of Detroit sophomore who ignored the African-American boycott of the 1968 Olympics and led the United States to the gold medal, signed with the Denver Rockets, reportedly for over a million. Haywood, whose style resembled Hawkins's, overshadowed all competition, as he led the league in scoring (30), rebounding (19.5), and average minutes played (45). By 1971 Hawkins and Haywood had jumped to the older league, but the ABA replaced them with three and a half men who would be the prototypical ABA players: the seven-foot Artis Gilmore, the ABA's first intimidating shot blocker; George McGinnis, a muscular yet fluid player who was an intense rebounder blessed with Baylor-like moves; and Julius "Dr. J" Erving, a man with unmatched hang time and a still growing overall game. The half a player was Darnell Hillman, noteworthy for one thing only—fierce tomahawk dunks. When Hillman and Indiana teammate McGinnis were on court together photographers and front-row fans were in constant danger of being buried under an avalanche of patriotic slam dunks. In 1973 second-year man George Gervin emerged with a 25.4 point average. "The Ice Man" started the season with the Virginia Squires, a franchise started in 1970, but was sold to San Antonio by owner Virginia Earl Foreman, who destroyed a potentially great team in order to pay his bills. Gervin began his pro career as a 6´7˝ forward, but as a Spur he'd spend most of his time at guard, where, while Earvin Johnson was still a schoolboy, he showcased the offensive advantages of a big guard. The ease with which Gervin shot over shorter guards and rebounded off the offensive glass made his type of game a harbinger of future backcourt play.

Marvin Barnes entered the ABA in 1974, establishing himself as one of basketball's great talents and one of its most obstinate head cases. He'd skipped out of Providence College for the Spirits of St. Louis (an unstable franchise known previously as the Carolina Cougars and before that the Houston Mavericks) for $2 million. That same season Moses Malone, a taciturn, tenacious player recruited out of a Petersburg, Virginia, high school, passed up a scholarship to Maryland for a contract with the Utah Stars. In the next, and final ABA season, Moses, Barnes, and another bruising bonus baby forward, Maurice Lucas, united for one of the meanest front lines ever. Barnes, with his appetite for one-upmanship and self-destruction, epitomized some of the worst aspects of the Black urban ethos. Malone's and Lucas's tactics, in contrast, represented the less flamboyant part of African-American ball: intimidation as psychological weapon and relentless force to wear down opponents mentally and physically. During their distinguished NBA careers, Malone and Lucas would be stellar rebounders, particularly off the offensive glass, where desire is essential. Each also grew into an intimidating force—Lucas used verbal threats and Malone a menacing look to bogart their space on court. These qualities later made both men crucial cogs in NBA winners.

The ABA's final disciple of elevation was David Thompson, perhaps the only player of his generation who could soar with a creativity that rivaled Erving's. From North Carolina State, where the 6 foot 4 guard was the most valuable player on the 1974 NCAA title winner that ended the UCLA dynasty, to Denver and the Rockets, Thompson brought a sweet jump shot and a gift for rapid elevation that earned him a 26.0 average in 1975–1976. Thompson could rise so high that during one college contest he flipped over onto his head after catching a foot on an opponent's shoulder.

Symbolic of the ABA's legacy was the annual slam-dunk competition inaugurated at its 1976 All-Star Game. Appropriately, the battle was staged in Denver, mile-high home of thin air, and the winner was (and you know it!) Dr. J. Ira Berkow wrote in the *New York Times,* "When Erving won, his final fling was a wild windmill. He took a running start at 3/4 court—dribbling isn't required—and then, as he drew nearer the basket, 'took off,' as he described it, 'and began to soar.'" During his 5 ABA years (two in Virginia, 3 in New York) Erving seemed an irresistible force of nature, an embodiment of all that was innovative and exciting, of the ability to intimidate through his improvisations. "Erving [dunked] with such power, force, grace and originality," wrote David Halberstam in *The Breaks of the Game,* "each move seemed invented at the very moment he made it, that it was not simply a matter of scoring two points. His moves electrified, not just his teammates, but the crowd as well, and they often changed the tempo of the game." But there was more to number 6 than just ability. "Both as an athlete and as a man, intelligent, proud, respected [Erving] was so important to black players. He was to them an almost mythic figure, the epitome of the black game," Halberstam observed.

Reared in the working-class New York suburb of Roosevelt, Long Island (also the home of Eddie Murphy), and recruited by the athletically underwhelming University of Massachusetts, Erving had neither a ghetto pedigree or the basketball-factory stamp of approval of most of his Black superstar peers. He left college early to earn money because of his mother's medical bills and was invited to the Virginia Squires' tryout camp with little fanfare—at the time no one in management had ever even seen him play in person.

Immediately, everyone noticed his enormous hands. The next thing that caught everybody's attention was when, during a rookie scrimmage, he leaped over five other players for a dunk. "The gym went silent," recalls former Virginia broadcaster Johnny Kerr. "All the players just stopped for a few seconds."

Later, during the regular season when Dr. J was tearing up the league, Kerr remembers "a young Julius Erving was like Thomas Edison. He was inventing something new every night." While in the ABA, his team won two titles and garnered three most valuable player awards, building a legend that forced the NBA to take a merger seriously, if only to bring Dr. J into its arenas. The image of Julius Erving, bushy Afro blowing back against wind resistance, goatee glistening with sweat, left arm stretched out for balance, and the red, white, and blue ball held high in his right palm awaiting that instant of rapid descent, is the perfect way to remember that long-gone league of free-form freakiness.

FALLOUT

In June 1976 it was announced that Denver, New York, San Antonio, and Indiana paid $3.2 million to join the NBA (with the Nets paying another $4 million to the Knicks). Kentucky, St. Louis, and Virginia disappeared, along with the red, white, and blue ball. The battle to seal this merger took as many turns as Earl Monroe did dribbling. It started in 1970 when both leagues realized that only a union would prevent the owners from spending themselves into extinction.

Problem one was that, as noted earlier, salaries had exploded with no ceiling in sight. Problem two was the NBA's shaky relationship with that pro sports' cash cow, network television. An early sixties deal with NBC had generated so little interest that Nielsen reported ratings as IFR (Insufficient for Reporting) numbers so small they couldn't be measured. In 1965 ABC agreed to broadcast games of the then nine-team league for $600,000 a year. If the relationship went on five years the league would make $1 million a year. By highlighting big-city teams (New York, Los Angeles, Boston) and stars (Chamberlain, Monroe, Frazier, Jerry West), by 1968–1969 the games averaged a respectable 8.9 rating.

Unfortunately, ABC and the league constantly argued over expansion. The NBA grew from nine to seventeen teams during those five years, primarily because the old-line owners could get large entry fees for new franchises. The price of this growth was diluted competition and waning fan interest. These two factors, plus the ABA's existence (part of the expansion was to beat the ABA to certain cities), meant a basketball glut. NBA owners, tired of ABC's unwanted advice and seeking bigger fees, switched to CBS in 1973. The owners got more money, but the damage done by the salary wars and expansion was profound. Ratings sagged. ABC's strategy of counterprogramming with trash sport activities, for example, pitting a bunch of athletes and stars against each other on an obstacle course, generated higher ratings. Poor strategic planning and greed had hurt the NBA, and the merger was viewed as a way to address all these ills.

But the players, led by its Black stars, challenged the merger. The NBA Players Association and its president, Oscar Robertson, filed a class action suit in New York District Court on April 16, 1970, claiming the proposed merger constituted a violation of the Sherman Anti-Trust Act because it restricted player mobility and made pro basketball a monopoly. Robertson and company didn't stop there: the suit called for the abolition of the player draft and the option clause that bound players to teams. In short, Robertson sought to exploit the chaotic situation and gain total freedom of movement for players. "We just felt in a nutshell that the playing conditions were totally unjust," said Robertson later. "I remember years ago when I was playing basketball certain players were blacklisted from playing. If I were an owner and you were on my team and I said, 'I was going to give you $10,000 and you may be worth $100,000—but if you don't accept my conditions, then I could have you blacklisted forever.' We felt that was totally wrong."

The Robertson case resulted in a preliminary injunction against the merger, with the court leaving the door open to ABA-NBA representatives for a Sherman waiver similar to that which existed for baseball and football. Bill S.2373, introduced by Nebraska senator Roman L. Hruska, would have cleared the way for the merger. But S.2373 ran into several roadblocks, the most prominent of which were North Carolina senator Sam Ervin, who, in this period just before his Watergate Hearing heroics, opposed the waivers (as he had the NFL-AFL agreement), and the Players Association, which lobbied against the bill because the NBA hadn't negotiated an agreement with it regarding the move. The salary wars for untested college stars "will inexorably end in ruin," said ex-California senator Thomas Kuchel on behalf of the league.

During Senate hearings on S.2373 the Brookings Institution completed a report on professional sports. Its findings said that clubs in both basketball leagues suffered not from salary inflation but from insufficent revenues due to playing in arenas too small to support them. Only the sharing of home-gate receipts with visiting clubs, plus the end of compulsory option clauses, could save them. The NBA response? Speaking for the owners, NBA commissioner Walter Kennedy said these provisions "wrecked the chance of merger."

Finally, on February 3, 1976, the NBA and ABA settled the Robertson suit with the Players Association. The agreement ended the option clause: teams that drafted a player only owned his rights for one year if he didn't sign immediately with them—the old contract had been for two years, college underclassmen could be drafted if they renounced their college eligibility, and a right-of-first-refusal rule was introduced, giving teams a chance to match offers made by other teams for their free agent players. Though modified many times, this settlement is still the backbone of the relationship between the NBA and its players. Salaries continue their upward spiral, and truly exceptional college players can jump to the pros more rapidly. The dark side of this deal is that it still encourages the idea that basketball is a great goal for African-American kids, especially the impoverished, and that college is no longer the goal but just a brief resting place on the journey to big bucks.

When the merger was complete, the NBA had twenty-two teams, including the four ABA additions and expansion teams in Buffalo, Portland, Cleveland, New Orleans, Milwaukee, and Phoenix. The San Diego Rockets were now in Houston and the St. Louis Hawks in Atlanta. In this new environment African-Americans reached significant positions of authority in pro basketball yet to be matched in most other segments of our national life. Sy Gourdine, a Black attorney, was hired as the NBA's vice president of administration, making him the highest-ranking person of African descent in integrated sports history. Many spoke optimistically about Gourdine one day becoming commissioner. Wayne Embry, who retired as a player in 1972, became the general manager of the Milwaukee Bucks and would go on to assemble one of the league's most intelligent teams. Player-coach Lenny Wilkens took over Seattle in 1969 and, after retiring, would coach in Portland before returning to take the SuperSonics to the title in 1979. Earl Lloyd and Ray Scott in Detroit, John McLendon in Denver, Al Attles in Golden State (NBA champs in 1975), Wilt Chamberlain with the ABA's San Diego Conquistadors, K. C. Jones with that same San Diego team and the Washington Bullets, Elgin Baylor in New Orleans, Zelmo Beaty in Virginia, all broke into NBA coaching in the seventies.

Bill Russell, ever the pioneer, became the first regular

African-American sports announcer on national television. His commentary on ABC's Sunday afternoon "NBA Game of the Week" was highly regarded. *Life* magazine commented in 1972, "Russell's commentary on the last six NBA games has been as loose, confident, skillful, and precise as his play at center for the Celtics. You know exactly when he's disgusted, exactly when he's bemused, exactly when he's bored. No fright, no panicked floundering or beating of gums on 'dead air,' just professionalism, authority."

In 1975 Seattle SuperSonics owner Sam Schulman, who had already had one Black coach in Lenny Wilkens, gave Russell $125,000 to become that club's coach-general manager. While holding these positions for four seasons he laid the groundwork for Seattle's 1979 champions.

Unfortunately, during Russell's tenure in Seattle he would as coach set the tone for a profound asethetic debate that pitted pre-ABA/ premillionaire pro ball athletes of his era against the monied funk 'n' dunkers of the seventies. Aside from inducing Russell back into coaching, Schulman spent millions in court battles and salaries to wrest forward Spencer Haywood, guard John Brisker, and center Jim McDaniels from the ABA. To Russell, a man whose outlook was molded by discipline and desire, these were all flawed players who didn't deserve or work hard enough to earn their salaries.

"When I was playing"—a phrase NBA old-timers used often in the post-ABA years—"and we lost a bad one, I'd have to walk the streets at night. You think everybody has pride and self-respect, and you find that you're wrong," he said. He abhorred the no-cut contracts that guaranteed players cash and a job no matter how slovenly they performed.

Because of guaranteed money and the individual quirks of their personalities (Haywood never did truly fit into any system for long in his NBA career), Russell grew distant from the players, the press, and ultimately Schulman. He'd later write, "Once the challenge of rescuing a franchise had worn off, winning basketball championships was not worth enough to me to tolerate being around people I didn't like or respect. Since it is my habit simply not to talk to people I don't like, I found it harder and harder to have discussions with many of the players. It was obvious to them that I didn't like them, and naturally they didn't like me either."

Russell's message that players of the late seventies were spoiled, unmotivated because of their contracts, and plain-old overpaid took on another texture when championed by others. With the league now overwhelmingly Black, with coaches and even referees brown-skinned, white fans and writers complained that their style was ruining the game. The media depicted the game's best player, Kareem Abdul-Jabbar, as a sullen giant who believed a weird (possibly un-American) religion. If he wouldn't open up to sportswriters he automatically had to be a bad guy, right? White stars were few and far between—the Celtics' John Havlicek and Dave Cowens, Portland's Bill Walton, and Atlanta's Pete Moravich. Television ratings shrunk, as if the hectic multiplication of teams, the constant movement of players and franchises, and, yes, the color of these tank-topped millionaires was simply too much for white ticket buyers to digest.

Not that all of this criticism was unwarranted. Many players did themselves and the game a disservice with their attitude. Philadelphia guard and Brooklyn schoolyard legend Lloyd "All-World" Free (soon to be known legally as World B. Free) was sharply dissected by Clayton Riley in the *Village Voice:* "The aptly named Free is a street-ball run-and-gun-fighter, the artist as entertainer, lofting stratospheric jump shots that fall to the hoop like portraits when he makes them, bricks when they miss. More than any single player in the NBA, Lloyd represents the new urban consciousness of the seventies, a spirit that recognizes no authority but its own appetites and remains perpetually indifferent to any requirements beyond immediate personal gratification." In the words of Free, upon the Sixers being flown out of a crucial playoff game: "I got my double figures. I'm doing my job." In the eyes of many observers, Black as well as white, many brothers were living out the decade's selfish ethos to the max.

But, thankfully, they didn't abandon that will to entertain and innovate. The qualities of genius and aggression had, just for a time, been overwhelmed by the sudden flush of big money. The phrase "Go for it!" spoke for the destructive greed that manifested itself throughout all levels of the pro game. What the NBA needed was not fewer Blacks but a more tasteful application of their style. Free, and others like him, had exploited the new atmosphere as if they were dancers and playing ball were just hanging out at some jive-ass disco. True funk was needed, and it was coming.

WHEELIN' 'N' DEALIN'

Not only did Black men change how the game was played, they also changed how it was described. The give-and-go, pick 'n' roll, and backdoor play are all products of textbook, classroom basketball that dates back to the early twentieth century. They describe passing plays executed in a half-court offense. Coaches use them, love them, and will intone them to their players well into the twenty-first century.

In the seventies the language of brothers talking about each other injected itself into all ball conversations because they were freaky, funky, and fly. Bad shots became "bricks." The goal wasn't merely to beat your man but to "burn" or "take" or "do" him. A "chump" or "turkey" or "sucker" (a lousy player) was easy prey for a "chucker" (see World B. Free), though it would be great if the chucker learned to "wheel" (dribble), "deal" (pass), or "dish" (pass off the drive) the "pill" or "rock" (ball). Anybody can stuff. Some can dunk. Few can "jam," and only the lucky can perform "a 360" (turn completely around in the air before slammin'). Bob Cousy passed pretty. So did Marques Haynes and Goose Tatum. But if they had come up in the last two decades all three would have "wheeled 'n' dealed." Perhaps because it so aptly described the game's new attitude, "In your (yo') face," the confident boast of a deadeye shooter, became the single most popular phrase of the new style. It was also known as "face" or, as whites put it, a "facial."

One of basketball's greatest lexicologists, Darryl Dawkins, toiled in the NBA during the seventies. Few have enriched basketball language like the man known as Chocolate Thunder. Dawkins entered the league in 1979 as one of its biggest players (6´11˝, 260 pounds) and youngest (nineteen). Like Moses Malone, the imposing young Dawkins was recruited right out of high school and brought a boyish enthusiasm (and inconsistency) to the game. On a team with the artistic Dr. J., Dawkins craved his own niche in dunkin' lore. Where Erving floated and soared, Chocolate Thunder crashed and destroyed. "I dunked every chance I got," Dawkins said. "I saw it as the ultimate form of expression on the basketball court." Dawkins did more than dunk—he gave his dunks names. There was the Earthquake Shaker, the Turbo Delight, the Sexophonic, the Go-Rilla (because "I swatted it in just like King Kong pawing airplanes"), the Greyhound Bus ("where I went coast-to-coast"), the infamous In Your Face Disgrace, and the world-renowned Rim Wrecker.

Dawkins's celebrity was built on more than talk. He became the first NBA player since the Bullets' Gus Johnson to break a backboard when jamming. And he did it twice. On November

13, 1979, at Kansas City's decrepit Municipal Auditorium, thirty-eight seconds into the second half Dawkins went up. Broadcaster Neil Funk reported, "He didn't just break the rim off the backboard—that backboard exploded ... There was broken glass, flying shards of shrapnel flying all over the place. It was a wonder that nobody got seriously hurt. Poor Bill Robinzine, the Kansas City center who had the misfortune of being victimized by Darryl's dunk, cut his hand." Darryl, immediately a Philadelphia cult figure, landed a column in the Philadelphia *Journal,* and in it he named the dunk a "Chocolate Thunder Flying, Robinzine Crying, Teeth Shaking, Glass Breaking, Rump Roasting, Bun Toasting, Wham Bam, Glass Breaker I Am Jam."

Three weeks later, home in the Spectrum, Dawkins jammed and broke the rim right off in his hands with his Candy Slam, single-handedly prompting the introduction of the collapsible rim into the game. Hampered by poor fundamentals and a penchant for fouling, Dawkins never totally refined his prodigious strength into a consistent approach. Still, Dawkins was a lot more fun than many steadier players. By word and deed Dawkins articulated seventies funk, a hard-core polyrhythmic Black music genre, with the same flair as the band Parliament/Funkadelic. "Funk is not a bad word," Dawkins wrote in *Chocolate Thunder.* "Funk is just being jazzy. As a matter of fact, there are two kinds of funk: Jazzy Funk and Funk Beyond Control. I am the only person who has ever harnessed Funk Beyond Control and that's why only I have Close Encounters of the Funkiest Kind."

POST-UCLA NCAA

With the fall of John Wooden's UCLA dynasty in 1974 the world of Division I basketball was thrown into a whirl of democratic chaos from which, thankfully, it is yet to recover fully. The recruitment of African-American athletes had, by now, utterly changed the NCAA. Now schools from Michigan down to Alabama not only competed for a few blue-chip African-Americans but would start five of them—even at home. Marquette's Al McGuire is an apt symbol of the changed philosophy. In the fifties, his Uncle Frank, coaching at North Carolina, couldn't use his New York contacts to recruit Blacks. Al, free of any pressure other than winning, became an acknowledged master at recruiting and keeping African-American players happy. He specialized in utilizing not only hardcore New Yorkers like guard Butch Lee from the Bronx but tough guys from all over. Maurice Lucas of Pittsburgh, for example, enrolled at Marquette because of McGuire's rep for respecting brothers.

The range of outstanding African-American talent was imposing: the agile forward David Greenwood of UCLA, the speedy North Carolina point guard Phil Ford, the long-range jump shooter Otis Birdsong of Houston, and the devastating turnaround pop shot of Tennessee's Bernard King. By the late seventies the opportunity for an education at white schools via sports, something new just a decade before, was now commonplace. At many schools these athletes constituted the first large group of African-Americans on campus. Often there were few or no African-American professors or female students. Teams kept their players in athletic dorms, taking the same classes, isolating them from a true college experience. Being Black and a sports star made them doubly visible, and every misstep, accidental or criminal, was headline fodder.

Bernard King, native of Brooklyn's gang-ridden Fort Greene neighborhood and a New York City schoolyard legend, enrolled at the University of Tennessee in 1976 and immediately became one of the best players not just in the school's history but in the entire history of the once all-white Southeast Athletic Conference. Obviously, King stuck out in Knoxville. It didn't help that early on in his stay King openly discussed declaring "hardship" to turn pro before graduating. It also didn't help that five times within fifteen months he was arrested for possessing a small amount of marijuana, prowling after dark, and burglary. Four cases against him resulted in no convictions. In the fifth he was fined for possessing marijuana and given a suspended sentence. Between his on-court adventures and off-court arrest this twenty-year-old was, for a time, the most visible Black man in the state. It was no surprise then that before his senior year King signed a five-year $800,000 deal with the New Jersey Nets. King's misadventures in the fishbowl of college stardom were similar to incidents involving brothers all around the country.

If Division I's romance with African-Americans was a mixed blessing for many individual players, it was a major blow to the Black colleges. The loss of top athletes, as well as coaches and scouts, to large white schools paralleled the negative impact integration had on African-American athletics. The children of parents who attended Fisk, Tennessee A&I, Tuskegee, and Virginia Union now could, and often did, walk through these recently opened doors and away from Black colleges. From the seventies on, the percentage of NBA stars who attended all-Black colleges would steadily decrease.

But the cupboard wasn't bare. One of basketball's little-known dynasties was Kentucky State University from 1970 to 1973, as under coach Lucias Mitchell the Thorobreds won three straight NAIA titles. Mitchell was wooed from Alabama State to Kentucky State in 1968 to turn around a program that had fielded a 2–9 team the year before. Six-three and well conditioned, Mitchell had the lean grace of an athlete, though his image as coach was probably defined by trademark black horn-rimmed glasses, à la John Wooden, that gave him a scholarly look. His father had been an army master sergeant, and that disciplined background influenced his coaching style. In his first season at Kentucky State Mitchell had to battle some players and school administrators over control of the program. He told Mike Embry that many players "didn't want to practice, they didn't want to work on fundamentals, they didn't want to run, they didn't want to study. They wanted to tell the coach what to do and I wasn't about to stand for that." One popular player became a discipline problem, so Mitchell suspended him for several games. On-campus sympathy for the players was high. Typical of the era, some students threatened a sit-in. School administrators feared the sit-in would turn ugly, yet Mitchell wouldn't reinstate the player and, eventually, the off-court controversy subsided.

It didn't hurt Mitchell's position one bit that Kentucky State improved in 1969–1970 to ten and fifteen and that he successfully recruited two future NBA draftees to the Frankfort, Kentucky, campus. Elmore "Big E" Smith, a seven-foot center from Macon, Georgia, and Travis "The Machine" Grant, a 6'8" forward from Clayton, Alabama, provided Mitchell with a nucleus. Smith, athletically a late bloomer, didn't play organized basketball until his senior year in high school. Under Mitchell's guidance Smith developed strong low post moves to accompany an innate feel for rebounding and shot blocking. His defensive presence, in the traditional Russell mode, allowed teammates to funnel opponents into the middle, where a block, turnover, or forced shot keyed the Thorobred fast break.

Often Smith kicked the ball out to Grant, a great pure shooter with unlimited range and a willingness to pump it up. He earned his nickname The Machine in the first game of his sophomore season, 1970, as, with Mitchell's kind permission,

Grant took seventy shots—thirty in the game's last 12:54—
hitting thirty-five baskets from the floor and totaling seventy-
five points in a 141–93 win over Michigan's Northwood Institute. Note that despite a wide-open style Kentucky State held
its opponent to under 100 points, showing that Mitchell didn't
just roll out the ball in practice. In fact, his blend of wide-open
ball, tough interior defense, and Black athleticism was a synthesis that anticipated the NBA of the late seventies.

Supported by guards Jerry Stafford and Jerome Brister and
forward Mike Bernard, Smith and Grant led the Magic Men to a
28–3 record, including their NAIA play-off wins, in
1970–1971. Some attempted to stop the Thorobreds by slowing
the tempo, such as Central State of Ohio, which almost upset
them, 66–65. Others, like the all-Black Guilford squad that featured future Piston and Celtic M. L. Carr, tried to outrun the
Thorobreds but were outclassed, 108–90. Though they beat
Eastern New Mexico only 79–71 in the title game, Kentucky
State led most of the way and never felt threatened. After it was
over Mitchell stopped just short of predicting a repeat. "We
hope to make it two in a row," he said. "We have the horses."

Kentucky was actually better in 1971–1972. William Graham, aka "Bird," previously a sixth man, replaced the graduated
Bernard in the starting lineup. Considered a better all-around
player than Bernard, Graham excelled at crashing the offensive
boards. No one was surprised when Mitchell's team went 26–2
during the regular season with Grant averaging 30.9 points
and Smith 26.5. The center also took down twenty-four
rebounds a game and Graham seventeen, so that the team's two
big men combined for more than forty rebounds per game,
which generated a slew of fast breaks and second shots.

The NAIA play-offs offered two challenges, though only one
was on the court. Kennedy McIntosh, a 6′7″, 220-pound senior,
was the anchor of an Eastern Michigan team that had bested

Kentucky State in regular-season games three times in three seasons. In the last two contests McIntosh had dominated Smith, so Big E and his teammates clearly had something to prove. The club also had a dream. Mitchell felt that by winning the NAIA again his team might earn a National Invitation Tournament slot and a chance to display their gifts at Madison Square Garden. Despite their obvious greatness few outside small college circles knew of Kentucky State. On court all went well. McIntosh outscored Smith 21–11, but Smith still grabbed fifteen rebounds and was a defensive demon in the middle. Grant rose up to score forty-three points, twenty-four by the end of the first half, when Kentucky State led, 57–40. After the victory Mitchell claimed there was "not a better front line anywhere." But despite back-to-back NAIA titles, Kentucky State was never invited to New York.

To add to Mitchell's pain, after the season Graham graduated and Smith joined the NBA's expansion franchise, the Buffalo Braves. This should have been the end of the Kentucky State title run, but there was one more year to come. With Sam "The Leaper" Silbert at center, Stafford still at point guard, and an offense geared toward setting screens for Grant, the Thorobreds recovered from a rocky start to win their last eighteen games. Offensive production was way down, but the defense remained solid and Grant's shooting took Kentucky State to its third straight NAIA title.

The difference in the three championship teams is that in the 1972 final Grant, with thirty-nine points, was the only Thorobred in double figures. He averaged 31.2 points and had a 64.8 shooting percentage in 1972 (throughout his four years he averaged 33.4 points and shot 63.8 percent) and was named college basketball player of the year. The only other team to have won three consecutive NAIA titles? John McLendon's Tennessee A&I squads of 1956–1959. The final gasp of this great Kentucky State team came in 1974 when Mitchell and company lost in the NAIA semifinals to West Georgia, 79–75.

The flash and funk of the late 1960s and 1970s had helped transform the sport. Pro teams dotted the national landscape, many with Black coaches and a majority of Black players. At large colleges everywhere white alumni embraced the school's Black stars, marveling at their huge Afros and tomahawk dunks, while too many of these players neglected their studies for dreams of emulating Dr. J's adventures above the rim. The profile of basketball in the African-American community was at a new high—money, fame, and, for the level-headed, an education made possible through ball. In the 1980s the bill for this roundball mania came due.

GLAMOUR PROFESSION

At the dawn of the 1980s basketball had a full-fledged rep—one perpetuated by coaches and media and believed by way too many Black families—as the fastest way out of the ghetto. "The life" (aka street hustling in general and drug dealing in particular) had this rep, too. So did the music biz. The narrowness of these options is testimony to the alienation so many young people felt toward the more traditional, socially acceptable means of personal empowerment.

It's important to note that the emphasis was on the fastest, not the best or surest way to elevate oneself. For many poor kids escape, not necessarily from the ghetto, but from poverty was the crucial goal. In hip-hop parlance "livin' large" and "gettin' paid" were not automatically linked to leaving the 'hood. In fact, the great goal of many young African-Americans was to be large *in* the 'hood. And basketball, it became clear as the decade progressed, couldn't guarantee you a reputation, cash, and/or the American Dream extolled by European-Americans and mainstream African-American media like *Ebony* (in cover stories on entertainers' multimillion-dollar homes) and epitomized by a consume-till-you-drop philosophy. In numbers larger than at any time in history, young African-Americans found hustling, sparked by the creation of crack—the Big Mac of drugs—a surer bet than music or basketball since it required no skills other than tenacity, raw desire, and the willingness to cultivate a contempt for the dignity of others.

The balance of power between drugs and sports shifted because after three decades of integrated basketball, Black kids now understood the deal. They'd seen local high school legends recruited to out-of-state colleges with dreams not of a degree, but of the NBA in their heads. Colleges, usually through boosters, provide sex (access to accommodating women, often white coeds), transportation (access to spanking-new sports cars or jeeps), housing (either off campus or in special athletic dorms), and money (or its equivalent, such as athletic gear, tickets, and warm-ups that can be bartered for cash). All this largess continued to accrue while the players maintained eligibility. As soon as their eligibility was up, it was almost uniformly "see ya later" at a great many institutions of higher learning. Lacking cars, girls, a pro contract, or a degree worth anything in today's marketplace, the brothers wandered back to the 'hood. Most returning players don't turn to drug dealing, but too many do. The failure of these players following years of work at (and exploitation by) schools lets folks back home know these men were just pawns in a game. Where once access to a college was an end in itself, the basketball salary explosion of the 1970s blurred that vision. Greed and ego led too many brothers in search of a false dream, a dream that led many—even well-meaning athletic programs—to exploit Blacks for the glory of their schools and the money that glory generated. "When you go to college, you're not a student-athlete but an athlete-student," Isiah Thomas told *Newsweek.* "Your main purpose was not to be Einstein but to be a ballplayer, to generate some money, put people in the stands. Eight or ten hours of your day are filled with basketball, football, etc. The rest of the time you've got to motivate yourself to make sure you get something back."

Crack's ascendance has helped erode the role of basketball players as a resource for binding together the African-American community. Whether it is through the color-coded gangs of Los Angeles or the more loosely organized teen posses in New York, crack has turned neighborhood bullies into a national network of Uzi-armed killers. In many cities gangs prevent teens from playing ball, seeing the camaraderie of sports as a challenge to gang allegiance. In neighborhoods overrun by stifled materialism and the crack culture, sporting activities are far from sacrosanct. For example, in New York City in 1991 many high school basketball games are held in isolation, with no fans present, due to the fear of violence. Fourteen-year-old Chicagoan Ervin Barker had a sadly typical experience in the fall of 1989 while he was playing basketball with some friends. In between games a schoolmate asked, "When are you going to start serving?" (i.e., selling drugs) and then told Ervin he could be supplied with quarter bags of cocaine retailing for $25. Though many of his playmates were making $125 a week, Ervin just said, "No." His schoolmate's reaction was to refuse to play with him, and most of Ervin's peers agreed. This child's decision not to deal didn't make him a hero but a social outcast.

Equally disheartening is that in areas bereft of businesses committed to their customers, drug dealers often sponsored tournaments: when an angry drug dealer shot a referee at a mideighties Queens summer-league game, it finally became common knowledge nationally. Some were surprised when wholesome New York guard Mark Jackson was subpoenaed to appear as a character witness at the trial of an accused drug dealer, Tommy Mickens. Jackson had, while at St. John's University, played in a summer league Mickens had financed. Though the 1987 rookie of the year was accused of no wrongdoing, Jackson's association with an alleged drug dealer suggests what a familiar presence dealers are in the world of inner-city athletics. For all of basketball's character-building pluses the sport was as helpless in blunting the drug onslaught of the 1980s as other American institutions. Given the environment, no one should be surprised at the extensive drug use among athletes. Maybe Len Bias's cocaine-induced death gave a few pause, but not enough. Shortly after the Maryland star's death, extra-potent crack was labeled "Len Bias" in D.C. in a sick tribute to the dead hoop star. In fact, the 1986 draft, in which Bias was selected number-one pick by the Boston Celtics, was one of the most drug-scarred ever. Four 1986 number-one draft picks (Bias, Chris Washburn, William Bedford, Roy Tarpley) had careers eventually destroyed or curtailed by drug use.

The drug culture is so ingrained in Black communities as a source of income and prestige that it is rare an inner-city kid doesn't have an acquaintance, friend, or relative in some way involved with the trade. In our cities drug dealers' money and athletes' celebrity status granted both groups entry to the same exclusive clubs and parties. They date the same fly girls—beautiful women who define their existence by the clout and/or cash of their boyfriends. Drug dealers populate the VIP sections at almost every NBA contest.

A vivid example of the contemporary tangle of drugs and sports occurred in Washington, D.C., around 1989. Georgetown freshman Alonzo Mourning, one of the nation's most sought-after recruits, and John Turner, a capable big man who served as the team's power forward, were friends with Rayfield Edmond III, who, according to D.C. police, was one of the biggest dealers in a city saturated with crack. Knowing that guilt by association is the norm in our media and society, Coach John Thompson tried to end these unfortunate friendships. He met with his players and, surprisingly, with Edmond as well. It was reported that at his meeting Thompson offered Edmond Georgetown season tickets in exchange for leaving his players alone and telling him if any of them were flirting with cocaine. Mourning heeded Thompson's warning, but Turner continued hanging with Edmond at after-hours clubs. In the spring of 1989 Thompson announced Turner was leaving Georgetown for academic reasons. Yet in truth it was Turner's inability to pry himself from bad associations that forced Thompson to send him packing. So it wasn't really a shock when in July 1989 Turner and four others were arrested at a recreational center near his Glen Gardens, Maryland, home on charges of cocaine possession with intent to distribute. As the *New York Times*'s William Rhoden said, "It seemed at the time that Turner was destined to become yet another inner city tragedy." Fortunately for Turner, the charges against him were dropped by prosecutors on the grounds that the arresting officers were out of their jurisdiction. Division I schools shied away from the tainted player, so Turner ended up at Phillips University in Enid, Oklahoma, where he averaged 22.5 points and 14.2 rebounds against NAIA opposition. In December 1989 Edmond received a life sentence for conspiracy in running a local drug syndicate around D.C.

The kicker to the story is that a year after being forced to exit from Georgetown, Rhoden asked Turner why he didn't simply stay away from Edmond. Turner answered, "He was just a friend, and I don't feel he was doing anything wrong when I was around him." That's the kind of wrongheaded thinking all too prevalent among American youth in the 1990s. It points out the troubles even the best role models have in dealing with the mentality of players raised in an era where drug dealing is the real glamour profession.

Turner, in essence, valued his friendship with drug lord Edmond more than basketball, Big East glory, or lessons taught by the most successful Black coach in big-time college ball history. Despite losing Turner and a few other young men to the streets during his nineteen years at Georgetown, John Thompson has persevered as a powerful, positive presence and architect of his own powerhouse brand of Black basketball.

BIG JOHN

I first saw John Thompson at Madison Square Garden in December 1978. As an intern at New York's Black weekly, the Amsterdam *News,* I talked my way into covering the holiday tournament, and, as a student then attending St. John's University, the tournament favorite, my interest was more than journalistic. My only knowledge of Georgetown was that it had an African-American coach, was based in D.C., and had a star guard named John Duren and a promising one, Eric "Sleepy" Floyd. Then, during the pregame warm-ups, Thompson walked across court. That a Black coach headed a Division I basketball program was striking enough—until then my idea of a big-time college coach was defined by frantic Italians like St. John's Lou Carnesecca and Villanova's Rollie Massino or slick, well-dressed "educator" coaches epitomized by North

Carolina's Dean Smith. It didn't occur to me that a bulky, 6´8˝ Black man could land such a gig. Thompson's physical size (and the fact that he towered over most of his players) shocked me. Immediately, my loyalty toward the Redmen was tested and found wanting. No way I could root against an over-whelmingly Black squad coached by an imposing Black man from Chocolate City, U.S.A. Just the sight of Thompson standing across the court from me sent a spasm of pride through me.

Then the Hoyas started playing. Aggressive, tenacious, and quite mean, Thompson's Georgetown squad had a steely edge. St. John's won the tournament, and the school's David Russell was the most valuable player. But Georgetown's attitude, the silky moves of Floyd, and Thompson's large glowering presence remains locked in my mind. In the pressroom a white sportswriter mentioned to me a seven-foot kid from Boston named Ewing ("They say he's the new Bill Russell") was being recruited by Georgetown. Sounded good.

Years later, after Sleepy, Reggie Williams, Michael Graham, Michael Jackson, David Wingate, John Spriggs, Fred Brown, Charles Smith, and Patrick Ewing, a new "next Bill Russell" named Alonzo Mourning wears Ewing's number 33, cruising the lane for the Hoyas. Between that holiday tournament and now, Thompson has gone from being an anomaly to one of the nation's best-known sports personalities and certainly the sport's most visible Black authority figure. To others, including countless white journalists, he's a lightning rod of antagonism. Black male authority figures—as opposed to stars—were few and far between during Ronald Reagan's presidency, but Thompson filled that role with gusto, expressing thoughts fearlessly and receiving reactions that ranged from hostility to outrage to shock.

With the exception of the obnoxious George Steinbrenner, no one has gotten as consistently negative a press as Thompson and his Georgetown program. And, unlike Steinbrenner, Thompson has never attempted to court the press. Like all Black achievers over forty Thompson's will was molded by the bittersweet struggle against segregation and the racial indignities of his youth. If there is anger in the man—and I believe there is hostility against the white sports establishment in him—he has funneled it into a coaching style that irritates not just opponents but observers as well.

In the years before the civil rights movement transformed the South, Washington, D.C., was as racially divided as any town in the nation. John Thompson, son of a laborer who couldn't read or write, was raised there, absorbing all the slights inflicted on African-Americans during the years of legal segregation. One kind of racism that affected Thompson, and still hampers Black children to this day, was the negative attitude of white teachers. Minor learning disabilities or simply poor study habits are customarily interpreted as "stupidity" by their instructors, and Black children are too often discarded early in life by an educational system with no faith in their future. After experiencing scholastic difficulties in a Catholic school, teachers there decided Thompson was retarded and told his parents, "This boy isn't educable." For many African-American youths those words would have led to the exile of slow-moving classes and neglect. But Thompson's mother taught him to defy those evil expectations and to maintain his self-esteem.

As a teen Thompson grew to 6´10˝, and in the process he found basketball. As the center of the Archbishop Carroll High team he took the school to fifty-five straight wins and D.C. high school championships in 1959 and 1960. Red Auerbach, Boston Celtic boss and D.C. native, influenced the high school senior to attend Providence College because under the NBA's territorial draft teams had first choice of players attending schools within a fifty-mile radius. Thinking ahead, Auerbach saw Thompson as a backup for Russell. Under future NBA coach Joe Mullaney Providence was a New England power which had already had one Black star, guard Lenny Wilkens, who had graduated the year before Thompson's arrival. As at most white schools then, athletes constituted a large percentage of the Black males on campus. Still, in an overwhelmingly white environment Thompson fared well socially and athletically. Though the media tends to portray Thompson as perpetually hostile, one-on-one he gets along well with people of all kinds and has a sharp sense of humor. In fact, it's been said he was tighter with his white teammates at Providence than his Black ones, which suggests he judges people on character as much as color. During his three varsity years Providence made the NCAA tournament once and the NIT twice. Thompson's assets were a nice touch and good "court sense," but his slow-footedness became a liability in the pros. With bulk and determination as his chief tools Thompson's Celtic career was short and undistinguished. As Bill Russell's caddy for two NBA champs Thompson played in seventy-four games and averaged 3.5 points.

But Thompson absorbed the philosophies of Auerbach and Russell. He watched as defense won titles and the team's two leaders cultivated the "Celtic mystique" to fuel the team's consistent excellence. The Hoyas' emphasis on defense and insistence on players fitting into designated roles are Celtic echoes. So is a distant public persona that Auerbach has said, "[Thompson] picked up from me and Russell—take control, stay in control, put everyone else on the defensive."

The Chicago Bulls selected him in the 1966 expansion draft, while the New Orleans Buccaneers claimed his ABA rights, but Thompson decided he didn't want to be a journeyman player on bad clubs. Instead, he returned to D.C., where he worked for the United Planning Council and the National 4-H Council before beginning his coaching career at St. Anthony's Catholic High School. Drawing on friendships in the area and contacts made working for 4-H, he built a program at St. Anthony's that attracted the attention of the administration of Georgetown, an overwhelmingly white Catholic school located in one of the city's most fashionable neighborhoods. Thompson immediately recognized the allure of operating in an elite school environment surrounded by a predominantly Black, working-class city. In this time, before Black history courses and affirmative action became neoconservative targets, the university sought a way to reach out to the rest of D.C. During the 1971–1972 season Georgetown's Hoyas won only three of twenty-six games. So its president, Robert Heale, asked Thompson if he would take over the program. In accepting the job Thompson vowed he would emphasize athletics and academics. To that end he hired assistant coach Mary Fenlon to monitor his teams' in-class performance.

During the 1974–1975 campaign, his third as head Hoya, Thompson withstood a racially motivated challenge to his authority. His top scorer, Jonathan Smith, was caught cutting classes and Thompson benched him. Following a seven and two start the Hoyas lost six straight with Smith sitting. In response, some white students unfurled a banner at a home game that read, "Thompson, the Nigger Flop, Must Go!" Thompson was unintimidated, pulling his players together to win eleven of its next twelve to capture the ECAC championship and qualify the school for its first NCAA tournament in thirty-two years, an achievement that enabled him to develop a powerful local recruiting network. From St. Anthony's he recruited his first nationally celebrated star, guard John Duren. Later, he'd begin a fruitful friendship with Bob Wade, coach at Baltimore's Dunbar High, who would help him woo Dave

Wingate and Reggie Williams, key players on Georgetown's 1984 NCAA winning team. (Thompson later repaid Wade by recommending him for Maryland's head coaching job.)

Thompson's career was changed forever in 1981 when he successfully recruited Patrick Ewing. Born in Jamaica and raised by a doting mother in Boston, Ewing was the dominant high school center in Beantown history while attending Boston Latin. The seven-footer was shy and had some difficulty in school, so Patrick's mother was adamant her son would attend a school that made its athletes study. The story goes that one evening in the Ewing living room the youngster asked Thompson about social life in D.C. According to legend, Thompson said, "With your schoolwork and the athletics, you won't have much time for social life in Washington, D.C.," and with that Mommy Ewing made her decision. True or not, Patrick Ewing enrolled at Georgetown, immediately transforming the school into a national power and inaugurating a period of intense off-court controversy and on-court achievement.

Thompson had a policy of allowing the media limited access to his players. After the game reporters could slip inside the Georgetown locker room for postgame quotes, but only for fifteen minutes. After that the media were ushered out. Freshmen weren't allowed to be interviewed at all. On-camera television interviews were kept to a minimum. Reporters seeking to profile Ewing, expecting access to his dorm room, photos of him in class, and anecdotes of him at play, had no chance. Like John Wooden at UCLA, Thompson shut them out.

"It's not that I'm intentionally trying to make anyone's job harder," he told *Sport* in 1985. "It's unfortunate that the rules and regulations that I have are inconvenient to the media. That part I am sorry for. But I have no intention of changing. I'm taking the time to talk now, but during the season it's just not my priority. I can't spend this kind of time talking when I've got 15 kids with almost every kind of problem you could imagine, including basketball ... who has the media educated? Who has the media made better able to do something? John Wooden didn't let out interviews at all when Alcindor was there. They make more out of me having limited interviews than they did out of him having none with Alcindor."

To the media, hungry for backstage access to the ascendant Georgetown program, Thompson's policy was a horror. Some sharp-tongued media type termed it Hoya Paranoia, and the phrase was subsequently replayed in hundreds of headlines and broadcasts. The spoiled sports media, used to having colleges suck up to them, handle rejection as well as a lovesick fifteen-year-old. Moody stars, close-mouthed teams, or coaches that are just plain quiet try the patience of reporters. That natural hostility toward poor sources was certainly exacerbated by the fact that Thompson, as well as Ewing, were towering Black men whose disinterested attitude toward interviews clearly irritated an overwhelmingly white male media.

But the issue was not simply one of Black subject versus white reporter. While at the Amsterdam *News* and later at *Black Enterprise* magazine, I had the opportunity to interview Thompson. In each case he was initially quite intimidating, clearly a man with low tolerance for those he perceived as foolish. He warmed up as we talked, but not, I think, because I was Black but because I neither patronized nor attacked him. Contrary to the image projected about him, Thompson didn't strike me as a knee-jerk nationalist. Just because I was a Black journalist didn't mean I automatically got more time or courtesy than a white writer. It was my impression, however, that if you were Black and, in his judgment, good at what you did, it was definitely a plus. Thompson's been criticized for having all-Black squads and rarely going after white athletes. But if Thompson was racist Mary Fenlon wouldn't be his academic counselor or Dean Smith a friend and mentor.

The combination of Thompson's negative press and the Hoyas' on-court aggression made them the Oakland Raiders of the hardwood. Ewing, tough and relentless, with a warrior's heart, repeatedly got into staring contests and even fights with opponents and was the chief target of racist fans. During the 1982–1983 season students at Providence College held up "Ewing Can't Read" signs. At the Meadowlands Seton Hall supporters unfurled a banner that read, "Think! Ewing! Think!" while in Philadelphia Villanova fans wrote "Ewing Is a Ape" on placards. T-shirts were sold at the Big East schools declaring, "Ewing Kan't Read Dis." Several Georgetown games were interrupted by bananas thrown on the floor. Twice during the 1982–1983 campaign the Hoyas and chief rival St. John's engaged in fistfights partially attributable to the Big East's ultraphysical style—a style Thompson's team helped inspire— as well as the racial slurs from St. John's student body. Far too many of the school's white working-class Catholic student body used Ewing as a sounding board for their own latent racist attitudes. I am a St. John's alumnus, and I saw and heard things from them that brought dishonor on the school. "Ignorance has no color," Thompson told *Time*. "The point isn't that this season has been degrading to a black man, it has been degrading to any man. On the airplane last week I asked Pat again how he was holding up. He told me, 'I've grown accustomed to it. I got so much of it in high school.' That made me saddest of all."

It should be said that Georgetown's approach did sometimes result in questionable judgments. In that year's title game against North Carolina, Ewing tried to intimidate Sam Perkins, James Worthy, and freshman Michael Jordan by goaltending the Tarheels' first six shots. It was a wildly assertive physicalization of the Black ball ethos and, in this context, it was silly. When Jordan hit the game-winning basket with just seconds left he won the game—but if Ewing hadn't provided North Carolina with those free points early on the outcome would have been different. A year later the Hoyas, more mature and emotionally focused, gave Kentucky an unforgettable ass-whipping in the NCAA semifinal. Adolph Rupp was long gone from the Blue Grass State's bench, but the perception among Blacks was that the university favored the recruitment of light-skinned Blacks, for example, center Sam Bowie and forward Kenny Walker, or those with a decidedly nonflamboyant approach. Fair or not, Kentucky's image and school approach made it, for many Blacks, Floyd Patterson to Georgetown's Muhammad Ali. Ewing, along with the muscular, menacing forward Michael Graham and tenacious guard Gene Smith, keyed a stifling, belly-to-belly "D." That Saturday, with my girlfriend holding my space in a movie line, I slid into McGlade's on Columbus Avenue to watch the game. The bar was overwhelmingly white and completely anti-Hoya. The bartender was telling customers, "None of Georgetown's players can read" and "Thompson is a fraud" as a coach. I bit my tongue and then watched as the ball was tossed up for the second half. Kentucky led, 29-22, when Thompson's team began playing with incredible defensive intensity. The Hoyas held Kentucky to three for thirty-three shooting for the game's last twenty minutes. Three for thirty-three! Throw in five free throws and you have eleven points in an NCAA tournament game for a team boasting two future first-round draft picks. McGlade's customers weren't merely stunned into silence. They were clearly overwhelmed. The sight of Graham with his razor-cut short hair glistening with sweat, the ball clutched tight after snatching a rebound, sneering contemptuously at Bowie, will linger in my mind as an image of unbridled Black passion. As *Newsday*'s Joe Gergen said, "That's about as close as any college team in the contemporary era has come to ground zero, the ultimate defensive accomplishment."

The championship win against Houston wasn't as dominating a performance, but it was just as aesthetically pleasing. The Hoyas' particular contribution to Black style was to update the old Celtic defensive philosophy with Ewing as Russell, Gene Smith as K. C. Jones, Graham as Sanders, and Reggie Williams and David Wingate as Sam Jones. Watching the Houston Cougars was like attending an ABA All-Star Game. They were labeled "Phi Slamma Jamma" because when they went to the hole the last thing they wanted to do was lay it in. Cougar stars were Hakeem Olajuwon, a seven-foot product of Lagos, Nigeria, who'd only been playing ball a few years and already was being touted as potentially the best center ever, and Clyde "The Glide" Drexler, a guard as quick above the ground as he was on it. Along with Benny Anders, Alvin Franklin, Michael Young, and Larry Micheaux, the Cougars, under Guy Lewis's loose reign (he also coached Elvin Hayes), usually outleaped and outran the competition. Physically, they were probably more gifted than Georgetown and Kentucky. In later years both Olajuwon and Drexler were acknowledged members of the NBA elite. Yet, with the exception of the early moments when Houston hit its first seven shots, Thompson's players were in control. The game's tempo was set by Georgetown's defense and careful shot selection. Never did Houston have one of those slam-dunking, crown-exciting flurries that had been characteristic of its season. The final score was Georgetown 84, Houston 75, and it really wasn't that close.

As the first African-American to coach a team to an NCAA title John Thompson became a national figure of Black achievement and Georgetown the "official" Black team. Georgetown jackets, baseball caps, and T-shirts became the most popular gear in the street. Thompson's every move, positive and negative, was of national import. When Michael Graham had scholastic difficulties at Georgetown Thompson suggested he leave, even though it weakened his team, but it was a strong statement about where Thompson's priorities lay. Though the Hoyas lost to Villanova in the 1985 finals, Thompson still had the honor of taking a team to the final three straight seasons. In 1988 he coached the U.S. Olympic team, again irritating the press with his close-mouthed style. Unfortunately, he lost to the Russians and the United States earned only a bronze medal. The criticism of Thompson's attitude increased again. Luckily for Thompson, that same year he'd recruited Alonzo Mourning, a 6'10" center whose shot blocking and competitiveness recalled Ewing. He was doubly blessed when a local mailman put him in contact with Dikembe Mutambo, a seven-foot Nigerian who gave Georgetown an even more fearsome big man duo than its combination of Graham and Ewing.

Thompson's visibility translated into dollars. Between his regular salary, summer camp, Nike endorsements, a D.C. area television show, speaking engagements at $15,000 a shot, and national advertising (such as for Transamerica Insurance), Thompson reportedly earns a half million a year. His affairs are managed by Pro Serv, the same multipurpose management-marketing company that handles Ewing, Moses Malone, and Michael Jordan. It's not hyperbole to state Thompson has probably made more money than any Black basketball coach in history. But in addition to cashing in on his visibility Thompson has also used it to publicize his position on, aside from drugs, the most controversial issue in American collegiate sport—eligibility.

The failure of African-American athletes to finish school or even remain eligible from semester to semester was one of the ongoing travesties of integration. At Georgetown the graduation rate of Hoya players was 90 percent, but the Division I average was 27 percent. For Blacks that average in the revenue-producing sports of football and basketball was only 20 percent: eight out of ten don't graduate in the two high-profile sports. In a 1989 survey only 31 percent of Black athletes thought their coaches encouraged them academically. But 44 percent of those athletes apparently didn't care since, with stupefying optimism, that percentage of Black football and basketball players thought they'd sign an NFL or NBA contract.

The most famous illustration of college sports' exploitation of Blacks is the sad tale of Kevin Ross. In 1982 it was discovered that Ross played three years at Creighton University in Omaha without the ability to read or write. "They promised me an education but they used me by putting me in these bonehead courses," he said later. "I stayed eligible by taking three required courses and courses such as the theory of basketball, theory of ceramics. I made D's in the required courses and A's in the others." Years later Ross attended Black educator Marva Collins's private school in an attempt to make up for a lifetime of poor teaching.

The NCAA responded to this situation with two far-reaching rule changes. The first was Proposition 48. The 1986 rule mandated that all incoming college freshmen score 700 on the Scholastic Aptitude Test, 15 on the American College Test, or have a 2.0 grade point average in a college prep curriculum. If an athlete failed to meet either the test or grade standard he could keep his scholarship but couldn't compete his freshman year. Three years later the NCAA got tougher with Proposition 42, which extended the test score/grade point criteria of Proposition 48. In essence, a freshman who didn't meet the criteria was denied an athletic scholarship and potentially four years of eligibility. Black educators, at traditionally Black colleges and at white institutions, rallied against both rulings, seeing them as unfairly putting the educational burden on athletes and their high school teachers or schools.

Moreover, minorities of every persuasion, including women, have long complained about the inherent bias in standardized testing. As Temple coach John Chaney, a chief critic of both propositions, pointed out, "Most universities consider SAT scores along with other variables in their admissions screening. They will, for example, discount a poor performance on the SAT if it is offset by good high school grades or recommendations from educators. However, a Proposition 48 student-athlete must meet all of the rule's standards in order to play ball." People as different in philosophy as Dale Brown, LSU's outspoken white coach, and Black sports activist Harry Edwards, felt these new rules were racially biased.

But it was Thompson who dramatized the opposition on January 14, 1989, before a game between Georgetown and Boston College. The game was thoroughly overshadowed by an event that occurred just before the tip-off: Thompson took his trademark white towel off his shoulder and walked across the court of the Capital Center back to the Hoya locker room from whence he came. He was involved in his own mini-two game boycott, vowing, "I will not be on the bench in an NCAA-sanctioned Georgetown game until I'm satisfied that something has been done." Following a meeting with NCAA officials in Kansas City, Thompson ended his protest after getting assurances that Proposition 42 would be reviewed.

Thompson's walk took the Proposition 42 issue off the sports page onto the front page. It was another blow in the battle over educating Blacks and the ongoing saga of John Thompson.

JOINING THE CLUB

Thompson's prominence is why, in the summer of 1990, the owners of the Denver Nuggets offered him millions and a percentage of the club in exchange for becoming general manager. For successful college coaches to be wooed by the NBA owners wasn't unusual; the color of these particular owners was. Bertram Lee and Peter C. B. Bynoe, two Chicago-based businessmen, were the first African-Americans to own a major-league sports franchise. (Other Blacks had an interest in NBA clubs, such as hair-care manufacturer Edward Gardner, who has a piece of the Chicago Bulls.) Lee had long sought a pro franchise. A childhood tennis partner of Arthur Ashe and the owner of several major-market radio stations, Lee had previously bid on the NFL's New England Patriots, the American League's Baltimore Orioles, and the NBA's San Antonio Spurs. In May 1988, with the support of NBA commissioner David Stern, he had almost captured control of the Spurs, but the deal fell through.

Unfortunately, Lee and Bynoe's brief tenure as owners has been stormy. There have been several confusing front-office shifts, and the franchise's two cornerstone players, Alex English and Fat Lever, left, as did popular coach Doug Moe. The pair were even accused of racism by a fired white assistant coach, a charge belied by the hiring of white head coach Paul Westhead and the installation of his controversial run-and-gun offense. In the first full season of their stewardship, 1990–1991, Denver had the league's worst record, and near the season's end Lee left the operation. So far these pioneering owners have been quite unimpressive.

The recruitment of Bernie Bickerstaff as general manager in 1990 was the only major stride Lee and Bynoe made toward stabilizing their operation. Bickerstaff, while not the national figure Thompson is, presents a more representative image of how Black on-court dominance has created off-court opportunities. An assistant coach at Washington under several coaches for over a decade, before working four years as the SuperSonic's head coach, Bickerstaff is the kind of well-liked mediocrity that would only have been so consistently employed in baseball or football if he was white. In most big-time sports, both pro and college, an old boys' network of old teammates, coaches, alumni, and friends impact on who gets jobs. The NBA is the only pro league with enough Black behind-the-scenes clout to have its own old boy network and Bickerstaff is one of those old boys.

In the NCAA's Division I, in May 1989, there were twenty-five Black head coaches in men's basketball, which constituted 9.1 percent of the overall 263 positions. Considering that 57 percent of the players were Black those numbers aren't overly impressive, that is, until you notice that only 9 of 263 women's basketball coaches are Black, 4 out of 175 coaches in football are Black, 5 out of 200 in track, and none—zero, *nada*, zip—in baseball. At the pro level, where the desire to win can overcome the racial intolerance of administrators and alumni that can impair Black hiring at the college level, there have been at least two Black head coaches in the NBA every season since the mid-seventies. During 1989–1990 eight coaches were on the bench in Charlotte (Gene Littles), Cleveland (Lenny Wilkens), Houston (Don Chaney), New Jersey (Willis Reed), New York (Stu Jackson), Seattle (Bernie Bickerstaff, K. C. Jones), and Washington (Wes Unseld). Some were lousy, some were rookies, and a couple did excellent jobs. Most were ex-players or ex-assistant coaches, and all benefited from the game's openness to Black authority figures.

But the Black infiltration of the NBA old-boy network didn't end there. In that same 1988–89 season African-Americans were in many powerful decision-making positions: Players Association head (Charles Grantham), general manager-head of basketball operations (Cleveland's Wayne Embry, the Clippers's Elgin Baylor, Sacramento's Bill Russell), and head of player personnel (Minnesota's Billy McKinney), as well as 13 assistant coaches, 8 announcers, and 10 director/vice-president level were employees in areas as diverse as broadcasting (Sacramento's Mike McCullough), ticket sales (Charlotte's Clayton Smith) and finance (Denver's Walter Richards). Symbolic of the gulf between basketball and the other major sports was that when in 1989 Art Shell was named coach of the Los Angeles Raiders, it was front-page news. Yet the same year, when Littles was installed at Charlotte, a large Southern city, sports editors yawned across the land. And don't hold your breath waiting for a Black to enjoy the same broad powers in baseball or football that Embry or Russell did. While the NBA could do more, no other competing sport (and few other American industries) have a better record of empowering Blacks.

Much of this forward motion is due to the Boston Celtics. Because they were so successful as players, Black and white, many who wore the jersey have since been recruited into coaching. Don Nelson has been the ex-Celtic most effective in coaching, but African-Americans have greatly benefited from the Celtic mystique. Don Chaney, Paul Silas, Tom Sanders, K. C. Jones, and Russell have all worked at the pro level—the most Blacks from any single source—while Sam Jones and Thompson both worked at the collegiate level.

Most impressive, Russell backup Wayne Embry became pro sports' first Black general manager when he was hired by the Milwaukee Bucks in 1972. While Russell has a spotty track record as an administrator—his late-1980s sojourn in Sacramento was a disaster—Embry has been one of the league's shrewdest executives. After eight years as an all-star-caliber center in Cincinnati and two in Boston, Embry played his last campaign with the expansion Bucks in 1969. After the Bucks' ownership offered him the job, Embry was faced with the daunting task of dealing with a disgruntled Kareem Abdul-Jabbar. In 1977 Embry engineered a six-player deal with the Lakers that could have set back the Milwaukee franchise for a decade. Instead, Embry picked up players who would become Milwaukee mainstays and in 1976 talked Don Nelson into coming on as coach. That Nelson became one of the NBA's best is evidence of Embry's vision.

Just as important was Embry's eye for on-court talent. While never winning a league championship Milwaukee was one of the NBA's quality clubs from 1977 to Embry's exit in 1986 because he focused on acquiring strong, unusually bright players. It's no coincidence that three NBA Players Association heads, Quinn Buckner, Junior Bridgemen, and Bob Lanier, played for the Bucks during those years. Along with Sidney Moncrief, a great guard with a deep commitment to community involvement, the Bucks' team nucleus was probably the smartest, on and off court, in the league.

Toward the end of Embry's tenure in Milwaukee Nelson began receiving most of the credit for the team's success and also sought more control of its operation. So in the spring of 1986, when Gordon and George Gund, owners of the woeful Cleveland Cavaliers, approached him about rebuilding the team, Embry responded positively. Even before formally taking the job he advised them on a key draft deal that brought the rights to North Carolina center Brad Daugherty. In that same draft Cleveland, at Embry's urging, selected Ron Harper and obtained the rights to guard Mark Price from Dallas. Daugherty, Harper, and Price were the core of the league's best young team, a squad that in 1988–1989 compiled the NBA's best record.

To coach the Cavaliers Embry hired Lenny Wilkens in a nice example of Black old-boyism. Wilkens, who'd coached in Portland and won a title in Seattle, brought experience to his young players. Born in Brooklyn, he went on to stardom at Providence College in 1957 and was named to nine All-Star teams. In 1990 Wilkens, a stellar point guard before the term came into vogue, was elected to the Basketball Hall of Fame. Embry and Wilkens were peers who brought a rare combination of Black clout of experience to Cleveland.

Yet the Embry-Wilkens stewardship is not without its irony. After building a powerhouse in 1988–1989, they saw the Cavs racked by injuries in 1989–1990. Together they made a controversial decision, one that will determine the club's destiny and their employment in the 1990s. In exchange for the stylish guard Harper they obtained the rights to basketball's great new white hope Danny Ferry, who'd played a year in Italy rather than join the Los Angeles Clippers, who had drafted him. Because of his passing, shooting, and court sense Embry and Wilkens gambled that Ferry can be to Cleveland what Larry Bird was to Boston. In choosing Ferry's classroom game over Harper's well-schooled schoolyard athleticism these two African-American men set the stage for years of comparisons between Ferry and Harper, the relative success of the Cavaliers and Clippers, and critiques of their judgment.

BIRDLAND

What's already clear is that young Ferry, who played expertly under pressure at Duke University, will be under immense scrutiny as he attempts to bridge the NBA's white-boy gap. He's got a big job since Larry Joe Bird is easily the best European-American to perform in the league since the brothers bumrushed in the 1950s.

Before Bird, Dave Cowens, John Havlicek, Rick Barry, "Pistol" Pete Maravich, and Bill Walton all labored under the burden of representing white competence in a game gone dark. Every one of them was of Hall of Fame caliber and none, for different reasons, was as good as Larry Legend. Maravich had the "blackest" game—he's probably the closest thing we'll see to a combination of Marques Haynes and Earl Monroe—but he never had the generosity of spirit to match Bird's. He passed spectacularly but not often enough and too often only when forced by the defense.

Walton, nearly Jabbar's equal as a UCLA center, played only eight years in the league—in two he played less than fifteen games and in two other less than thirty-five. Compare that to Bird's durability and Walton comes up lame. Cowens had Bird's relentless winning desire but none of his well-rounded skills. Havlicek was a better one-on-one defender but not as creative a passer and, because of the three-point shot, Bird displayed his shooting touch from greater range. Barry, underrated today because he spent much of his prime in the ABA or contractual limbo, was as versatile as Bird—he even had a similar knack for passing fancy—but for turning the Celtics around when he arrived in 1979 and leading them to three titles in the 1980s, this French Lick, Indiana, native gets the nod for leadership.

To be as slow and earthbound as Bird in this age of elevation, then to dominate African-American skywalkers for a decade testifies to his greatness. It's not Bird's fault that he was pale by birth and that a sporting press, desperate for white sporting hopes, heaped more praise on him than Isiah Thomas or Karl Malone or Charles Barkley. Nor can Bird be blamed for the fact that Boston's citizens, often indifferent to Black stars (see Bill Russell or the Red Sox's Jim Rice), and hostile to the perceived threat of African-American advancement (see school busing battles of the seventies), and suspicious of young brothers (see the Charles Stuart murder case of 1990), made Bird a major deity. Nor can he be faulted for accepting the huge endorsement deals that made brothers jealous.

After all, it was Black racism that led the press to label the eighties Celtics "a white boy's team," which ignores the key contributions to the franchise by Gerald Henderson, Tiny Archibald, Cedric "Cornbread" Maxwell, and, in particular, Dennis Johnson and Robert Parish. Parish was a tower of strength in the middle of the Boston dynasty, yet many dismissed his dignity and determination in their hatred of Danny Ainge and Kevin McHale. True, the Celtics' half-court offense, anchored by Parish, Bird, and McHale seemed a throwback to the pre-Black aesthetic era, especially compared to L.A.'s inside grace (Jabbar) and outside speed. But the Celtic style was dictated more than anything else by the fact that Parish and McHale were demons close to the basket. Did anyone who watched the K. C. Jones-coached Celtics think otherwise? Unfortunately, yes. Attacks on Bird, Ainge, McHale et al. too often degenerated into Black racist monologues against the team, which had nothing to do with what happened on the hardwood. If Thompson was a white whipping boy, Bird and Boston were targets for Black venom.

The central question of the age was, "Who was better, Bird or Magic?" At times during their first six years in the pros Bird definitely had the edge. But over the course of their entire careers when you consider championships won (Magic five, Bird three), the impact of injuries (Magic has never missed more than a quarter of Laker games any season, while Bird has seen his last three seasons haunted by back and foot problems), and the ability to improve (Bird's outside shooting has grown erratic, while Magic has become a better free throw and three-point shooter), Johnson, over all, has to be given the edge. That he broke Oscar Robertson's all-time NBA assist record in 1991, while Bird will probably hold no all-time league records, makes one lean toward this future Hall of Famer. That still means Bird was better than 99 percent of the NBA most of his career. Not bad for a white boy. Or anyone else.

NEW JACK SWINGERS

In the late eighties a hybrid form of Black music emerged from New York City that blended elements of traditional rhythm & blues harmonies and melodies with the intense street beats of rap music. Vocalist Al B. Sure!, Keith Sweat, Johnny Kemp, GUY, Bobby Brown, and producer Teddy Riley managed to inject youthful energy into R&B and make rap more palatable to adults. "New Jack Swing" was a sound that bridged a generation gap among African-Americans. The phrase, coined by Black journalist Barry Michael Cooper, was, like the music itself, a blend. "New Jack" was the equivalent of a young blood or a kid with fresh attitude or style as opposed to old jacks or veterans. "Swing" was Cooper's description of the New Jack groove, usually created by using the swing beat program on drum machines.

Coinciding with this latest trend in Black music and slang came a brilliant new generation of players who, through physical gifts, determination, and intelligence, redefined basketball much as Russell, Chamberlain, Robertson, and others had in the fifties and that the ABA's above-the-rim crew, led by Julius Erving, had during that league's existence. Until the previous decade it was thought that championships were won by teams with dominant centers (Russell, Chamberlain, Reed, Jabbar,

Walton). Power in the paint was what teams sought more than any other commodity. But players at other positions, particularly at both guard spots, and small forwards had grown taller overall, and greater passing and speed was being displayed by power forwards and centers. The increasingly popular three-point shot and trapping defenses spread action on the court. All of these changes came together at the decade's end to alter the game profoundly. Trapping defenses (really covert zones) made quickness and anticipation as important as size. The three-point shot meant small men with long-range jumpers could become vital to an offense. Forwards who could pass and, in some cases, dribble like a guard—something the Trotters had emphasized in the forties—broke down defenses and increased the offensive options of a team. Guards were bigger and more versatile than at any time in basketball history. For example, Fat Lever, a 6´3˝, 175-pound guard, regularly led his Denver Nuggets team in rebounding throughout the eighties. The Detroit Pistons won back-to-back NBA titles with most of their points and leadership coming from an amazing three-guard rotation (Isiah Thomas, Joe Dumars, Vinnie Johnson).

Many historians feel the 1979 NCAA final between Larry Bird's Indiana State team and Magic Johnson's Michigan State squad was the event that previewed NBA ball in the eighties, that it was surely a preview showdown of superstars. However much more crucial to this text is game six of the 1980 NBA finals. Sparked by the addition of rookie guard Johnson, the Lakers and Jabbar had risen from competence to near greatness. At 6´9˝ Johnson was as tall as Bill Russell and weighed nearly as much. Yet his dexterity and court vision made him seem more a big Walt Hazzard or Oscar Robertson. His ability to "see" the whole court, analyze the action, and make the correct play was improvisation of the highest level. His presence also made clear that Jabbar, for all his ability, needed a guard who understood how to complement his low post game (as Robert-son did during Milwaukee's championship year of 1971) to win titles. Though lacking exceptional leaping ability, in every other way Johnson embodied the brilliance and tradition of the Black athletic aesthetic.

The Lakers had a three-to-two advantage against the Philadelphia 76ers bomb squad of Julius Erving, Darryl Dawkins, Caldwell Jones, and Lloyd Free, when an injury meant Jabbar would be unavailable for game six. In an inspired bit of strategy coach Paul Westhead matched Johnson at center against the 76ers duo of Dawkins and Caldwell Jones. Both were bigger and stronger than Johnson, but in every other way Johnson was the superior player. In this title clincher Johnson scored forty-two points, had fifteen rebounds and seven assists, one of the most amazing single-game performances in NBA finals history.

With that game Johnson set the tone for the decade. Boys just entering puberty in 1980 would, by the time they'd enter college, have spent ten years watching and then emulating his approach. Big men like the 6'9" John Williams of Louisiana State and the Washington Bullets, and Sean Elliott of Arizona and the San Antonio Spurs, as well as Derrick Coleman of Syracuse and the New Jersey Nets, and Billy Owens of Syracuse, both over 6'8", had before their eighteenth birthdays mastered the floor game. Where Russell reinvented basketball defense, Magic Johnson destroyed all stereotypical notions of how size dictated positions and, along with Bird, glorified creative passing and teamwork. The Russell-Johnson parallel doesn't end there. When you include his NCAA championship Johnson was the key to six titles during a ten-year period—success of Russellesque dimensions.

Johnson's New Jack Swing peers all had their own idiosyncrasies, but each, through their intelligence and athleticism, changed perceptions of how their positions could be played.

New Jack Star Charles Barkley puts it, "There are only a few guys who don't have a position. We're not forward or guards. We go beyond what one guy is supposed to do. I can play power forward, small forward, go against some centers. Nobody else can do that." There are others who could fit that multipositional bill—Clyde Drexler, Karl Malone, Akeem Olajuwon—but nobody epitomizes New Jack ball better than Johnson, Barkley, Dennis Rodman, and Michael Jordan. Defying established stereotypes of Black players, none of them are from major urban centers (Barkley and Jordan are from the South, Rodman from the Southwest, and Johnson from the midsized Northern city of Lansing), most come from nurturing, though not necessarily traditional, families, and all are celebrated for their work habits.

THE B-BOY

"Throw down like Barkley!"
—"Bring the Noise," a 1987 rap classic by Public Enemy

Charles Barkley leaps and snatches a rebound from seven-foot Patrick Ewing and 6'10" Charles Oakley during a 1988 play-off game at Madison Square Garden. Sweat pops off his round, closely cropped head when he lands. His jersey, mauled throughout the game by Oakley's aggressive defense, is sliding off his shoulder. Heedless of the disarray, the crowd noise, and Knick Johnny Newman's hand smacking his wrist, Barkley moves downcourt. Knicks lunge at him, trying to angle him off toward the side, trying to make him pass off. Instead, Barkley switches hands on the dribble and shifts around defenders like a running back fooling linebackers. Barkley arrives at the Knick foul line with Gerald Wilkins at his side. Then Barkley takes off, his crimson jersey a blur, the ball held with two hands over his head. A half second of hang time. Blam! The ball rips through the net. Barkley lands. Then he turns and sneers at the Knicks, the courtside fans, and the vast building of people who booed him when he was introduced. "My dream," he once said, "is for a fan to come at me in an alley and grab me—and be pounded through the concrete."

Listed at 6´6˝, though really 6´4˝ and change, and weighing anywhere from 300 pounds in college to a bulky 260 pounds as a pro Barkley is a highly combustible blend of power, speed, and agility. He regularly outpositions or skys over bigger men for rebounds while outrunning and outsmarting smaller men in the open court, all of which would be enough to make him an all-star. But Barkley is more than another quality player. Barkley, like fighter Mike Tyson and slugger José Canseco, plays and talks in the spirit of the boastful music known as rap music. Barkley sells wulf tickets by the bushel, and there's enough arrogance in his game to back up his lip.

In college he was hardheaded enough to balloon up to 300 pounds (thus his collegiate "Round Mound of Rebound" nickname) and still take Auburn to the NCAA tournament. In his rookie year he called a team meeting without consulting 76er captain and leader Julius Erving in a major breach of protocol. Even after Erving retired and Barkley was the team's star, he didn't lead by diplomacy but by haranguing teammates ("wimps" and "complainers" aren't unusual Barkley nouns). "I wouldn't want to be a diplomat," he says. "I wanna be Charles, I'm gonna be real. I'm what life is about. I don't play games or put up fronts. I don't tell people what they wanna hear. I tell them the truth."

Raised by his mother and grandmother in Leeds, Alabama, Barkley is filled with the absolute conviction in his correctness, an attitude one associates with a spoiled kid. Yet it is that certitude that helps elevate his game. In his bragging and toughness Barkley plays as if he were trying to match the pounding beats and high-pitch wailing of the era's most potent rap group, Public Enemy. It was a connection the rappers acknowledged on "Bring the Noise." The sonic intensity of Public Enemy's records and Barkley's noisy game are two powerhouse examples of Black male potency transformed into art.

THE WORM

Dennis Rodman is a poor dribbler. Twenty-foot jumper? Please. When the Detroit Pistons bring the ball up in a half-court offense the man guarding number 10 isn't working to deny him the ball. He'd like it if Rodman had the ball out by the three-point line. It would mean Rodman wasn't, thank God, anywhere near the backboard. You see, before a shot goes up nobody worries about Dennis Rodman.

But when Isiah Thomas or Joe Dumars or Vinnie Johnson puts up a "J" from outside suddenly the gawky 6'10" man with the big ears known to fans and foe as "The Worm" becomes the most dangerous Detroit Piston. Though only 210 pounds, Rodman is the most menacing offensive rebounder in the game. Rodman usually sneaks around opponents on the baseline or jumps over them to tap-tap-tap-tap the ball to himself, a teammate, or off the glass. If you're fortunate enough to control a defensive rebound against him the danger increases. Bill Russell was a defensive wizard in the lane, but Rodman has the ability to harass from baseline to baseline. Quick feet, sprinters' speed, and a total dedication make Rodman the defensive equivalent of Jordan and Johnson on offense. In Detroit's back-to-back title seasons of 1989 and 1990 Rodman checked Jordan, Johnson, Patrick Ewing, Clyde Drexler, Scottie Pippen, and every other aggressive scorer in the league.

Rodman regularly shuts down ordinary players. This doesn't just mean simply no points for his opponent; on occasion his man gets off no shots at all. Rodman literally eliminates players completely from their team's offense. Rodman attempts to force great players to dribble into a double team, pass off before they want to, or commit an offensive foul.

On a team so notorious they were labeled "The Bad Boys," Rodman has his own unique niche. As *Rolling Stone* noted in a Piston profile, "[Rodman] is the quintessential Piston: tightly coiled, self-combustible, relentless ... With his energy set to burst his skin, he shares it with fans and teammates, pointing a finger skyward after each gliding dunk, pumping his fist for hysteria's sake." After a dunk Rodman has been known to jump on the scorers' table and scream in celebration. It drives fans at the Pistons' Auburn Hills home crazy—and opponents to anger. In 1987, the then rookie forward created a national controversy when he said Bird was "overrated" because he was white. He weathered the fire storm of indignation (a storm shared with Isiah Thomas, who seconded Rodman and should have known better) and emerged a wiser interview subject.

By his third season Rodman was only causing on-court headaches. Recall the fourth game of the Piston-Knick conference semifinals in May 1990. The Knicks were down 2-1 in the series and were giving the defending champs a battle into the fourth quarter. Knick guard Mark Jackson led a fast break with teammates on either side. Jackson looked left. Jackson looked right. But behind him danger lurked. A long-legged streak in a blue jersey bore down on Jackson and before he could hear teammate Trent Tucker's warning Rodman had flicked the ball away. That extra effort stopped a Knick rush and sealed a win. It was a play typical of how Rodman, in the tradition of Russell and K. C. Jones, has turned defense into titles.

B-BALL BUPPIE

Michael Jordan, still in his twenties and already the creator of a million memories of shots, blocks, and moves. Hang time. Suspended animation. Damn, did you see that! Sixty-three points against Boston in the 1986 play-offs. Last-second play-off buzzer-beaters that knocked out Cleveland in 1989 and the Knicks in 1990. As a freshman at North Carolina he hit the winning shot in the NCAA final against Georgetown in 1983. He's scored one third of all the Chicago Bulls' points in a season twice, which tied him with George Mikan and placed him just behind Wilt Chamberlain on a very exclusive list of scorers. Of the five largest scoring margins between the first and second leading scorers on an NBA team, three are held by Chamberlain—from 1961 to 1964 Wilt scored at least 23.4 points more than the next Philadelphia Warrior. In 1987–1988 and 1986–1987 Jordan averaged 22.6 points more than the next Bull scorer.

Comparisons between Jordan and the game's first two dominating offensive big men are quite apt since all three dominated NBA scoring in their eras. Jordan will never average fifty a game for a season, but in only six seasons he's made a Chamberlainesque dent in the record book. If all he did was score Jordan would merit respect. Yet whenever he's been asked to play point guard it has been clear that if he concentrated on that position, he'd be in the class of John Stockton and Magic Johnson. Moreover, Jordan defends so well he was once named the league's top defensive player and to the All-Star defensive team three times. In essence if one could select the best aspects of all his New Jack peers—Johnson's passing, Rodman's defense, Barkley's all-court intensity—you'd have a reasonable facsimile of Michael Jordan.

Even among the all-time greats Jordan has few peers: he

hangs as long and high as Elgin Baylor and Julius Erving, he combines rebounding and passing like Oscar Robertson but is quicker and more deceptive, and his will is as steely as Russell's or anyone else who has laced up sneakers. Evidence of this will was supplied early in the 1985–1986 season, his second campaign, when Jordan sustained a serious leg injury. Bulls management asked him to sit out the rest of the season. Jordan refused. Risking further injury and millions of dollars Jordan suited up after missing eighteen games and pushed his sorry teammates to an undeserved play-off spot. "In taking on management, he was the first guy who came out in the media and said he felt he could play," said then Bulls coach Stan Albeck. "In doing that, it elevated him to superstar status. Most players are told by their agents that if there's any doubt, don't play. But Michael has an intense love of the game."

Jordan, of course, is not simply a player. Through a series of endorsement deals Jordan has risen above the game to become a video age myth, a Black face with the mass appeal to sell goods (and himself) rivaled only by prime time's favorite sepia pitchman, Bill Cosby. Upon graduation from college Jordan signed with Pro Serv, one of the top athletic representation agencies. Jimmy Connors, Patrick Ewing, Arthur Ashe, James Worthy, John Thompson, and Jordan's college coach, Dean Smith, are among its clients. After being named *Sporting News* college player of 1983 and 1984, leading the Olympic team to gold in 1984, and being the Bulls' number-one draft choice in 1984, only two companies approached him for endorsements: Nike and Converse (which is the sneaker he wore in college). Nike wasn't looking to make Jordan a trademark. The initial offer was your typical jock-athletic shoe hookup—some cash, some posters, and an unlimited supply of footwear.

But Pro Serv pushed hard on what it believed was a unique product. Playing the game spectacularly yet somehow unselfishly and playing the media with his cool Southern charm, Jordan became basketball's Arthur Ashe. Jordan defied the stereotypes of the street-hardened inner-city player. He was reared in the peaceful Sunbelt state of North Carolina in a solid nuclear family. Religious, well-spoken, and with none of the wariness of whites that hamper many young African-American men, Jordan is the flip side of the crack dealers who populate the local news broadcasts of big cities. With the exception of Julius Erving no previous Black ball star has had the same balance of tremendous talent, poise in public, and personal charisma. But Ashe is an even truer parallel because his background, in terms of how and where he was reared, is similar. Ashe was the Sidney Poitier of tennis who blended in with the country-club set. Jordan, as clean-cut as a starched shirt, epitomized Black athletic style on court while not reminding viewers of the conditions that helped nurture it—something Jabbar's Islamic name and Barkley's arrogance never disguised.

Within a year of his graduation Pro Serv had convinced Nike to move on its idea of a "signature shoe" called Air Jordan. This revolutionized the endorsement game, bringing Nike approximately $130 million Air Jordan's first year, opening the door for the Ewing collection and the Mugsy Mobile, a special-edition Ford Fiesta sold only in the D.C.-Baltimore home turf of the 5´3˝ guard Tyrone "Mugsy" Bogues.

Jordan's Nike deal was the catalyst for an explosion of sportswear chic among African-American youth. In his solo commercials and in several directed by and costarring Spike Lee, Jordan used his mystique to glamorize Nike gear. In the streets Nike sneakers and Chicago Bulls jackets became among the most prized possessions of young Blacks—and often dangerous to wear. Much-publicized shootings led many to point a finger at Jordan and Lee as instigators of this murderous fashion mania.

Unfortunately, the problem wasn't that simple. Since I was in high school in the seventies certain pieces of desirable clothing have instigated kids to envy and thievery. In the seventies it was suede coats called quarterfields. Just prior to the Nike mania, Adidas sneakers (popularized by the rap group Run D.M.C.) and European designer glasses called Cazal's were the gear to wear and steal. The Cazal's were a particularly mindless item since they were often worn without glass—it was the expensive frames that were desired. Right after the excitement over Nike and starter sports jackets peaked, multicolored jackets with the eight-ball logo were hot items to rob. No Michael Jordan—Spike Lee ads inspired this fad—it was a street sensibility that made them hot. Jordan took a lot of heat for the import his ads had in instigating crime, but the roots of the Nike sneakers crimes were in the misdirected materialism of many kids and, only partially, in Jordan's salesmanship.

Jordan became a Coca-Cola spokesman, according to Neva Richardson of Chicago's Burrell Advertising, the nation's largest Black-owned agency, because the company needed help. In the wake of the New Coke fiasco, the soda makers hooked onto Max Headroom as their new commercial symbol. Problem was, Black folks—a huge part of Coke's market—hated the computer-generated talking head. Here came Mr. Jordan. "Michael Jordan legitimatized Max with a Black audience" by interacting with him in a spot, according to Richardson.

But Jordan's ultimate challenge was getting signed with Mickey Dee's. "It took Pro Serv a year to turn McDonald's around," the company's Bill Strickland says. Three times Ronald McDonald said no to Jordan, citing as the major impediment the fact that Jordan played a team sport in which individual identification wasn't as high as in boxing, tennis, or golf. But Pro Serv kept up the pressure, and as Jordan went from man to pop icon McDonald's bought in.

With his well-honed talents, shrewd advisers, and carefully cultivated smile Jordan had, to quote the title of C. L. R. James book about blacks in cricket, gone beyond a boundary. On-court he is, in his time, the equal of the Big O, Russell, Wilt, The Pearl and Dr. J. Off-court, though, Jordan is something new, something peculiar to his time.

More than any other contemporary African-American athlete, his ability to thrive in the pressure cooker of corporate endorsements (his off-season is packed with appearances at various company conferences, charitable events, and golf tournaments sponsored by advertisers and shooting commercials), while never making any embarrassing "I'm not black, I'm universal" comments or selling his soul rather than just his visage, makes him a major symbol of nicely assimilated black America. Michael Jordan—commodity, pop star, all-African-American guy—is a true basketball buppie (a Black yuppie). And he did it all in the eighties without a nose job.

FINAL SCORE

PROFESSOR HENRY LOUIS GATES: There's no single relationship between the representation of images of ethnic groups and social relationships. I read an article recently that said the most popular TV show in South Africa was "The Cosby Show." And "The Cosby Show" is the most popular TV show in the United States precisely when we have the highest black unemployment rate, the highest black birth-out-of-wedlock rate, that we've had in my lifetime. There was a time in Afro-American cultural history when we thought if only we could have an image represented to the bulk of Americans that showed a refined Afro-American doctor married to a refined Afro-American lawyer, who's a partner in a Wall Street law firm—

PROF. ALVIN POUSSAINT: That would cure us all.

PROFESSOR GATES: And obviously that hasn't happened.

—*New York Times*, August 7, 1989

In many ways Jordan exemplifies the values of the muscular Christian movement and the willfulness of the Delta bluesmen. As a clean-living, God-fearing, sports-focused man, Jordan speaks to the dreams of Gulick, Naismith, and the coaches, Black and white, who envisioned sports as a force of personal fulfillment and social good. Yet for all his off-court courtesy, on court Jordan is a warrior constantly outwitting opponents (and even slow-thinking teammates) with a catalogue of shakes, stutter steps, and leaps that sum up and extend a century of basketball. Jordan can't really fly, but he can jam after elevating 360 degrees in the vertical plane, an act that in the blues tradition defies rules of logic, decorum, and gravity in one amazing motion.

Inspired by Jordan, younger players like Kevin Johnson, Kenny Anderson, David Robinson, Billy Owens, Gary Peyton, and Alonzo Mourning will extend the Black athletic aesthetic into the nineties and into the next century in the tradition of Russell, Chamberlain, Robertson, Baylor, and Hawkins. Yet there is, if not a hollowness, certainly a deep aura of melancholy, that hovers over the NBA and big-time college games in the nineties. For the scores of moneyed NBA superstars there are literally hundreds of Connie Hawkinses—African-American men who are undereducated by teachers yet advanced so their school can reap financial or promotional benefit. They are used until the educational charade is ended either by failing marks or the end of four years of eligibility. For decades many Black colleges directed their athletes toward academic excellence as a tool to achieve equality. But that philosophy has been corrupted by the hypocrisy of too many large white universities and abandoned by African-American players and families who've grown as mercenary as any college recruiter.

One of the saddest results of Black ball success is the economic isolation of the players. Blacks get jobs as coaches, scouts, recruiters, and broadcasters due to the proliferation of African-Americans in the NBA. But the players themselves rarely employ Black agents, attorneys, or accountants. Despite three decades of on-court excellence, off court only one Black agent, ex-UCLA center Fred Slaughter, has a high profile, but in no way is he in the class of Pro Serv. Moreover, player investment in Black-owned businesses is always noteworthy because it's so rare. In the mideighties, for example, ex-Laker Bernard King and Norm Nixon invested in a play by Pulitzer

Prize–winning playwright August Wilson, *Joe Turner's Come and Gone.*

In business, as in the sport, Magic Johnson is an important exception. In 1991 he went into business with *Black Enterprise* publisher Earl Graves in purchasing a Pepsi Cola bottling plant and other ventures. Current Piston star guard Isiah Thomas and former Piston star guard Dave Bing are involved in various investments in Detroit. These are, however, exceptions that prove the rule. The idea that these well-heeled Black men would one day make a profound financial contribution to the well-being of their fellow Blacks in the nineties seems like another civil rights era dream deferred.

Furthermore, the visibility of these, in many cases, multi-millionaires has not made white Americans more tolerant of the average Black man. Nor has it, in any measurable way, overtoned the tide of low self-esteem that has overwhelmed the morality of too many of their brothers. In fact, the triumph of a gifted elite has only bred a frustrated fatalism in those left behind.

Drug abuse, for example, is not a cause of crime, it is a by-product of personal idiosyncrasy *and* the lies of America's shared national wealth that NBA stars embody.

For every Jordan there have been thousands—in the years since World War II maybe millions—of Black men whose promise was destroyed by drugs as was Earl Manigault's. "The Goat" is still a legend in New York, a subject of mythology and possible movie deals, but all his prowess could not shield him from drug addiction. The roll call of drug-related defeats in basketball is long, stretching from the heroin jones of Manigault to that of Len Bias two decades later. But these men are not alone. America is caught up in a web of its weakness. In every state, city, and home we are all affected by the deadly obsession that drives neighbors, friends, ourselves to drugs for pleasure and escape. To still believe a sport alone can carry a child safely above this sickness is to overstate the game's vitality and ignore how insistently this society preaches the need for instant gratification.

It would be wonderful to say 100 years after basketball's inception and several decades after Blacks began their dominance that Jordan represents the culmination of this story and that this Black aesthetic—our music put into physical motion—has forced European-Americans to give Black men their due respect. Jordan, ultimately, is just one big success story in a nation of souls so long abused that many have embraced their own self-destruction. The sad truth is that despite all the innovation, flair, and magic African-Americans have brought to basketball, racism and self-delusion still bedevil them. Greatness is a gift from God, though it isn't always rewarded. In America geniuses don't always prosper and survive. For Black geniuses, whether on the hardwood, the bandstand, or the speaker's podium, the gap between celebration and survival is even wider. This has been proven so often by American history that it can no longer be viewed as a tragedy but as a matter of sociological inevitability.

The reality is that the existence of African-Americans in the twenty-first century depends not merely in rechanneling the energy of their male offspring into nonathletic activities but taking the strongest, richest aspects of our aesthetic and translating it into actions that run counter to capitalist standards. Make the goal not just to enrich oneself but to give back to the culture and people that spawned you. Without such a mentality, not only on the part of the players but the overall community, the next 100 years will see stellar athletes increasingly divorced from their cultural roots, rows of men defeated in their quest for professional dollars and ill equipped to find another dream, and a mass of African-Americans who view basketball stars not as role models but as actors in athletic soap operas utilized to keep them numbed to the social chaos engulfing them. Or as Earl Manigault once said, "For every Michael Jordan, there's an Earl Manigault. I didn't hurt anybody but myself."

Finals 1956 Basketball: Crispus Attucks vs. Lafayette (Indiana High School Athletic Association), 1988.

Greatest Sports Legends: Bill Russell (GSL), 1986.

Greatest Sports Legends: Wilt Chamberlain (GSL), 1985.

Home of the Brave: '86–87 Season plus Sweet Sixteen: '85–86 Championship Season (CBS Fox), 1990.

Hoosiers (Hemdale), 1986.

Madison Square Garden's All-Time Greatest Basketball Featuring the Harlem Globetrotters (Congress Video Group), 1985.

NBA Awesome Endings (CBS Fox), 1990.

New York's Game: History of the Knicks (CBS Fox), 1989.

Pride & Passion: The 1983–84 NBA Championship Film (Embassy), 1984.

Texas Style: 1986 All-Star Weekend (CBS Fox), 1980.

The Drive for Five: Lakers '87 (CBS Fox), 1987.

Come Fly with Me: Michael Jordan (CBS Fox), 1989.

History of the NBA (CBS Fox), 1990.

The following periodicals were of great help in writing this book:

Ebony, Jet, Black Enterprise, Village Voice, New York Times, New York *Daily News,* Boston *Globe, Newsday,* the New York *Post,* Los Angeles *Times,* Washington *Post,* Philadelphia *Inquirer,* Boston *Phoenix, Sporting News, Sports Illustrated, Sport,* Amsterdam *News, Philly Sport, Players, City Sun, Life, Time,* Chicago *Tribune,* Atlanta *Constitution, Basketball Digest, Pro,* sundry team yearbooks and media guides, and especially that defunct experiment in athletic cultural consciousness, *Black Sports,* which I subscribed to as an adolescent and whose conception eventually inspired this work.

BIBLIOGRAPHY

Abdul-Jabbar, Kareem, and Knobler, Peter. *Giant Steps.* New York: Bantam, 1983.

Anderson, Dave. *The Story of Basketball.* New York: Morrow 1988.

Ashe, Arthur. *A Hard Road to Glory: The History of the African-American Athlete, 1619–1918.* New York: Warner Books, 1988.

——— *A Hard Road to Glory: The History of the African-American Athlete. 1919–1945.* New York: Warner Books, 1988.

——— *A Hard Road to Glory Since 1946: The History of the African-American Athlete.* New York: Warner Books, 1988.

Assante, Molefi Kete. *Afrocentricity.* Trenton, N. J.: African World, 1988.

Auerbach, Red, with Joe Fitzgerald. *On and Off the Court.* New York: Macmillan, 1985.

Axthelm, Pete. *The City Game.* New York: Penguin, 1970.

Barlow, William. *Looking Up at Down: The Emergence of Blues Culture.* Philadelphia: Temple, 1989.

Beckham, Barry. *Double Dunk.* Los Angeles: Holloway House, 1980.

Bennett, Lerone, Jr. *Before the Mayflower: A History of Black America,* 3 vols. New York: Penguin, 1985.

Berkow, Ira. *The DuSable Panthers.* New York: Atheneum, 1978.

Bill, Bob. *The Amazing Basketball Book.* Louisville, Ky.: Devyn, 1988.

Bird, Larry, with Bob Ryan. *Drive: The Story of My Life.* New York: Doubleday, 1989.

Boskin, Joseph. *Sambo: The Rise and Fall of an American Jester.* New York: Oxford, 1986.

Bradley, Bill. *Life on the Run.* New York: Bantam, 1986.

Campbell, Nelson, ed. *Grassroots and School Yards. A High School Basketball Anthology.* Lexington, Mass.: Stephen Greene Press, 1988.

Carr, M. L. *Don't Be Denied.* Boston: Quinlan, 1987.

Cole, Lewis. *Dream Team.* New York: Morrow, 1981.

———. *Never Too Young to Die: The Death of Len Bias.* New York: Pantheon, 1989.

Cousy, Bob, and Hirshberg, Al. *Basketball Is My Life.* Englewood Cliffs, N.J.: Prentice-Hall, 1957.

———, and Ryan, Bob. *Cousy on the Celtic Mystique.* New York: McGraw-Hill, 1989.

Cripps, Thomas. *Slow Fade to Black: The Negro in American Film, 1900–1942.* New York: Oxford, 1971.

Cruse, Harold. *Plural But Equal.* New York: Morrow, 1987.

Dawkins, Darryl. *Chocolate Thunder.* Chicago: Contemporary, 1986.

Drake, St. Clair, and Cayton, Horace R. *Black Metropolis.* New York: Harper, 1945.

Drape, Joe. *In a Hornet's Nest.* New York: St. Martin's, 1989.

Ellis, Dock, and Hall, Donald. *Dock Ellis in the Country of Baseball.* New York: Fireside, 1976.

Embry, Mike. *Basketball in the Blue Grass State: The Championship Teams.* New York: Scribners, 1983.

Feinstein, John. *Dream Team.* New York: Villard, 1990.

Frazier, Walt. *Walt Frazier: One Magic Season.* New York: Harper & Row, 1988.

Gabler, Neal. *An Empire of Their Own: How the Jews Invented Hollywood.* New York: Doubleday, 1989.

Gallner, Sheldon M. *Pro Sports: The Contract Game.* New York: Scribners, 1974.

Gayle, Addison, ed. *The Black Aesthetic.* New York: Anchor, 1971.

Goldpaper, Sam, and Pincus, Arthur. *How to Talk Basketball.* New York: Dembner, 1983.

Gutman, Bill. *The Pictorial History of Basketball.* New York: Gallery, 1988.

Guttmann, Allen. *A Whole New Ball Game: An Interpretation of American Sports.* Raleigh: University of North Carolina Press, 1988.

Halberstam, David. *The Breaks of the Game.* New York: Knopf, 1981.

Hawkins, Connie, with David Wolf. *Foul!* New York: Warner Books, 1972.

Haywood, Spencer. *The Spencer Haywood Story.* New York: Tempo, 1972.

Heeren, Dave. *The Basketball Abstract.* Englewood Cliffs, N.J.: Prentice-Hall, 1988.

Heinsohn, Tommy, and Fitzgerald, Joe. *Give 'em the Hook.* Englewood Cliffs, N.J.: Prentice-Hall, 1988.

Holzman, Red. *Red on Red.* New York: Bantam, 1988.

Hoose, Phillip M. *Necessities: Racial Barriers in American Sports.* New York: Random House, 1989.

James, C. L. R. *Beyond Boundary.* New York: Pantheon, 1963.

Johnson, Earvin, and Johnson, Roy S. *Magic's Touch.* Reading, Mass.: Addison-Wesley, 1989.

Katz, Milton, and McLendon, John B. *Breaking Through.* New York: 1987.

Krugel, Mitchell. *Michael Jordan.* New York: St. Martin's, 1988.

Lapchick, Richard E., and Slaughter, John B. New York: Macmillan, 1989.

Lazenby, Roland. *Championship Basketball: Top Coaches Present*

Their Winning Strategies, Tips and Techniques for Players and Coaches. New York: Contemporary, 1987.

Leab, Daniel J. *From Sambo to Superspade: The Black Experience in Motion Pictures.* Boston: Houghton Mifflin, 1975.

Lemon, Meadowlark, with Jerry B. Jenkins. *Meadowlark.* Nashville: Nelson, 1987.

Levine, David. *Life on the Rim: A Year in the Continental Basketball Association.* New York: Macmillan, 1989.

Levine, Lawrence. *Black Culture and Black Consciousness: Afro-American Folk Thought from Slavery to Freedom.* New York: Oxford, 1977.

Lipsyte, Robert. *Sportsworld: An American Dreamland.* New York: Morrow, 1975.

Marcus, Greil, ed. *Stranded: Rock and Roll for a Desert Island.* New York: Knopf, 1979.

Mellen, Joan. *Bob Knight: His Own Man.* New York: Donald I. Fine, 1988.

Michener, James. *Sports in America.* New York: Ballantine, 1976.

Monroe, Sylvester, and Goldman, Peter. *Brothers: A Study of Courage and Survival Against the Odds of Today's Society.* New York: Morrow, 1988.

Morris, Willie. *The Courting of Marcus Dupree.* New York: Doubleday, 1983.

Murray, Albert. *Stomping the Blues.* New York: McGraw-Hill, 1974.

Neft, David S., and Cohen, Richard M. *The Sports Encyclopedia: Pro Basketball.* New York: St. Martin's, 1988.

Nelli, Bert. *The Winning Tradition: A History of Kentucky Wildcat Basketball.* Lexington: University Press of Kentucky, 1984.

Novak, Michael. *The Joy of Sports: End Zones, Bases, Baskets, Balls, and the Consecration of the American Spirit.* Hamilton, 1988.

Ostler, Scott, and Springer, Steve. *Winnin' Times: The Magical Journey of the Los Angeles Lakers.* New York: Macmillan, 1987.

Packer, Billy, and Lazenby, Roland. *The Sporting News College Basketball's 25 Greatest Teams.* St. Louis: Sporting News, 1989.

Parks, Gordon. *Voices in the Mirror.* New York: Doubleday, 1990.

Pasteur, Al, and Toldson, Ivory. *Roots of Soul.* New York: Doubleday, 1982.

Peterson, Robert W. *Cage to Jump Shots: Pro Basketball's Early Years.* New York: Oxford, 1990.

Powers, Richie, with Mark Mulvoy. *Overtime.* New York: McKay, 1975.

Rashad, Ahmad, and Bodo, Peter. *Rashad.* New York: New American Library, 1988.

Reynolds, Bill. *Big Hoops: A Season in the Big East Conference.* New York: New American Library, 1989.

Riley, Pat. *Show Time: Inside the Lakers' Breakthrough Season.* New York: Warner Books, 1987.

Roberts, Randy, and Olson, James. *Winning Is the Only Thing: Sports in America Since 1945.* Baltimore: Johns Hopkins, 1989.

Russell, Bill, and McSweeny, William. *Go Up for Glory.* New York: Coward-McCann, 1966.

————, and Branch, Taylor. *Second Wind: The Memoirs of an Opinionated Man.* New York: Random House, 1979.

Rust, Edna and Art. *Art Rust's Illustrated History of the Black Athlete.* New York: Doubleday, 1985.

Ryan, Bob, and Raphael, Dick. *The Boston Celtics: The History, Legends, and Images of America's Most Celebrated Team.* Reading, Mass.: Addison-Wesley, 1989.

Salzberg, Charles. *From Set Shot to Slam Dunk: The Glory Days of Basketball in the Words of Those Who Played It.* New York: Dutton, 1987.

Schron, Bob, and Stevens, Kevin. *The Bird Era.* Boston: Quinlan, 1988.

Seymour, Harold. *Basketball: The Early Years.* New York: Oxford, 1960.

Sobel, Lionel S. *Pro Sports and the Law.* New York: Law-Arts Publishers, 1977.

Susman, Warren I. *Culture as History: The Transformation of American Society in the Twentieth Century.* New York: Pantheon, 1984.

Tarkanian, Jerry. *Tark: College Basketball's Winningest Coach.* New York: McGraw-Hill, 1988.

Thomas, Isiah, and Dobek, Matt. *Bad Boys: An Inside Look at the Detroit Pistons 1988–89 Championship Season.* Masters, 1989.

Viorst, Milton. *Fire in the Streets: America in the Nineteen Sixties.* Touchstone, 1979.

Wielgus, Chuck, Jr., and Wolff, Alexander. *The In-Your-Face Basketball Book.* New York: Wynwood, 1989.

Wooden, John, and Tobin, Jack. *They Call Me Coach.* Contemporary, 1988.

Wright, Richard. *Black Boy.* New York: Harper, 1945.

———. *Native Son.* New York: Harper, 1940.

Douglas, Robert L., 34, 46
Drew, Charles, 24–25
Drexler, Clyde "The Guide," 214
Drucker, Norm, 101
Drugs, 77–78, 201–5
Duer, Al, 88
Dukes, Walter, 110
Dunk shots, 192–93
Duren, John, 205
DuSable Panthers (Chicago), xvii,
    68–71, 99

Eastern-style basketball, 75
Edmond, Rayfield III, 204
Education
    college performance and, 215–18
    federal aid to, 8–9, 17
    sports vs., 188, 201–2
Embry, Wayne, 152, 188, 220–22
Erickson, Keith, 143
Erving, Julius "Dr. J," 74, 182–84
Ewing, Patrick, xiv, 210, 212–13
Exploitation, 201–2

Fast break, 71, 78, 86–87
Fetry, Danny, 222–23
Fisk University, 82, 92–94
Flournoy, Harry, 135
Floyd, Eric "Sleepy," xiv, 205
Forwards, domination of, in ABA, 181
Frazier, Walt, 89, 174–77
Free, Lloyd "All-World" (World B.
    Free), 190–91
Free-lancing, 69
Freshmen, testing scores and, 216–17
From Set Shot to Slam Dunk (Salzberg),
    59
Frontcourt, speed in, 143
Full-court press, 71

Gabler, Neal, 45
Gaines, Clarence "Big House,"
    168–71
Gambling, 128–30
Gant, Charlie, 25
Gardner, Willie, 119

Garvey, Marcus, 33–34
Gates, William "Pops," 36, 39–40,
    64, 67–68
Georgetown Hoyas, 205–17
Gervin, George, 182
Gibson, Josh, 19
Gilmore, Artis, 182
Glover, Melvin, 26
Goaltending rule, 113
Goodrich, Gail, 177
Gossett, Lou, 48
Gotthoffer, Joel "Shikey," 38
Gottlieb, Eddie, 37, 46, 55
Gourdine, Sy, 188
Graham, Michael, 215
Graham, William "Bird," 197–98
Grant, Travis "The Machine," 196–98
Grantham, Charles, 220
Gulick, Luther, 2–3

Hacken, Joe, 129
Halas, George "Papa Bear," 43
Hamilton, Ronald, 91
Hammond, Joe, 77
Hampton Institute, 23, 26–29, 92
Hardnett, Charlie, 170
Harkness, Jerry, 134
Harlem Globetrotters, 41–56, 67, 96,
    100, 109, 115
    clowning and, 48–51
    early history, 42–46
    guards' role, 51
    innovations of, 51–56
    naming of, 43–44
    in 1940s, 50–54
    in 1950s, 56
    as Original Chicago Globetrotters,
        43–44
    as Tommy Brookins' Globetrotters,
        43
    the "Trotter way," 50–51
Harlem Magicians, 55–56, 98, 101
Harlem Renaissance ("Rens") (team),
    25, 33–40, 46, 64, 67, 100
Harlem Yankees, 39
Harp, Dick, 113